LABOUR IN BRITISH SOCIETY

LABOUR IN BRITISH SOCIETY

AN INTERPRETATIVE HISTORY

RICHARD PRICE

ROUTLEDGE
London and New York

First published in 1986 by
Croom Helm Ltd

Reprinted as a University Paperback in 1990 by
Routledge
11 New Fetter Lane, London EC4P 4EE
29 West 35th Street, New York, NY 10001

Printed and bound in Great Britain by Mackays of Chatham PLC, Kent

British Library Cataloguing in Publication Data

Price, Richard
Labour in British society : an interpretive history.
1. Great Britain. Working classes
I. Title
305.5′ 62′ 0941

Library of Congress Cataloging in Publication Data

Price, Richard
Labour in British society : an interpretive history/Richard Price
p. cm. —
Includes bibliographies and index.
1. Working classes — Great Britain — History. I. Title.
[HD8388.P75 1990]
305.5′ 62′ 0941 — dc20 89-35548

ISBN 0-415-04453-7 (University paperback)
ISBN 0-85664-736-5 (cased)

CONTENTS

To Marshall

ACKNOWLEDGEMENTS

Writing this book has been made easier by the assistance I have received from many people and institutions. I would like particularly to thank James Cronin. There is scarcely an idea in this book that has not benefited from his advice. He saw the manuscript at an early stage of its preparation and his comments and criticisms were always helpful and usually right. It is also a great pleasure to acknowledge Ira Berlin, my colleague at the University of Maryland. Ira was kind enough to read the book when it was most in need of a distanced eye. His commentary was invaluable both for its stylistic and editorial remarks and for the perspective of an American social historian. If this book is comprehensible to any beyond the narrow world of British social historians, it is due to Ira Berlin. Others who deserve public notice of my gratitude include my former colleague Harvey Smith who patiently listened to my early ideas, James Cockburn who excised many solecisms from the manuscript, and Geoffrey Crossick of the University of Essex under whose aegis this book was originally conceived. I also benefited from the comments of various audiences at scholarly gatherings who listened to early versions of parts of the work. In particular, I should mention the audience at the Social History Society's 1981 meeting in Winchester, England. My publisher, David Croom has been most generous, not least in his understanding of many unmet deadlines. Needless to say, I alone am responsible for the errors in the finished product.

I have received help from many institutions and libraries. Both Northern Illinois University and the University of Maryland supported my research with welcome financial assistance. The American Council of Learned Societies awarded me one of their grants and I received a similar award from the American Philosophical Society. The interlibrary loan department of Founders' Library, Northern Illinois University, was of great assistance in meeting my demands for huge stacks of obscure nineteenth-century trade journals – an incredibly rich and still underutilised source for the study of the history of social relations. And it is a great pleasure to acknowledge the assistance of St Bride's Printing Library in addition to the indispensable sources of the British Library and their newspaper collection at Colindale.

I must also thank my typists Yvette Williams and Padma Seetharam for their skill on word processors. Finally, but not least, I wish to thank my family. My wife's ruthless editorial assistance helped make this book more readable. Most important of all, however, was her support and love. This book is dedicated to my son, as a token of my appreciation for the difference he has made to my social being.

ABBREVIATIONS

AEU	Amalgamated Engineering Union
ASE	Amalgamated Society of Engineers
ASRS	Amalgamated Society of Railway Servants
CBI	Confederation of British Industry
CWC	Clyde Workers' Committee
Ec. Hist. Rev.	Economic History Review
EWO	Essential Works Order
ILP	Independent Labour Party
JPC	Joint Production Committee
LRC	Labour Representation Committee
NEB	National Enterprise Board
NPLA	National Power Loading Agreement
NSO	National Service Order
NUBSO	National Union of Boot and Shoe Operatives
NUR	National Union of Railwaymen

INTRODUCTION

Organised labour has occupied a particularly important place in the history of modern Britain. Ever since the first industrial revolution produced the first working class, the relationship between class and society has been the subject of endless debate and enquiry. This book is part of that enterprise. In the pages that follow the reader will encounter many of the well-established themes of labour history and my argument owes as much to the rich literature produced by other toilers in this field as it does to my own researches. I am not concerned, however, to travel again paths well worn by general histories of trade unionism, industrial relations, or the Labour Party. My intention is to provide an interpretative history of the relationship between labour and society from the eighteenth century to the present day.

The prominence of labour in British society has been displayed through the parallel influences of working-class organisation in industry and the representation of labour in politics. Over the past 200 years these twin elements have registered many variations, but their persistent ubiquity has shaped the changing history of labour in society. For labour historians, therefore, the affinities between the industrial and political perspectives of labour's history are of central importance. Thus, two themes recur throughout this book: first, how the pattern of social relations in British industry has developed since the industrial revolution; and second, how these patterns have been affiliated to national political and economic developments.[1]

There is nothing particularly unusual about that agenda. It resembles the original schema for labour history as it was defined at the beginning of this century by Sydney and Beatrice Webb, J.L. and Barbara Hammond, and G.D.H. Cole. Their task was to account for the rise of labour to industrial and political maturity, which they conceived as an unproblematical response to the course of economic and social change. By the 1950s, however, this framework had been disturbed. The work of Marxist-oriented historians such as Eric Hobsbawm, John Saville and Edward Thompson shifted the focus away from the history of labour's growing institutional and political presence. Attention was drawn to the economic and social conditions that underpinned the structures of labour organisation. The conceptual approach also changed. Whereas earlier historians had generally regarded the rise of labour as an unqualified story of ultimate triumphs, these historians were intrigued by the enigma presented by the working class. Two mutually opposed tendencies seemed to be combined within the British working class. A strong sociological and cultural sense of class identity coexisted with a political practice which had failed to raise a serious ideological challenge to the capitalist organisation of society. The central problem for labour history was to explain that contradiction.

Initially, the matter seemed straightforward enough. Class development in Britain could be seen to follow from the structural consequences of Britain's economic development. In particular, attention was directed to the way a labour aristocracy emerged out of industrialisation with a privileged relationship to the rest of the working class and an ambiguously co-operative relationship to the dominant classes. This situation encouraged and allowed the development of reformist, labourist politics.[2] Even when the ambiguities of the labour aristocracy's position were granted greater prominence and its integrity and 'independence' accorded fuller recognition, the main lines of argument were merely elaborated and refined rather than altered.[3] This feature of the working class, it was argued, was susceptible to the deep commitment to constitutionalism that carried over from the radical tradition of the eighteenth century to the new labour movement in the nineteenth. Thus radicalism never managed to break out of this mould to develop an economic and social critique of class relations. The end result was to produce a politics that, in the mid-nineteenth century, was virtually devoid of ideology; and in the late nineteenth century, when politics did change, the socialism that emerged remained firmly trapped within the limitations of its own parliamentarianism. The subsequent course of labour politics could be seen in large part to demonstrate the logic of a politics that failed to incorporate any theory of social change beyond a naive belief in the evolutionary growth of enlightened opinion and social progress.[4] Thus, an interest in theory and ideology was not part of the labour movement tradition, and the encounter between Marxism and native cultural traditions at the end of the century produced a series of curious hybrids like the ethical socialism of the Independent Labour Party and early labour leaders. This encounter also helped produce Fabianism, of course; but although some Fabians possessed a broad social and cultural vision, the core of their prescriptions for social change boiled down to technocratic administration by the professional experts beloved by the Webbs.

Working-class politics was thus divorced from working-class economics. Industrial militancy, a deep sense of class distinction, a sociological class identity, and a certain autonomy of culture and society all were viewed by historians as, to some extent, contradicting the nature of labour's representation in politics. Taken together, however, these forces produced a working class whose collective action was ultimately instrumental and economist. Whereas French workers could be seen to possess a radical, even revolutionary, ideology and oriented their class action towards politics, British workers were more militant at work but supine when it came to politics.[5]

For many years this general view of the dynamics of labour's history remained quite secure. In recent years, however, the assumptions and categories of analysis that labour historians traditionally accepted have been cast into doubt. Ironically, it is likely that this development was a consequence of the publication of E.P. Thompson's *The Making of the English Working Class* which reopened the question of how working-class history should be theorised. Thompson's classic reconstruction of the origins of modern class relations disrupted the conventional Marxist and non-Marxist paradigms of working-class history. Its portrayal of the working class as an active participant in the making of its own history offered a more sophisticated conception than any previous work. But the vision of the working class as the carriers of an alternative social and political organisation remained implicit in Thompson's emphasis upon the autonomous and oppositional tendencies in working-class consciousness. Inspired by Thompson's example, subsequent research into the details of working-class culture and society has not necessarily confirmed this bias. A more complicated picture has begun to emerge which emphasises how the failures of labour's history were inherent from its very beginning.

The intellectual origins of this version of labour's history go back to the 'peculiarities of the English' debate in the mid-1960s. In that debate, Perry Anderson and Tom Nairn assailed what they saw as the romanticised, heroic view of the working class portrayed by Thompson. In its place, they offered an interpretation of working-class history as determined by the ruling class. The politicisation of labour in the Chartist movement was a 'premature' development; it occurred in the absence of a Jacobin tradition from which it could learn because since the Civil War the bourgeoisie had been absorbed into the cultural hegemony of the aristocracy. This unfractured ruling class offered labour no alternative model of politics but to replicate bourgeois culture in its own culture and politics.[6]

Throughout much of the 1960s and 1970s this view stood essentially isolated as a theorisation of working-class history. But it may not be coincidental that as the political climate began to change in the late 1970s, a highly charged debate on the theoretical basis of Thompson's work revived the themes that underlay Anderson and Nairn's original critique.[7] At more or less the same time a parallel – though not dependent – shift in the emphasis of empirical research began to be manifest. A revived debate on the labour aristocracy, for example, questioned its adequacy as an explanation of working-class reformism, and came to revolve entirely around the relative importance of the external and internal structures that ensured the subordination of the working class. The vulnerabilities of the working class to capitalist domination in industry and to bourgeois cultural hegemony began to be stressed as the main determinant of the nature of the working-class social and political presence. Alastair Reid, for example, pointed out that defeat was the normal condition of the working class which could be attributed to the sectionalist fragmentation that was a general characteristic of the class.[8] The absence of a genuinely class politics followed from this natural tendency towards social and industry disunity.

In addition, a renewed attention to the historical processes of work yielded ambiguous results. Whilst it could be shown that conflicts over job control were an important influence on the nature of production relations, exactly how to assess their meaning remained problematic. It could be argued that these conflicts possessed limited scope, were apolitical, did not contradict the 'real subordination' to capitalist domination and, finally, did not signify a uniquely militant property of the rank and file.[9] Labour's vulnerability in the labour process encouraged tendencies within the working class which made co-operation as equally characteristic as conflict within the structure of class relations. In a powerful study of mid-nineteenth century Lancashire textile workers, Patrick Joyce argued that social relations were dominated by paternal reciprocities with employers. A total subordination at the work-place and the replication of the factory hierarchy in the structures of the working-class family led the modern factory working class to internalise a paternalistic conception of class relations. Co-operation rather than the opposition of class consciousness and conflict thus came to characterise class consciousness.[10] The conclusion that might fairly be drawn from all this, therefore, was that the peculiarities of the British working class followed quite naturally from the social and economic structures of the subordination that conditioned class formation.

By the early 1980s the direction of labour historiography no longer seemed certain. An impasse had emerged between those who – to oversimplify – saw the dynamic of labour in society as a function of its oppositional tendencies and those who saw it as determined by its openness to subordination. This impasse was not merely a reflection of different kinds of evidence, nor of how that evidence should be read; neither was it a function of different conceptual approaches – both sides rooted their explanations in the details of economic and social structure. The impasse lay more in the fact that both flowed from the same teleology. Implicitly or explicitly, the defining paradigm of labour history remained its failure to fulfil an expected trajectory. Originally defined by Marx, this trajectory did not necessarily have to be conceived of as a revolutionary process, but it did assume some kind of social and political progression that would proceed in a linear way, driven by class attributes and consciousness. The fact that this can be shown to have happened in a way that is full of contradictions and inadequacies remained the problem to be explained. Those who emphasised the attributes of class solidarity in labour's history tended to seek explanation in the obstacles and difficulties that have dogged the realisation of this goal – the obstacles presented by the nature of class formation, or the stultifying effects of an ideology of labourism, for example. On the other side, those who rejected the very assumptions of 'class' as generally conceived may point to the fact that the structures of class and class consciousness – its sectionalism, for example – are themselves major impediments to the working class's exercising an autonomous power and influence. Powerful arguments may be mustered in support of both sides, but labour history will remain in this contradictory state unless the divergencies can be reconciled into a synthesis that transcends the various limitations of each. What is to be done?

Considerations of this sort have led to the search for new procedures and assumptions. Much of this revisionism remains implicit because great emphasis has been directed towards an empirical erosion of common assumptions rather than the development of new paradigms. But a book of essays by Gareth Stedman Jones may serve as one example of an attempt to evolve a new angle of vision. Like most labour historians, Jones traditionally operated within a framework that emphasised the importance of understanding labour's history in terms of its social base. His early work was concerned to explain the links between working-class action and the structures of working-class life. In particular, he was concerned to address the 'gulf between the predictions of the Marxist explanatory model and the actual assumptions that appear to have guided the activities of the groups of workers with whom I was concerned'. But the difficulties he encountered in explaining the cultural, political or ideological formations of labour in the context of social determination have led him to admit disillusionment with the procedure itself. A more fruitful line of approach, Jones now suggests, is to reverse the explanatory priorities and approach social being through the discourses of the language of politics itself.[11] Since Jones has applied this procedure only to a study of Chartism and to a much shorter essay on the Labour Party, it is hard to know exactly how it can be used to reinterpret our understanding of labour's history. Jones's writings are always worth serious attention and there is considerable merit in his call for a better understanding of the dynamics of political relations. But in its current formulation it may be doubted whether it provides an adequate answer to the impasse that has developed.

Specific criticisms could be made of his conception of Chartism and the Labour Party as formations in some way detached from their social bases. In the light of recent research into the local origins of the Labour Party which show quite precisely how the timing of its emergence was closely related to economic and social changes, it hardly seems appropriate to describe the Party as a 'vacant centre . . . defined primarily from without'.[12] But this is secondary to the main weakness which lies in the way the procedure represents just another way of addressing the problem that first created the impasse. That is, the specific problem his procedure is designed to address remains the failure of the relationship between the economic and the political spheres of social being to result in a certain trajectory of labour history. In a sense it is curious that it is the fact of this link – at least *from* social base *to* politics – that is now being questioned, rather than reconceiving the nature of the relationship proposed by the original model. Thus, in place of seeking the answer to this question in the social structuring of labour's history, the answer is now to be sought in the elevation of politics both as the dominant category of analysis and as the determinant of social being itself. At its simplest, most basic level, then, what is being proposed is a reversal of priorities: labour historians should seek the meaning of labour history in the discourses of politics rather than in the structures of everyday life.

This book is an attempt to address the conceptual impasse of labour history in a different way. It cannot pretend to be anything more than a particular study which has been informed by an interest in how best to understand the broad course and dynamic of labour's history. The issues discussed in this introduction remain rough hewn and speculative. But they are intended to be suggestive of the general conceptualisations that underlie my purpose, which is to find a way of approaching labour history that will pay proper regard to its divergencies but still retain the notion that labour has been an agency in the making of its own history and in shaping the history of society. As I see it, there are four considerations relevant to that task.

First, it is necessary to try to avoid the teleology of writing labour history as either conforming to or deviating from a certain trajectory. This tendency has pervaded the historiography since its beginnings; it is not the perversion of a Marxist influence but was as much employed by the Webbs as by Lenin. In the work of the Webbs, for example, it took the fairly harmless form of writing the history of labour as the evolutionary product of a maturing consciousness and organisation which would eventually secure the trade unions a place as the functional representatives of labour in the society. Within this teleology (which, of course, reflected, in part, the Webbs' involvement in a main theme of their time) certain things were excluded and others included. The most obvious example is the way the history of organisation was placed at the centre of labour history. More debilitating are what might be called the Leninist assumptions that underlie much of the historiography. Lenin, it will be recalled, formulated a distinction between trade union and revolutionary consciousness in the context of an intra-party squabble.[13] But this distinction rapidly became attached to the historical analysis of labour as part of the explanation of why labour's history had failed to confirm the expectations originally placed upon it by Marx. Conceptually, this influence has been all-pervasive. The 'economism' of trade-union consciousness implied a view of the historical logic of labour's action that left no choice between consistent opposition and revolutionary consciousness and a purely reactive function to capitalist strategies and economic imperatives. An alternative typology – apart from the alternative of no typology – within which one can understand the engagement of labour in the historical process has not been forthcoming. This problem was not resolved by Thompson whose concentration on the way the working class made its own history did not address how this labour presence had influenced, for example, the course of economic progress or the structuring of social relations. Indeed, it must be said that the main theoretical trends have been to reinforce the conceptual trap expressed by Lenin.

As an example we turn again to Gareth Stedman Jones and review the main argument of his article on working-class culture and politics at the end of the nineteenth century.[14] Like most commentators, Jones saw the reconfiguration of social and political relations during this period as a defensive reflex by labour to an aggressive and rampant capitalism. But he went even further than writers like Henry Pelling who tended to view this response simply as an instrumental reaction by the trade unions to the employers' counterattack; for Jones it was structurally rooted in the nature of working-class culture. Although there had been a time when this culture (and he was particularly concerned with London) had been oppositional, a series of developments in the mid-nineteenth century created an impermeable but conservative, defensive and consolatory culture. Within this context, nothing could make a difference: 'The rise of the new unionism, the foundation of the Labour Party, even the emergence of socialist groups marked not a breach but a culmination of this defensive culture.'[15] This profoundly pessimistic view of the process of social and political change has largely gone unremarked – in this version even the socialist societies were butterflies caught in the web of capitalist hegemony. But the main thrust of the argument is to insist that the vulnerabilities of labour ensure a historical determination that lies in initiatives from groups and forces outside the working class. The logic of this position is that the working class is an agency only in its own subordination. What I shall argue in this particular case is that the events of the late nineteenth century can indeed be understood as a remaking of the working class, but one in which labour's role was active and not merely reactive. This requires some emphasis.

Whilst this book is not specifically about class formation, I have been led to think about how it should be conceived. I see the process of class formation as an ongoing process, not as one that is finite. One of my implicit theses is the way class formation is constantly being remade. This is true both at the social structural level – by which I mean the divisions in class structure – and at the level of social relationships. It is both helpful and factually accurate for historians to periodise this process because particular characteristics do predominate at certain periods. But the emergence of a different configuration of class structures and relations is a process in which the prior formations – those that are being decomposed – continue to inform and condition the character of the new. This book pays more attention to the relationships that mark these different stages than it does to the precise ways in which the social structural features are different. In part, this is because much research remains to be done in this latter area. But it is mainly because of my belief that labour history needs to place at the centre of its concern the active processes that conditioned labour's relationship to the making of the history of society. I also believe that this must be done without slipping into a typology whose categories of analysis tend to be idealist and external to the historical process, which leads to my second general point.

In order to avoid such a typology it is necessary to move away from the post-Thompsonian focus upon the autonomous internalities of working-class history and toward an approach that attempts to link the various levels of experience not only within the working class but also between the class and 'society'.[16] A major part of this effort must obviously be to readdress the conception of the relationship between social base and politics. It is now fashionable to reject the vulgar assumption of a directly readable and determinant relationship between economics and politics in favour of their 'relative autonomies'. But this healthy tendency has gone too far; it has discouraged attempts to deploy empirical historical material in order to describe how linkages may be understood. This still remains a critical question for labour historians not only because of the actual situation of the subjects of their studies, but also because the way labour history is read depends largely upon how this relationship is conceived. The approach taken in this book places particular attention upon the way the disruptions of prior orderings of social relations serve to alter political possibilities. The advantage of this conception is that it seems to be a way of reconciling the relationship between economics and politics without assigning an absolute primacy to either. It allows for the role of structural change without denying the 'autonomy' of politics. Part of the problem, however, has been our conceptions of what is required for changes in political structures to occur.

One of the key criticisms that can be raised against reading politics from social bases is the argument that structural change proceeds slowly with ambiguity and is, therefore, seldom consistent with shifts in political relations. Indeed, it may be the case that 'structure' remains the same while political perceptions undergo radical change. But if structure remains unchanged, social relationships may still be disrupted.[17] Aside from major external disruptions such as wars, for example, minor alterations in production such as changes in plant layout or method of wage payment may be enough to disrupt a prior structure of social relations and demand a renegotiation of their organisation and mediation. On a more general level, changes in 'structure' may turn out to be changes primarily in the *nature* of production. The initial process of proletarianisation during industrialisation, for example, is now increasingly seen more as an alteration in market relations than as a reordering of the means and methods of production.[18] Clearly such changes alter relationships both within the working class and between the working class and other groups even if they leave the economic structure – the tools of production, place of production, hierarchy of production – unchanged in their essence. Other influences have the same effects. The 'abdication of the governors' from their paternal responsibility in the early nineteenth century, or the retreat of the patrician élites from town government in the late nineteenth century altered social relations and obliged their reordering. Such changes will inevitably spill over into politics, especially because they usually tend to cluster together. In the nineteenth century, they did so first at the local level because they were essentially a local phenomenon – even though they could coalesce to assume a national aspect, as in Chartism or Labour Party politics. In the twentieth century, the disruption of social relations frequently involved state intervention – as during the First World War or the 1960s and 1970s – which inevitably brought them into the political debate. But whatever the exact process, shifts in the bases of social relations inescapably involve questions of how power, authority and hierarchy are to be organised, mediated and represented. And it is at this point that 'politics' enters, for such matters are political questions. The ultimate nature of that politics does not assume a predetermined course – the consequence of the disruptions of the 1970s was populist conservatism – and will owe much to Jones's political discourses which may themselves change perceptions of social being. But it is when these changes in social relations come together with a widespread debate about how social being should be represented in politics that structures of political relations change.

If the formation of social and political relations is neither the product of a predetermined teleology nor a reflex of social base, it is, nevertheless (and this is my third point) a process that reflects the active engagements of labour. This engagement takes a variety of forms, but it is the actual *process* that must be the key focus of historians. As I see it, this process is not to be comprehended by teleologies that presume a predestined course for labour history, nor by the application of such abstract notions as a 'class acting for itself'. A more useful approach is to see it as resulting from a negotiation between what is demanded of labour and what labour is willing or able to accept or reject. The dimensions of this bargaining have varied enormously over time. And, furthermore, it is largely a sectional process in which different groups participate not according to some clear common end but in the context of the particular circumstances they face. Each resulting set of broad compromises creates contradictions and tensions of its own which influences later stages of the process. Thus, in the early and mid-nineteenth century, the need to mobilise labour to serve the demands of an expanding economy was partially met by the development of structures that represented a 'paternal' expression of social relations. Such a system represented a reciprocal negotiation between what capital could reasonably expect to secure given the techniques of social control at its disposal and the aspirations of labour to an 'independence' from domination that was amply demonstrated in the great social movements of the early nineteenth century. But the compromise thus reached conditioned the possibilities for changing social relations in the late nineteenth century as the system became obsolete. This occurred at a variety of social and political levels. My focus is on the sphere of production where the mid-Victorian compromise created obstacles to changes employers wanted to make in the labour process. But the net effect was to set in motion a dynamic between older structures, new initiatives and workers' responses that conditioned the emergence of the new configuration of political and social relations associated with the 'rise of labour'. The end result was to change the dimensions of the relationship of labour in society to create the enduring problem of the twentieth century: how should that relationship be expressed in labour politics and what role should labour play in the determination of national politics?[19]

Finally, my fourth point: it follows from the above that the process that creates the structuring of labour's relationship to society is composed of inherently ambiguous and contradictory elements. Categories of analysis such as class consciousness and subordination, co-operation and conflict, hegemony and independence are not only all useful and complementary categories of analysis, but they are also historically determined and not universal abstractions. The tendency of the historiography has been to place them either in opposition to each other or to treat them as something external to the history itself. But in fact it is the presence of differing quantities and types of 'subordination' and 'resistance', of 'class consciousness' and 'class co-operation', of 'hegemonical' influences and 'independence', that composes the character of the wider structures of social relations. And it is the tension and friction within these formations that provides them with their dynamic quality, so that, rather than being fixed, immutable expressions of equilibrium, they are in an almost constant state of movement and renegotiaton. The trick for the historian is to see how they operated as a process without losing sight of the historical transience of their particular forms.

To summarise the conception of labour history that underlies this book: the labour presence in society has worked through a constant series of negotiations and accommodations to create structures of social and political relations which themselves set the stage for a further series of negotiations and accommodations. It is through this process that labour has entered into the history of society. The advantages of this conception are threefold. First, it allows us to reconcile the divergent and contradictory aspects of that history which have formed the main points of contention within the historiography. Secondly, it is a conception that promises to break free of the stultifying hold of a teleology that, whatever its sophistication, ultimately reduces that history to a series of universal, absolutist categories of analysis. But, thirdly, it is also a conception of history that does not require us to retreat into a meaningless empiricism which would see no sense or dynamic to the course of that history. It has always been a strength of labour history to reject the idea that history is *merely* a series of unforeseen contingencies; it is just that labour history has been too long trapped in the wrong kind of model and prospectus.

Notes

1. Early attempts to formulate this problem may be seen in R. Price, 'Rethinking Labour History: The Importance of Work' in James Cronin and Jonathan Schneer (eds), *Social Conflict and the Political Order in Modern Britain* (London, 1981); Price, 'Structures of Subordination in Nineteenth-Century British Industry' in Geoffrey Crossick, Roderick Floud and Pat Thane (eds), *The Power of the Past: Essays in Honour of Eric Hobsbawm* (Cambridge, 1984); Price, 'The Labour Process and Labour History,' *Social History*, vol. 8, no. 1 (1983).

2. Eric Hobsbawm, 'The Labour Aristocracy' in Hobsbawm, *Labouring Men* (London, 1964); John Foster, *Class Struggle and the Industrial Revolution* (London, 1974); John Saville, 'The Ideology of Labourism' in Robert Benewick *et al., Knowledge and Belief in Politics* (London, 1973).

3. Geoffrey Crossick, *An Artisan Elite in Victorian Society* (London, 1978); Robert Gray, *The Labour Aristocracy in Victorian Edinburgh* (Oxford, 1976).

4. Patricia Hollis, *The Pauper Press* (Oxford, 1970); Trygve Tholfsen, *Working Class Radicalism in Mid-Victorian England* (London, 1976); F.E. Gillespie, *Labour and Politics 1850-67* (New York, 1966); Ralph Miliband, *Parliamentary Socialism* (London, 1965); David Coates, *The Labour Party and the Struggle for Socialism* (Cambridge, 1975).

5. Duncan Gallie, *In Search of the New Working Class* (Cambridge, 1978).

6. Perry Anderson, 'Origins of the Present Crisis', *New Left Review*, no. 23 (1964); Tom Nairn, 'The English Working Class', *New Left Review*, no. 24 (1964).

7. Richard Johnson, 'Edward Thompson, Eugene Genovese, and Socialist-Humanist History', *History Workshop Journal*, no. 6 (1978); Keith McClelland, 'Some Comments on Richard Johnson, "Edward Thompson, Eugene Genovese,

and Socialist-Humanist History" ', *History Workshop Journal*, no. 7 (1979); Gavin Williams, 'In Defense of History', *History Workshop Journal*, no. 7 (1979); Simon Clarke, 'Socialist Humanism and the Critique of Economism', *History Workshop Journal*, no. 8 (1979); Gregor McLennan, 'Richard Johnson and His Critics, Towards a Constructive Debate', *History Workshop Journal*, no. 8 (1979); Richard Johnson, 'Against Absolutism' in Raphael Samuel (ed.), *People's History and Socialist Theory* (London, 1981); Edward Thompson, 'The Politics of Theory' in Samuel, *People's History;* Thompson, *The Poverty of Theory* (London, 1979); Perry Anderson, *Arguments within English Marxism* (London, 1980).

8. H.F. Moorhouse, 'The Political Incorporation of the British Working Class: An Interpretation', *Sociology*, vol. 7 (1973); Moorhouse, 'On the Political Incorporation of the British Working Class: A Reply to Gray,' *Sociology*, vol. 9 (1975); Moorhouse, 'The Marxist Theory of the Labor Aristocracy', *Social History*, vol. 3, no. 1 (1978); Moorhouse, 'History, Sociology and the Quiescence of the British Working Class: A Reply to Reid', *Social History*, vol. 4, no. 3 (1979); Alastair Reid, 'Politics and Economics in the Formation of the British Working Class: A Response to H.F. Moorhouse', *Social History*, vol. 3, no. 3 (1978); Reid, 'Response', *Social History*, vol. 4, no. 3 (1979); Robert Gray, 'The Political Incorporation of the Working Class', *Sociology*, vol. 9 (1975); Gareth Stedman Jones, 'Class Struggle and the Industrial Revolution', *New Left Review*, no. 90 (1975); Jones, 'Working-class Culture and Working-class Politics in London 1870-1900: Notes on the Remaking of a Working Class', *Journal of Social History*, vol. 7, no. 4 (1974).

9. Richard Price, *Masters, Unions and Men: Work Control in Building and the Rise of Labour 1830-1914* (Cambridge, 1980); Mike Holbrook-Jones, *Supremacy and Subordination of Labour. The Hierarchy of Work in the Early Labour Movement* (London, 1982); Michael Burawoy, *Manufacturing Consent* (Chicago, 1979); Jonathan Zeitlin, 'Trade Unions and Job Control: A Critique of Rank and Filism', unpublished paper, Birkbeck College, University of London, 1982.

10. Patrick Joyce, *Work, Society and Politics. The Culture of the Factory in Later Victorian England* (Brighton, 1980); Joyce, 'Labour, Capital and Compromise: A Response to Richard Price', *Social History*, vol. 9, no. 1 (1984); Richard Price, 'Conflict and Cooperation: A Reply to Patrick Joyce', *Social History* vol. 9, no. 2 (1984); and Joyce, 'Languages of Reciprocity and Conflict: A Further Response to Richard Price', *Social History*, vol. 9, no. 2 (1984).

11. Gareth Stedman Jones, *Languages of Class. Studies in English Working Class History 1832-1982* (Cambridge, 1983), pp. 7-8.

12. Ibid., pp. 22-3; David Howell, *British Workers and the Independent Labour Party 1886-1910* (Manchester, 1983); K. Laybourn and Jack Reynolds, *Liberalism and the Rise of Labour 1890-1918* (London, 1984). See also John Foster, 'The Declassing of Language', *New Left Review*, no. 150 (1985).

13. S. and B. Webb, *History of Trade Unionism* (London, 1902); Industrial *Democracy* (London, 1913); V.I. Lenin, *What Is To Be Done?* (New York, 1973), p. 14. Jones, *Languages of Class*, pp. 179-238.

15. Jones, *Language of Class*, p. 237; Henry Pelling, *A History of British Trade Unionism* (Harmondsworth, 1976), pp. 123-8; Standish Meacham, *A Class Apart. The English Working Class 1890-1914* (Cambridge, Mass.,1977).

16. This effort is now underway; see James Cronin, *Labour and Society 1918-1979* (London, 1984).

17. Jones, *Languages of Class*, pp. 10-11; Margot Stein, 'The Meaning of Skill: The Case of French Engine-Drivers 1837-1917', *Politics and Society*, vol. 8, nos. 3-4 (1978).

18. Ronald Aminzade, 'Reinterpreting Capitalist Industrialization: A Study of Nineteenth Century France', *Social History*, vol. 9, no. 3 (1984), which

confirms the drift of Clive Behagg's findings quoted later in this book and soon to be published as *Politics and Production in Early Industrial Society*.

19. Keith Middlemas, *Politics in Industrial Society* (London, 1979).

1 ECONOMIC CHANGE AND PROLETARIANISATION 1780-1850

The Economic Process of Industrialisation

The legacies of the past dominated Britain's modern economic development from its very beginnings.[1] A prolonged and protracted gathering of the forces of industrial capitalism ensured that change was generated through traditional modes of production and accommodated within a social structure whose most important aspects were its continuities. The dynamic of economic growth in the period of industrialisation and urbanisation was as much – perhaps more – a function of expanding outworking hand-labour production than it was the consequence of 'machinofacture'. The extent to which Britain was peculiar in this respect could be a matter of debate. It seems reasonable to suggest that 'primitive' forms of production played a larger role in the process than they did elsewhere. But whether this is true or not, it is increasingly evident that the popular teleology of economic development as a growing sophistication in organisational forms, driven by the relentless logic of technology and expansion, needs to be rethought.

The superiority of one kind of economic technique or organisational form over another is not inherent. The adoption of particular technologies is the product of a complicated blending of the appropriate social, market and technical possibilities. The choice of technique is a matter of social decision-making, not the inevitable result of the technology itself. A trend to concentration in modern industry remains only a trend and, at the very least, tends to generate further segments of small-scale units of production. Thus, it is not the case that the archaic structures of production are residuals, doomed to be replaced. More likely, the process of economic change proceeds through a dynamic recreation of the mix between archaic and modern forms at each stage and within each stage of development. Outworking and domestic work exist within modern industry not as islands of the past but as integral to the core spheres of high technology and concentrated production. As a result of the essentially variegated nature of economic development, the nature of social relations within capitalist forms of production may similarly be marked by anomalies and contraditions. The second serfdom in Eastern Europe and the slave society of the southern United States illustrate how pre-capitalist structures of social relations may be perfectly capable of producing for capitalist economic relations.[2]

Britain's industrial revolution presents itself as one variant of this general pattern of economic and social development. It was able to take advantage of the growing pull of expanding markets in the eighteenth century because it possessed a long experience of 'organic' economic, social and political development. A literate, skilled and expanding labour force was available for industrial production, even if it was not fully acculturated to its disciplinary imperatives. Significant segments of the aristocracy and bourgeoisie were united in the pursuit of wealth maximisation and at least since the late sixteenth and early seventeenth centuries had joined together in commercial enterprise. From the mid-seventeenth century, the state willingly subordinated its foreign policy almost entirely to commercial ends. Except for the American War of Independence, all the wars of the eighteenth century were generated by the drive to carve out a market supremacy.[3]

By the time industrialisation occurred, Britain had conquered her markets and was largely devoid of external competitive pressures – as opposed to the pressure to satisfy those markets. These facts present a major point of contrast with later industrial revolutions. Elsewhere, the process had to be more actively forced and protected against the imperialism of Britain's free trade. This role was usually assumed by the state. In Prussia the drive to catch up with Britain began in the 1840s as a deliberate policy. The first ironworks and railways were essentially funded with state capital.[4] Thus, in other countries the drive to modernise was intimately associated with the necessity to secure markets and to utilise the most effective technical and organisational forms. By the late nineteenth century the contrasts between Britain and her major competitors in this respect were only too evident.

The accelerating pull of domestic and foreign markets in the eighteenth century could be adequately supplied without a wholesale reorganisation of the technical or organisational bases of British industry. The centres of innovation in technology and organisation were limited and narrowly based. Factory mechanisation was only one means by which the redeployment of capital and labour could occur to satisfy expanding domestic and world markets.[5] These had long been satisfied by 'proto-industrial' forms and in many cases continued to be served in this way. The cotton-spinning factory was correctly seen as a portent of the future, but it remained the only true factory industry throughout the initial period of industrialisation. Naturally, the fact that factories and machinery were successfully fused in this period was of enormous significance. Their contribution to growth statistics was out of all proportion to the scale of their presence. But it is well to remember that the historical experience of industrialisation was not one dominated by futuristic elements of production. And recent work in economic history is providing growing support for a view that places continuity and ambiguity at the centre of the industrialising process.

Growth was primarily market-driven; it was less a sudden spurt into take-off and more a function of steady acceleration throughout the second half of the eighteenth century. Capital formation was not only exceedingly primitive (though effective) but also occurred at the relatively low level of about 7 per cent of national income per annum. Only in the 1830s does it seem to have edged above 10 per cent, which was way below the 30 per cent figure reached in subsequent industrial revolutions. Similarly, the contribution of the 'leading sectors' to production should not be overemphasized. In the 1780s, the cotton- and iron-making industries contributed perhaps 3 per cent of manufacturing income. As late as the 1840s iron, cotton and steam power generated less than 25 per cent of income from manufacturing. Even the contribution of the steam engine – symbol of the technology of the first industrial revolution – needs to be kept in proper perspective. In 1800, 50 per cent of all stationary steam engines were used in mining and, as von Tunzelmann has shown, slow diffusion did not decisively alter the nature of production until at least 40 years into the nineteenth century. In the early 1860s, over a third of all textile factories used steam engines of less than 20 horse power and, as late as 1870, the textile industry alone used half of all steam power in manufacturing industry. Water power was finally displaced as the prime energy source only in the 1870s.[6]

In addition, the well-known persistence of small-scale units of production bears repeating. In 1838, the average size of engineering factories in the heartland of the Northwest remained under 100 employees. The same was broadly true of the textile factories in the 1840s where the early dominance of the single-process weaving and spinning firms established the pattern of textile industrial organisation for the rest of the century. The woollen industry retained its links with artisan production throughout the century. Large mills were the exception, 'more typical was the multitude of workshops, small mills and mill tenancies. Many were not factories in the proper sense, but processed materials for independent clothiers for a commission.' The worsted industry, on the other hand, grew in the 'classic' pattern of merchant capitalists becoming factory owners.[7] Outworking and sub-contracting proliferated in the period of industrialisation, reinforcing this pattern of small-scale organisation. Indeed, these were the truly typical organisational forms of the process of industrialisation. As late as 1830, outworking handloom weavers 'outnumbered all the men and women in spinning and weaving mills of cotton, wool and silk combined'. This expansion of outworking was not confined to textiles. The nail, chain-making, boot and shoe, and tailoring trades, to take just a few obvious examples, continued to be organised in this manner until the end of the century. Thus, as E.P. Thompson has pointed out:

> The characteristic industrial worker worked not in a mill or factory but . . . in a small workshop or in his own home, or . . . in a more or less casual employment in the streets, on building sites, on the docks.[8]

Work that was located in small-scale establishments generally also meant the predominance of hand labour; or, at most, the utilisation of a hand-driven, ancilliary piece of machinery. In the conditions of the period, of course, relatively primitive mechanical devices could be used to achieve impressive gains in output. But it is worth noting that contemporary economists in the eighteenth century, and into the early nineteenth century, tended to place most emphasis upon the division of labour as the source of productivity. There was considerable uncertainty about the moral or technical benefits to be derived from advanced technologies. And this debate within political economy was not resolved until the economist McCullogh 'chastised [Adam] Smith for giving all his attention to the division of labour and neglecting the breakthrough constituted by machinery'. It was left to the political economists of the 1830s and 1840s 'to integrate the machine and capitalist accumulation into their vision of economic progress'.[9]

The contributions of capital, labour and technology to the expansion of output in this period are very difficult to measure, in spite of the heroic efforts of recent economic historians. But it does seem clear that the contribution of labour-saving devices should not be overestimated. The doubling of investment over the last 50 years of the eighteenth century left the capital-labour ratio unaltered until about 1830, suggesting an enormous growth of hand labour. It has been estimated that until about 1860 over 50 per cent of the growth of production derived from the non-mechanised sectors of the economy. The building industry, for example, continued to contribute more to net capital formation than factory textiles. If no mechanised sector had existed, income per head would still have grown from £11 in 1780 to £22 in 1860: the additional contribution of machinery added another £6 to the latter figure. Even productivity rates did not differ sharply between sectors. The non-mechanised sector grew at 0.65 per cent per year until 1860; iron and woollens (which by 1860 was mechanised) grew by 0.9 per cent per year; coastal and foreign shipping grew by a large 2.3 per cent – but this industry still awaited the arrival of the modern steamship; and cotton textiles, the big exception, grew by 2.6 per cent per year.[10]

Whatever the precise balance of the various 'inputs', the fact remains that hand labour continued to reign supreme in the execution of production. Even in cotton and engineering – the two clear examples of machinofacture – the handicraft skills of the machine minder and turner were essential to the effective use of the machine. Indeed, machines often proved to be less efficient than hand labour. Charles Babbage told of a machine to point pins that was only one-fifth as efficient as handwork. In addition, machine production created an enormous demand for ancillary services performed by an increasingly specialised hand-labour force. The preparatory and finishing processes in textiles and the iron trades were examples of the peripheral sector of handwork to the mechanised factory core. The expansion of economic activity reverberated to the sound of the carpenter's hammer, the miner's pickaxe and the navvy's shovel.[11] In truth, the industrial revolution can best be understood as the vast expansion of prior modes of production and the large-scale redeployment of labour and capital within those modes.

This is not to suggest that the successful marriage of factory organisation and technology and the resolution of the social difficulties that had accompanied earlier experiments in the concentration of labour were insignificant. It would be foolish to deny the economic significance of these developments and it would be equally obscurantist to ignore their impact upon contemporaries as clear harbingers of the future. At a time when the exact course of that future remained a matter of doubt, however, the true significance of the factory and technology lay to a large degree in the way they epitomised but one version of expanding economic structures; they did not totally describe those structures. As Thompson has pointed out, for over 50 years after the technical and organisational breakthrough of the cotton mill, its workers remained a minority within the cotton industry. The threat and promise of the industrial revolution was the direct dependence of man upon machine; but this was not the dominant way the nexus of dependence was altered by the immediate experience of industrialisation. Indeed, a consideration of the process of proletarianisation during the industrial revolution will further emphasise the importance of continuities in the structures of economic and social relations.

The Process of Proletarianisation

The relationship between the history of labour before the industrial revolution and its subsequent development remains to be fully explored. But it is obvious that the structural formation of the working class was in progress long before industrialisation. As a class of workmen, for example, coal miners were a creation of the late sixteenth and early seventeenth centuries. Only very rarely did they contract as a group to mine the coal themselves; they were wage labourers from the beginning. And, as Rab Houston has recently demonstrated, the structure of labour relations, managerial strategies and industrial conflict remained essentially unchanged between the late 1600s and the early nineteenth century.[12] By the late eighteenth century, at the latest, wage labour was the dominant form of labour payment but it was frequently tied to a diversity of occupational tasks. A major unit of production remained the household, with women and children the main source of labour in the domestic system; and dual labour activity provided a degree of 'independence' from total reliance upon wage employment. Coal miners, again, worked at most eight hours a day and, like the Lancashire weavers, usually had access to small-holdings. Similarly, in the urban industrial crafts, the wage was not a purely monetary phenomenon but supplemented by a host of customary non-monetary benefits. The tailors got their 'cabbage,' the shipyard workers their 'chips' (sometimes amounting to enough to build small houses), the weavers claimed their 'thrums'.[13]

More centrally, perhaps, the separation of the worker from his or her product was well established. This was true both in terms of access to the supply of raw materials and to the product market. This was a long and fractured process which has yet to be properly explored by historians. But it is likely that the mid- to late seventeenth century was a key period. By 1681, for example, the appearance of the retail, shopkeeping tailor was deplored as a new development in London. By the early eighteenth century the London tailor was a lifelong wage earner with a well-established network of union-controlled houses of call to co-ordinate employment with the labour market. The central economic fact of social relations was the progressive tightening of this dependence upon market relations beyond the influence or control of either the urban craftsman, the rural artisan or the rural labourer. The threat of the machine was seen as lying less in the way it made labour into a mere appendage and more in the way it promised to accentuate the commodity status of labour. The agitation for reduced hours by the weavers and spinners in the 1830s, for example, was designed to stabilise the market conditions under which production was carried on against the threatened extension of the working day demanded by the machine.[14] To that extent, these movements were essentially continuous with the efforts of eighteenth-century artisans to regulate the market conditions of work through, for example, control of the labour supply by apprenticeship.

But if the objective conditions of production before the industrial revolution created a class that worked according to the rhythm of capitalism, the nature of its consciousness was quite distinctive. As Thompson has pointed out, eighteenth-century social relations revolved around 'class struggle without class' precisely because the economic forms of capitalism co-existed with reciprocities, obligations, cultural and social relationships that were customary and traditional in character. Some of these continued to be expressed in institutional forms, such as the dying practice of wage regulation by Justices of the Peace and the mediation of social relations through the law. When these reciprocities broke down they were frequently reasserted by crowd actions or, in the case of artisans, by efforts to restore their political and structural integrity. It was this broad structure of social relations that the industrial revolution decomposed. But, it did so by the enormous expansion of the traditional modes of production and by a consequent accentuation of structures of dependency whose elements were already visible by the late seventeenth century. Thus, the process of proletarianisation – of increasing dependence upon the dictates of capitalist relations – was not primarily a matter of subordination to a labour process that was technically driven. Rather, it was a process that occurred more in the sphere of market relations and involved an increased exposure to the vagaries of market forces. The process was essentially the same as it had been in the eighteenth century. The significance of the industrial revolution for labour, however, was that it marked the crescendo to the vast expansion of market demand (foreign trade increased by 800 per cent between 1780 and 1800) which finally shattered the remaining restraints of market regulation. There were three essential methods by which this increased dependency upon market relations was achieved: a closing of the access to markets, an extended specialisation of labour, and the related incursion of excess labour into an expanded labour market.

The growing gulf between workers and capitalists was represented less by the factory and more in those trades which continued to be organised on the putting-out system. This was illustrated by the nail trade, which in the later eighteenth century came to be increasingly dominated by the ironmongers' control over the supply and marketing of goods. It was during this period that the hated middleman fogger emerged to serve as intermediary between the urban ironmongers and the mainly rural small masters and artisans. Technical change was non-existent, but the growing competitiveness and specialisation of product markets encouraged an equivalent specialisation of labour and a consequent dependence upon the fogger for access to work and market. The balance of power had earlier rested in favour of the nailing smiths. It was a common complaint in the early eighteenth century that nailors would not respond to pressure from London wholesalers to reduce their prices, but by the 1790s, 'the workmen were less able to bargain with their employers than they had been in 1700. They were more dependent than before upon a single source of income and therefore had to work on any terms they could get.'[15]

This was a common experience in the second half of the eighteenth century. In hosiery, the growing role and function of middlemen expanded greatly during this period. Seldom working for one hosier alone, they 'received yarn with orders to get certain goods made and generally distributed the work as [they] pleased, sometimes giving out direct to journeymen stockingers and sometimes to small masters who, in turn, shared it among their workers'. Middlemen often were involved in the growing grievance of frame rents. Although the practice of frame renting existed from the inception of the industry, it only became a dominant feature from the mid-eighteenth century. This would seem to have been due to the fact that access to the markets for independent craftsmen was increasingly problematic. Thus, even if a producer could afford the cost of the frame, the supply of work and its distribution still remained in the hands of middlemen. Ironically in these circumstances an independent producer was more exposed to market forces than the journeyman who rented his frame. The reasons for this had to do with the economics of frame renting and owning. Independent producers had to find work to amortise the capital investment; thus, they acted as a downward drag on prices. On the other hand, the hosiers were eager to keep their frames running even in times of depression; thus, journeymen who rented frames were more likely to be constantly employed during downturns in trade. But, of course, this only tied the journeyman into an even closer dependence upon the hosier or middleman. The latter usually collected the rent – adding a percentage for his trouble. Frame rents were the one dependable source of profits and so tended to increase from the late eighteenth century even though the cost of production was falling. The rent was deducted from the wage, and in depressions the tendency to spread the work thinly must have put stockingers in the position of being obliged to work for fear of severing their lifeline with middlemen, while failing to earn a sufficient wage to cover the frame rent.[16]

Small masters were also affected by these kinds of development. It is, of course, very difficult to distinguish clearly between the artisan and the small master during this period. The number of small masters almost certainly increased partly as a function of the proliferation of subcontracting. At the same time, however, the small master found himself increasingly an appendage of the large employer, dependent upon him for credit and work, increasingly drawn into a particular relationship due to the growing specialisation of products. The ideal of the independent artisan or small master was assiduously cultivated and sometimes used to force a 'discount' on the price of the product these 'independent' producers sold to the merchant capitalist. But, gradually, the ideal possessed less and less substance.

Control of credit was the central instrument by which small masters were brought into a dependency upon the large. The terms upon which credit would be given were determined by those who were able to extend long periods of collection and had ready access to the banking system. Small producers were obliged to buy in the dearest and sell in the cheapest markets to remain afloat from week to week. They were unable to compete effectively with the larger masters and were thus increasingly reduced to performing certain limited stages of production as subcontractors for the large. In addition, competition between the small employers for the work handed out by the large encouraged a lowering of standards and wages and the adoption of a tightened discipline in the workshops. Indeed, this was actively fostered by the large employers and their factors frequently inspected the small workshops to assess the disciplinary conditions as part of the determination of credit-worthiness. As Clive Behagg has pointed out, the reorganisation of work in the small iron trades of Birmingham, 'was primarily a function of the market rather than a direct product of the machine'.[17]

The increased dependence upon those who dominated the market relations of buying and selling both encouraged and reinforced the growing specialisation of labour. It is virtually impossible to say anything very definite about the details of this in the eighteenth century. But it was clearly an ongoing process which almost certainly intensified during the industrial revolution. The trade of watch-making in the late seventeenth and early eighteenth centuries was, perhaps, one of the first to experience the emergence of what Marx called 'the detailed labourer' and was a prototypical example of the way mass production could be achieved through an intense specialisation of function. By the mid-eighteenth century 'the division of the labour was such that hardly any journeyman could have produced a whole watch'. In 1795 one 'maker' manufacturer 'employed over 100 men making the separate components in their Camberwell garrets'. When depression occurred, competition within the overstocked labour markets relentlessly drove wages and conditions down. In 1817-18, for example, watchmakers who had previously earned as much as 30s. a week were soon forced to accept one-third of that and to receive poor relief.[18]

A similar process of specialisation occurred in the Coventry ribbon trade where the rise of a small master class after the Napoleonic Wars disrupted the stable regulation of conditions by mutually agreed price lists. Like small masters elsewhere, those in Coventry were dependent upon wholesalers for credit and they injected a more competitive element into the trade by their adoption of cost saving techniques. They took advantage of the repeal of the Statute of Apprentices to evade customary standards, pay below the list price and alter the division of labour. An innovative small master named John Day, for example, began to employ others at a weekly wage to perform certain processes he had never learnt. Within a few years he had ten looms working on this advanced division of labour and was employing women and girls on the unskilled jobs. The male artisans 'hated the division of labour because . . . it condemned them to continuous work by removing from their weaving the intervals of picking up'. The replacement of piece wages by a weekly wage undermined their previous independence by ensuring regular attendance at work. The slump of 1829 brought high unemployment and drew attention to these proletarianising techniques. A campaign of violence against Day was launched and was followed by the demolition of the first factory in 1831. By these means the ribbon weavers halted for a while the 'degradation' of their craft.[19] But the pattern of these events mirrored on a smaller scale the protracted and agonising decline of the hand-loom weavers.

The story of the hand-loom weavers has become the archetypal story of proletarianisation in the industrial revolution. From their golden days in the 1780s and 1790s – when it was said every weaver owned a gold watch and ate beef every day – the hand-loom weavers had been reduced by the 1830s to a pitiful state of dependence. This was achieved without the direct intervention of the machine, although by the 1830s competition from machine weaving completed the process of degradation. Proletarianisation was a complex process of interaction between a growing subdivision of labour stimulated by market demand in the 1770s and 1780s, the consequent expansion in the labour market, and the decisive appearance of the trade cycle pattern of boom and slump by the late 1790s. Booms encouraged the movement of labour into the trade and the abandonment of customary protections like apprenticeship. Slumps allowed standards and wages to be reduced through labour market competition and increased dependence upon single masters through frame-rent indebtedness. As in so many other cases, the extensive deflation that followed the Napoleonic Wars decisively shifted the balance of dependence in the industry. One observer remarked in 1844 that there was a time when

> manufacturers hired rooms in districts . . . and the employer inquired after the employed; but the case is now diametrically the opposite, the labourer not only undertakes long journeys in quest of work, but is doomed to many disappointments.[20]

By 1820 at the latest, hand-loom weaving was overstocked with labour. And this – our third method of proletarianisation – was a problem that confronted virtually all the craft-based artisan trades. The expansion of the labour supply was the product of the growth in population (which doubled between 1750 and 1820), the greater specialisation of labour and the break up of the household economy which sucked women and children into direct competition with men. The process of deskilling commonly associated with the machine, in fact, was more a product of the invasion of excess labour into the artisan labour process. Indeed, in this period, the machine tended to be more an agent of male reskilling than the reverse. Male cotton-spinners displaced female spinners as the new mules replaced the jenny and reduced women to the status of unskilled. Within the dominant handicraft trades, however, it was the pressure of the excess labour supply that posed the greatest challenge to standards and the artisan division of labour. Once the barriers against that pressure were breached, proletarianisation rapidly followed. In no trade was it so rapid, Thompson tells us, as in wool-combing.

Before 1825 high wages had attracted many new workers into the trade and led to the abandonment of apprenticeship restrictions. The traditional, haughty independence of the wool-combers was, perhaps, adopted by these newcomers because union organisation remained continuous from the 1740s until 1825. But a strike in the latter year turned into a showdown over union recognition, and after nearly six months the wool-combers were defeated and their independent status as artisan craft workers was transformed overnight into depressed, sweated home workers. As in so many other handicraft trades, wool-combing machinery was kept in reserve for 20 years, more as a threat to reduce conditions than a relentless instrument to alter the work process.[21]

A similar, though more protracted, series of events characterised the breaching of stable standards in the tailoring and shoemaking trades of London in the 1820s and 1830s. In tailoring, for example, the division between the honourable and dishonourable sections – the flints and the dungs – had existed since the mid-eighteenth century. But at least until the end of the Napoleonic Wars favourable market circumstances allowed co-operation between the two sections and the effective regulation of conditions which blocked the expansion of home- and piece-work. The repeal of apprenticeship legislation in 1814, however, caused a tightened division between the honourable and dishonourable divisions as the skilled sought to protect themselves behind restrictive union organisation. A wedge was driven between the two sections which subsequent efforts failed to bridge and which allowed the unorganised, dishonourable trade to expand rapidly sometime after 1824. Efforts to equalise conditions in both sections led to a major strike in 1834. When this failed, the determination of conditions by the overstocked dishonourable sections was assured and the honourable sections shrank back to a small and inconsequential bespoke West End trade.[22]

The story of the shoemakers followed a similar trajectory. By the mid-1820s the organised men were beginning to be surrounded by a sea of unorganised dishonourable labour. Their position was further weakened by the movement of the trade to the outworking districts of Northampton and Staffordshire to escape the restraints of the London artisans. It was in these latter districts, however, that a final stand was made against the determination of conditions by the overstocked tail of the labour market. In 1825 and 1831 efforts were made by the Northampton shoemakers to control the rural labour supply in the villages by county-wide union activity. And, inspired by Owenite unionism, an incipient national union was formed in 1834 with the same purpose. But its brief life was snuffed out in the subsequent débâcle of general unionism.[23]

We may assume that the structure of the handicraft trades detailed by Mayhew in the 1850s was essentially a product of the early years of the century. It would seem that the 1820s and early 1830s were a critical time for the triumph of an uncontrolled and vastly expanded labour-market structure – although the hatters did not experience the creation of a dishonourable section until the 1840s. The process itself, however, and the methods employed to create dependence upon a complex structure of middlemen, subcontractors and garret-masters were not peculiar to this period; they were familiar themes in eighteenth-century social relations. But this was a period when the final assault was made upon the standards and structures of artisan production and it was also the period when the remaining theory and practice of the regulation of market forces was decisively rejected and undermined. These were the elements that made these years revolutionary in their economic and social implications.

Notes

1. See the remarks of Eric Hobsbawm, *Industry and Empire* (London, 1968), pp. 47-8.

2. See J. Rubery and Frank Wilkinson, 'Outwork and Segmented Labour Markets' in Frank Wilkinson (ed.), *The Dynamics of Labour Segmentation* (London, 1981); Charles Sabel, *Work and Politics. The Division of Labour in Industry* (Cambridge, 1981); Jairus Banaji, 'Modes of Production in a Materialist Conception of History'. *Capital and Class*, no. 3 (Autumn 1977); Charles Sabel and Jonathan Zeitlin, 'Historical Alternatives to Mass Production', *Past and Present*, no. 105 (Autumn 1984).

3. Lawrence Stone, *The Crisis of the Aristocracy 1558-1641* (Oxford, 1967), pp. 173-8; see also Hobsbawm, *Industry and Empire*, pp. 27-33, on markets.

4. Barry Supple, 'The State and the Industrial Revolution 1900-1914' in Carlo Cipolla, *The Fontana Economic History of Europe. The Industrial Revolution* (London, 1973).

5. See the remarks of Charles Tilly, 'Flows of Capital and Forms of Industrialization in Europe 1500-1800', *Theory and Society*, vol. 12, no. 2 (1983).

6. C. Knick Harley, 'British Industrialization before 1841: Evidence of Slower Growth During the Industrial Revolution', *Journal of Economic History*, vol. 42, no. 2 (June 1982), pp. 267-8; Hobsbawm, *Industry and Empire*, pp. 56-7; Peter Mathias, *The First Industrial Nation* (New York, 1969), p. 17; Dolores Greenberg, 'Power Patterns of the Industrial Revolution: An Anglo-American Comparison,' *American Historical Review*, vol. 87, no. 2 (December 1982); Mike Holbrook-Jones, *Supremacy and Subordination of Labour* (London, 1982), pp. 32-3; G.N. von Tunzelmann, 'Technical Progress during the Industrial

Revolution' in Roderick Floud and D. McCloskey (eds), *The Economic History of Britain since 1700*, Vol. 1 (Cambridge, 1981), p. 158.

7. V.A.C. Gatrell, 'Labour Power and the Size of Firms in Lancashire Cotton in the Second Quarter of the Nineteenth Century', *Ec. Hist. Rev.*, vol. 30, no. 1 (1977); Holbrook-Jones, *Supremacy*, pp. 36-7; Pat Hudson, 'Proto-Industrialization: The Case of the West Riding Wool Textile Industry in the 18th and Early 19th Centuries', *History Workshop Journal*, no. 12 (Autumn 1981), p. 51.

8. E.P. Thompson, *The Making of the English Working Class* (New York, 1964), pp. 92-3, 234.

9. Hobsbawm, *Industry and Empire*, p. 44; Maxine Berg, *The Machinery Question and the Making of Political Economy 1815-48* (Cambridge, 1980), pp. 90, 94, 110-11, 125-6; Maxine Berg, Pat Hudson, and Michael Sonnenscher, *Manufacture in Town and Country before the Factory* (Cambridge, 1983), pp. 56-7; Berg, 'Proto-industry, Political Economy and the Division of Labour 1700-1800', unpublished paper, University of Warwick, 1982.

10. See essays by C.H. Feinstein and D. McCloskey in Floud and McCloskey, *The Economic History of Britain since 1700,* pp. 138, 114-16.

11. Raphael Samuel, 'The Workshop of the World: Steam Power and Hand Technology in Mid-Victorian Britain', *History Workshop Journal*, no. 3 (Spring 1977); Charles Babbage, *On the Economy of Machinery and Manufactures* (London, 1832), pp. 189-90.

12. J.U. Nef, *The Rise of the British Coal Industry*, Vol. 2, (London, 1932), Chapter 4; Rab Houston, 'Coal, Class and Culture: Labour Relations in a Scottish Mining Community 1650-1750', *Social History*, vol. 8, no. 1 (1983).

13. R.W. Malcolmson, *Life and Labour in England 1700-1800* (London, 1981), Chapter 2; John Rule, *The Experience of Labour in the Eighteenth Century* (London, 1980), pp. 14, 126-8; Maxine Berg, 'Domestic Manufacture, Women and Community in the Eighteenth Century,' unpublished paper, University of Warwick, April 1984.

14. S. and B. Webb, *The History of Trade Unionism* (London, 1920), pp. 26-7; C.R. Dobson, *Masters and Journeymen* (London, 1980), Chapter 3; Berg, *The Machinery Question*, pp. 233, 252.

15. Marie Rowlands, *Masters and Men in the West Midland Metal Ware Trade Before the Industrial Revolution* (Manchester, 1975), pp. 80, 82, 150-4, 160.

16. F.A. Wells, *The British Hosiery Industry* (London, 1935), pp. 72-8, 94, 96.

17. This account has drawn entirely upon Clive Behagg's unpublished manuscripts. 'The Transformation of the Small Producer', pp. 35-65, is soon to be published as *Politics and Production in Early Industrial Society*.

18. Rule, *The Experience of Labour*, pp. 35, 202-3.

19. Peter Searby, 'Paternalism, Disturbance and Parliamentary Reform: Society and Politics in Coventry 1819-32', *International Review of Social History*, vol. 22, no. 2 (1977).

20. Thompson, *Making of the English Working Class*, p. 287.

21. Ibid., pp. 282-3.

22. Ibid., pp. 255-7; T.M. Parsinnen and I.J. Prothero, 'The London Tailors' Strike of 1834 and the Collapse of the GNCTU: A Police Spy's Report', *International Review of Social History,* vol. 22, no. 2 (1977); Eileen Yeo and E.P. Thompson, *The Unknown Mayhew* (New York, 1971), pp. 181-228; James A. Schmiechen, *Sweated Industries and Sweated Labor* (Urbana, Ill., 1984), pp. 8-9.

23. M.J. Haynes, 'Class and Class Conflict in the Early Nineteenth Century: Northampton Shoemakers and the GNCTU', *Literature and History*, vol. 5 (April 1973); Thompson, *Making of the English Working Class*, pp. 254-5; Schmiechen, *Sweated Industries*, pp. 9-11.

2 SOCIAL RELATIONS AND THE INDUSTRIAL REVOLUTION 1780-1850

Regulation and Laissez-faire

The nexus of tension in social relations throughout the eighteenth and early nineteenth centuries lay in the growing conflict between the principles of regulation and laissez-faire in market relations. Eighteenth-century social conflict was a complicated phenomenon which is only just beginning to be properly understood. The most likely moment of conflict was the point at which the logic of capitalism threatened to breach customary standard traditions and relationships. Price riots and struggles over rationalised use of land were the characteristic forms of this clash between the innovations of market forces and the assertion of a 'moral economy' of reciprocal obligations and responsibilities.[1] The same pattern dominated the more purely industrial relations of production. But here efforts to resist the depredations of laissez-faire could be legitimated by the presence of a tradition of legal protection and regulation of the conditions of production and the operation of the labour market. It is increasingly clear that this framework was by no means moribund in the eighteenth century, although it would be an equal mistake to regard it as a thoroughly coherent system. The practice of wage setting by Justices of the Peace, for example, had long been regarded with some disfavour in certain quarters. But it did not enter its terminal degeneration until the 1760s. In this, as in other spheres, the law was deeply intertwined with social relations in the eighteenth century. The growing sophistication and professionalisation of the law reflected its central place as an arbiter in society generally. It was virtually the only formal institution for mediating the growing numbers of industrial conflicts and disputes. And the constant intervention of Justices in employer/employee relations rested on and legitimated the well-established tradition of legal regulation of the conditions of employment. Even while an Act of 1726 prohibited combination amongst woollen workers, for example, it reaffirmed the principle of wage assessment by Justices. Subsequent collective action by the weavers of the Southwest aimed at the enforcement of this regulation against the attempts of employers to wrestle free from its implications.[2] As late as 1773, collective bargaining through rioting by the

Spitalfields weavers secured an Act that regulated their trade along traditional lines. Similarly, the Speenhamland decision, which ensured a cheap labour reserve for agriculture, nevertheless reflected a tradition of regulation that stretched back to the Statute of Labourers of 1341.

This was a tradition that died hard. It was not drowned by the cold douches of utilitarian individualism or the intellectual power of political economy. In the Coventry ribbon trade, for example, the honourable masters joined with the union in 1828 and again in 1838 to urge the parliamentary regulation of wages, and well into the 1830s it was possible to mobilise public support to enforce the list prices on recalcitrant masters. Not until 1848 did respectable opinion in the town begin to withdraw its support of union efforts to regulate the trade. On the national level, the balance of political forces shifted uncertainly and slowly in favour of laissez-faire. As late as 1835-7, it was possible for John Fielden to introduce to Parliament a Minimum Wages Bill which would deny 'the worst paying [weaving] masters the power which they now possess of regulating wages'. Even after the wholesale removal of protection between 1809 and 1814, the political possibilities remained as open as they had during the eighteenth century. The lengthy campaigns of framework knitters to secure parliamentary protection were underpinned by the support they were able to muster in Parliament. In 1779, for example, a committee of the House of Commons had reported in favour of a Bill fixing wages, and as late as 1812 and 1818 there was a base of support in the House for the regulation of production quality. The failure of these initiatives eventually turned the knitters to Luddism. But the effort to extend or reinforce regulation cut across class lines and was capable of mobilising community support. Although the statutory basis for general regulation by the Framework Knitters Company had been repealed in 1753, the tradition of regulation was kept alive by both masters and men. In 1765, for example, Nottingham masters secured a Bill protecting them from lower-quality work from the West of England and in 1818 they joined Leicestershire manufacturers and artisans in petititioning Parliament against cut-ups. At the same time, the incursions of unskilled labour and the destruction of standards that followed the revocation of the Company charter stimulated union organisation amongst the knitters, whose object was to restore stability to the labour market through regulation of apprenticeship and the quality of production.[3]

Indeed, in this industry as elsewhere, the original impetus to unionisation was not to realise modern class relations, but to enforce the restoration of a prior political economy which regulated and arbitrated the balance of power between groups. In 1799, the Lancashire cotton-weavers unionised to reassert laws that 'were being trampled under foot' by manufacturers' attempts to extend further the length of the standard piece of cloth. A year later, a Bill was passed which allowed for the intervention of Justices to set wages and resolve disputes over delivery and quality of goods. Employer hostility made this system of arbitration inoperative and led weavers to press for a Minimum Wage Bill and then the enforcement of apprenticeship regulation. Parliament's response was to begin the wholesale repeal of regulatory legislation in 1809.[4]

Perhaps the single most important issue in this tension between regulation and laissez-faire was the question of apprenticeship controls. The Statute of Artificers of 1563 had been passed the better to ensure the proper employment of skilled labour. But by the end of the eighteenth century it had become the central symbol of protections that artisans believed had been theirs in past times and were especially needed now. The law itself had always been of questionable value. As early as 1590 complaints were being voiced against its restrictions. Blackstone had pronounced it 'bad law' and throughout the century the trend of decisions weakened its provisions. Trades that had arisen since 1563 were not covered by the statute and Parliament enacted a widening sphere of exemptions from its coverage. In 1777, for example, both the dyeing and hatting trades were removed from its purview. In addition, the indentured craft apprenticeship of seven years envisaged by the Act was in full retreat throughout the eighteenth century. As we have noted, the demand for labour and the growing specialisation of work led to the willing abandonment of apprenticeship standards in many trades. In others, by the end of the century, apprenticeship had already assumed its modern meaning of five years' working at the trade.[5]

The importance of the issue, however, derived from the deepening relationship between an uncontrolled labour supply and the degradation of standards and conditions. In framework knitting, for example, the moribund Company continued to bind apprentices – often drawn from parish paupers – as a source of cheap labour, working mainly for their board and lodgings. In 1753 a parliamentary enquiry revealed that the trade was already overstocked with labour and this condition was worsened by the expansion and mechanisation of the early nineteenth century when the knitters made an effort to restore apprentice regulation. The reassertion of apprenticeship or its extension to new trades was, therefore, a major response to the uncontrolled spread of market forces.

In the 1770s and 1780s, trades like the Essex shoemakers and Manchester silk-weavers endeavoured to re-establish 'good Queen Betty's law'. In 1750 the cotton-check weavers tried to secure a recognised apprenticeship ratio and, between 1759 and 1761, the needle-makers of Warwick and Worcester fought a two-year struggle to force the dismissal of 'illegal' men. There was a growing intensity to these efforts by the 1790s. Between 1790 and 1814 the issue provided the main nexus of a growing trade-union organisation and agitation, a trend that was reinforced by the passage of the Combination Acts in 1799 and 1800. Apprenticeship remained the one legal basis of organisation. Thus, although the artisans of London were the most active and vocal in the campaign for the restoration of apprenticeship standards, the issue had nation-wide appeal. The calico-printers, who for 20 years had been complaining justly about the overstocking of their trade with boy labour, agitated in 1803-4 for an Act that would reintroduce apprentice limitation. A few years later the wool-weavers petitioned for the proper enforcement of the Statute of Artificers. Both pleas fell on deaf ears. Sir Robert Peel pointed out that industrial progress demanded freedom. The cloth-makers, less loftily but more to the point, argued that these kinds of rules 'operated as positive impediments to the increase of hands and to the maintenance of that subordination which is the life of all manufacturers, and at present so much wanted in this important branch of commerce'.[6]

But with or without parliamentary support, there is little doubt that a generalised movement to reassert apprenticeship gathered force from 1800. In London, shipwrights and caulkers passed more stringent rules; the Macclesfield silk-weavers did the same. The courts were delivering a series of contradictory rulings. In 1805 the framework knitters launched a campaign of prosecutions and succeeded in a series of rulings which imposed penalities upon employers for any breach of the apprenticeship regulations of the Company. Since the Company had been moribund from 1753, this probably had little practical meaning. More serious was the concerted litigation brought by a trades committee in London between 1809 and 1812 which was generally successful in forcing findings against employers who contravened the law. The judges had no choice: these were all trades covered by the Statute of Artificers. But judicial unease was reflected in the light penalties they imposed and their refusal to find costs. In 1813 this led the committee to launch a nation-wide campaign to appeal to Parliament for a more effective law. Over 70 towns and 60 trades were represented in the final petition. The employers were pricked into action. Engineering masters took the lead. This was hardly surprising; the pressures of expansion in this trade were severely restrained by the effective labour monopoly exercised by the millwrights. But they were joined by the fellmongers and others who argued against the restraints that were imposed by the statute and pressed the disciplinary advantages that would flow from an unregulated labour supply. It was explained that 'under the influence of the pretended privileges given by this Act, many masters are not permitted to hire their own workmen . . . the "shop committee" must be applied to'.[7]

The subsequent repeal of the Statute in 1814 by no means decided the issue of a totally free labour market. But it did change the terms of the debate. First, as the culmination of a fierce tussle within and without Parliament, it signalled the abandonment by the state of any claims to regulate the conditions of production. This did not imply the triumph of laissez-faire as a consensus within the political élite. But it did mean that the state would offer no protection against market dependence. State policy was neither consistent nor coherent – being prepared to intervene in the question of the labour hours of women and children, for example – and exactly what policies the state pursued depended upon a variety of immediate political circumstances. But its general direction and posture moved more clearly towards promoting the conditions for labour-market competition than before, as the New Poor Law and the refusal to mitigate the hand-loom weaver's plight demonstrated.[8] As late as the 1820s, the threat of prosecution was still being successfully used to intimidate uninformed employers, but the statute could no longer form the moral basis for collective action. If regulation was desired, it would have to be sought by the solidarity of trade-union organisation and not by reference to a wider political economy.

And this leads to a second point. The repeal of the Statute of Apprentices probably did assist in the destruction of certain craft labour markets. The millwrights' division of labour, for example, was reported to have been decisively breached because of the repeal. But as that same example suggests, the consequence was not necessarily a proletarian degradation. In the expanding trades where it was not possible to create a thoroughly unskilled division of labour, reskilling occurred or old skills remained important enough to permit a persistence of apprentice rules. Thus, although the Webbs were wrong to suggest that apprenticeship from this point steadily declines to a mere residual, they were right to point to an essential change in its status. It could no longer be justified on the grounds of market stability, nor for its role in ensuring quality of production. It also became a more casual formation, frequently extended to include 'improvers' and 'learners', and as something to be sought for its economic contribution to wages standards. It was one of the ways, therefore, that the working class was drawn to full participation in market relations, for it aimed to constrict the supply of labour for economic ends alone. Henceforth apprenticeship came to rest upon the ability of permanent unionism to reconcile restrictions in the supply of labour with the general state of the labour market.[9]

Some trades were able to effect this transition from regulating the labour supply in order to uphold a wider status of market stability and production relationships to a more modest manipulation of the labour market. The shipwrights, for example, managed to retain some control through apprenticeship regulation. In the mid-1820s the London shipwrights endeavoured to restore their threatened status as independent craft contractors against the shipowners' desire to bid freely for labour and prices in an unrestrained labour and product market. Similarly, the Dundee shipwrights established their own shipbuilding company in an attempt to escape the constant pressure upon traditional standards of apprenticeship and other conditions. Both these efforts failed. In London the question of labour supply remained unresolved after the great strike of 1825 and the Dundee shipwrights' company collapsed in 1831. But if the claim to a wider determination of market conditions was abandoned, the shipwrights' local unions fought bitter struggles in the 1840s and early 1850s in a generally successful attempt to sustain a fairly high degree of control over the labour supply.[10]

Production Relations in the Industrial Revolution

The outstanding fact of production relations in the industrial revolution is how little they differed from those of the past. Production continued to be secured by a variety of self-supervisory methods such as piecework, subcontracting and domestic work. One of the ironies of this general policy of devolution of the details of production was the tendency to force the small master to match his market dependence on the large master by adopting the discipline commonly associated with the large factory. It may be one of the paradoxes of the industrial revolution that the 'modern' tension between managerial authority and work-place autonomy was first located in the small trades where masters and men were in other respects poorly differentiated. As Clive Behagg has shown, slim profit margins and the need to prove their credit-worthiness made productivity and discipline absolutely critical. This surely explains the well-known association between chasing, driving and the bad industrial relations that were frequently encountered in the small-scale sector of production.[11]

But large-scale management remained a function of securing discipline and consent through systems of direct paternal control, and the consequence was the curiosity that the first industrial nation failed to develop a distinctive managerial ethos or ethic. Indeed, there was a singular lack of interest in the development of a managerial control that focused explicitly upon the execution of work in the labour process and a suspicion of innovation in the relationships of the factory hierarchy. Even political economy – the one area where one might expect to find an alternative body of belief – was generally silent on the 'implementation of capitalist control of the production process through [for example] the organization and pace of work and the redefinition and breakdown of skills'.[12] The one exception to this was the work of Charles Babbage; but his interest in the technical prescriptions for labour-process structuring was regarded as a marginal eccentricity and his advice was generally ignored. The archetypal exponent of managerialism was Andrew Ure, whose views confirm this void. His *Philosophy of Manufacturers* published in 1835 combined a complacency that self-acting machinery would ensure the subordination of labour with extensive homilies on the necessity for the behavioral and moral reform of the working class to secure obedience. Quite obviously, the factory demanded a closer attention to the systematisation of layout and organisation than had been necessary before. Boulton and Watt, for example, reorganised their Soho works in 1800 to secure a more rational division of labour, flow of production and accounting control. But it is interesting to note that this particular reorganisation was accompanied by the devolution of supervision on to the skilled men themselves who were switched from time- to piece-wages as the only way to guarantee reliable attendance and maximum output.[13]

Management's conservative approach to the details of production was reinforced by the painfully learned lessons of the past. The spectacular failures of seventeenth- and eighteenth-century joint-stock enterprises were remembered as the consequence of delegated managerial authority. Adam Smith himself endorsed this suspicion of any enterprise too large to be personally supervised when he pointed out that

> managers of other people's money rather than their own . . . cannot well be expected, that they should watch over it with the same anxious vigilance with which the partners in a private company frequently watch over their own.[14]

The delegation of authority was thus a difficult matter. The safest kind of delegation continued to be the division of departmental responsibility between the members of the family, and this tradition continued well into the nineteenth century. But a more extensive structure of supervision could hardly be avoided in the large concerns, even though vast areas were evacuated by systems of internal contracting. The overseers, foremen, or managers, however, were not seen as the agents of a rationally ordered structure with a distinct sphere of bureaucratic initiative. There was an arbitrary indistinctness to the spheres of authority. Decisions might be overturned on personal appeal to the higher paternal authority of the master himself, and most large employers insisted upon keeping this avenue open. Managers and foremen were regarded as *alter egos* of the owner and they were expected to behave with the same kind of sovereign responsibility as the master. In contrast to Germany, for example, where the bureaucratisation of authority had preceeded industrialisation and could readily be transferred to the organisation of the factories, the lessons of the British past pointed to the effectiveness of more personal and less formal hierarchies.[15]

Similar lessons were applied to experimentation with the organisation of production. The disruptive consequences of innovation were stressed above its potential for productive efficiency. The general consensus was probably represented by William Brown, a flax-mill owner in Dundee, who argued that 'a spinning mill is a complicated and ticklish kind of concern, and . . . is extremely liable to fall into disorder'. Thus, innovation must be second in consideration to the 'keeping of the mill in good order'. This sentiment was echoed 30 years later by James Montgomery, whose *Theory and Practice of Cotton Spinning* (1833) stressed organisational rationality but also warned that even if the arrangements proved inadequate, the interests of stability demanded that they not be overturned.[16]

There was practical experience to testify to the essential soundness of this position. The efforts of Samuel Bentham in the early 1800s to establish a tighter managerial control over the royal dockyards succeeded only in making management more difficult. His disruption of the traditional structures of work and organisation aroused resistance from the shipwrights when he tried to end their wasteful rights to wood chippings. But it also stimulated opposition from the vested interests of the dockyard officers. Efficient production was impeded not only by the sullen response to a reordered hierarchy, but also by the utilitarian rationality of the system itself. Thus, Bentham appointed a class of timber masters with delegated responsibility for the quality and supply of wood. Fearing for their jobs if any marginal timber was passed, however, they rejected such large proportions that timber merchants were soon voicing loud protests as erratic delays in the supply of wood obstructed the flow of production.[17]

In place of a rationalised supervisory hierarchy, then, reliance tended to be placed on the traditional method of paternal responsibility of the master. This meant that all responsibility tended to cluster in his hands alone and ideally it required an abiding presence. James Montgomery regarded it as essential to know the operations in detail and to monitor performances. Each day William Brown conducted a careful inspection of all aspects of his works. But it is interesting to note that only occasionally did he acquaint himself as 'to the number of workmen employed – their character – their attendance, the current wages etc.'. Robert Owen's mind was restlessly occupied in 'devising measures and directing their execution to improve the condition of the people and . . . to advance . . . the works and the machinery'. This intimacy between the owner and the intricacies of modern production left a deep legacy on managerial styles. It continued to underpin managerial attitudes and behaviour well into the nineteenth century. The personal control exercised by Joseph Whitworth, for example, was undoubtedly a major reason for his success in building the leading engineering company in the world by 1860. Even at that date his intimate grip extended

> to the smallest details of production and only things that he attended to got done. The result was lathe spindles loose in their bearing and turnings that were wildly inaccurate because not one dared bring the truth to the master.[18]

For the larger employers, whether in the factory or outworking, the problems of labour discipline did not relate primarily to the precision of supervision or how to ensure the most productive deployment of effort. Indeed it was production itself, not productivity (the notion of which was very poorly developed until the 1870s), that formed the main concern. The central question remained as it had for 150 years:

how to secure a general obedience and consent to the rhythm of capitalist production. Regular attendance at work was the prime example of these problems. Cotton spinners were frequently absent from the factory on Mondays and Tuesdays in the early days of industrialisation and the resistance to a regular week's work attendance was not overcome until the 1830s. In the South Wales mining and ironworks of the 1840s, it was reckoned that the week after the monthly pay distribution was virtually lost to production.[19] Saint Monday continued to be observed in many trades until the 1860s. On top of this were the absences occasioned by the many wakes and fairs. The central problem of management remained how to get labour to do the work in the first place.

Thus for all employers, but especially the larger ones trying to meet the pull of demand, control over the labour supply and time lay at the nexus of the production relationship. The question of labour supply was critically important because of its bearing on the division of labour and it was the division of labour, not the machine, which entrepreneurs like Boulton and Wedgwood used to ' "make machines of the Men as cannot err" '.[20] But labour supply was extremely problematic in this period – and made more so, one must assume, by the extended pressure of apprenticeship restrictions. The various constraints upon an open labour market were among the most troublesome problems employers faced during the industrial revolution. Apart from the continued relevance of apprenticeship restrictions enforced by trade-union presence, tight labour markets in trades like engineering led to rates of labour turnover as high as 100 per cent per year. Boulton and Watt's reorganisation of their labour process in 1800 had been delayed by a labour shortage which tilted the balance of power in favour of the men. Until then, wages were fixed by custom and the work habits of the men determined by their own rhythms. Thus, in 1797, it was reported of one man that 'he will by no means be fit to be left to himself, except he has piecework – for I know he has made very long hours . . . when the work might have been done without overtime'.[21]

These problems were nothing new and the strategies employers used to manage them were those endorsed by tradition. Renewed efforts were made to structure ties of dependence into the labour market. In Wedgwood's pottery works in the 1770s and in the cotton mills of the 1840s, core workers were hired for lengthy periods, sometimes with virtual security of employment. Yearly hirings were the norm in North-east coal mining until the 1840s and were adopted by the growing iron industry of western Scotland. They were a source of interminable tension in the pottery industry during the period 1760-1840. Patrimonial labour recruitment was another way of structuring labour supply, and it remained strongly entrenched in all the skilled trades until the twentieth century. Early industrialists like James Watt encouraged the system as a way to ensure an adequate supply of qualified labour. The railway companies pursued a similar policy, building schools to educate the children of railway workers.[22]

At its heart, therefore, the problem of industrial discipline was inseparable from the wider problem of social discipline generally. Social and cultural behaviour had to be moulded to the needs of the industrial system and, most of all, its tendencies to resist the authority of employers to respond to those needs had to be diminished. There was no question that this could be achieved through labour-process dependence; it had to be reached in more indirect ways. There were two strategies that traditionally had answered these requirements. The first, the use of the law, was coercive and specific. The second, a re-creation of paternal relationships, was orientated towards building compliance through structures of reciprocity and mutuality. Both were related: the law could only express the sovereign authority of the employer all the while social relations were represented paternally. And it is important to address both of these themes because throughout the period they provide the central elements which employers used to mediate social relations and generate co-operation in production.

We return to the law with a slightly different angle of vision than the one employed earlier. The law was deeply implicated in the dynamic of industrial relations and, as such, it served to mediate the duties and obligation of the groups within the social hierarchy. The status of labour's specific responsibilities to masters was progressively refined in the law of the eighteenth century. As the outworking textile trades expanded, from the 1740s, prodigious efforts were made to define the duties of weavers to the proper fulfilment of work schedules. Similarly, the rights of property ownership over the raw materials and finished products were more clearly established. Indeed, it was largely in this setting that the law on embezzlement as it related to work was first described. The most celebrated example of this were the Worsted Acts of the 1770s which allowed an inspectorate of masters to enter and search any weaver's cottage on mere suspicion of embezzlement. Similarly, the law on combinations had been expanded on a trade-by-trade basis, so that by the 1790s there were 40 Acts which defined combination for wages as conspiracy even if aimed at enforcing the Justices' decisions.[23] It was this body of law that was codified into the Combination Acts of

1799 and 1800. The repeal and subsequent modification of these Acts in 1824 and 1825 is commonly regarded as opening a new era in labour law. In fact, the continuities with eighteenth-century law remained virtually intact until the more radical displacement by the statutes of the 1870s.

For the first three-quarters of the nineteenth century, the nature of labour law expressed the essential continuities of social relations throughout the period of industrialisation. The act of 1824 repealed the Combination Laws and legalised trade-union activity. Its passage signified the temporary ascendency of the laissez-faire, free-trade party in politics who sneaked repeal through the House of Commons with the active aid of Francis Place and the silent acquiescence of William Huskisson and Sir Robert Peel. But the removal of legal restraints drew attention to a resurgent militancy (which had begun in 1823) and provoked a sharp backlash. Coal-mine owners in Scotland, for example, were confronted with demands for checkweighmen. Restriction of production and miners' control of labour supply effectively disrupted the market dominance of capital over labour. Shipwrights in London and elsewhere threatened a similar 'dictation of the . . . conditions affecting the conduct of business and manufacture'.[24] Huskisson and Peel backpedalled furiously. The former pleaded he had been too busy to notice the quite extraordinary nature of the 1824 Act and a Select Committee was established which recommended a reversion of the law:

> If the spirit of dictation now manifested is to prevail among the working class, if the application of capital is to be controlled, and the principle part of the process of manufacture and trade subjected to the judgment of committees, and every spirit of improvement by machinery or otherwise admitted or rejected at their discretion, the necessary consequence must be the withdrawal of capital and the collapse of commerce.

Thus, the 1825 Act returned the law to the main themes of the eighteenth century. Like previous statutes, it specifically asserted workplace hierarchy by establishing the rights of employers to manage and direct their businesses without interference. Similarly, it followed earlier prohibitions by denying the legality of any combination except those for specified purposes – in this case wages and hours. But this one window of liberalisation was promptly slammed shut by the adoption of language of the 1799 Act which prohibited any interference with the labour supply and regarded all combinations (except for wages and hours) as conspiracies at common law.[25]

Combinations had been increasingly subject to indictment as conspiracies in the eighteenth century. This connection was refined by the 1825 Act which brought a wide range of trade-union activities under the new crimes of intimidation and molestation. Thus, even if no act violating the statute had been committed, a mere agreement to engage in a certain activity – such as interfering with those who did not wish to join the combination – remained an indictable conspiracy. The basis for this dubious line of reasoning lay in the Poulterers case of 1611 which had been cited in some eighteenth-century conspiracy judgemments. But the 1825 Act made the connection explicit and the landmark cases of the following 50 years interpreted trade union action in this light. Thus, in *R* v *Bykerdike* in 1832 the dispatch of a letter to an employer warning of a strike unless certain men were dismissed was held to be an intimidation. The famous cases of Duffield, Rowlands and Druitt in the 1850s and 1860s all found peaceful labour activity a coercion of the liberty of mind of employers. Sir William Erle, who played a leading role in the development of this case law, expressed the logic of this deep defence of managerial authority to the Royal Commission on Trade Unions, 1867-69:

> I take it for granted that if a manufacturer has got a manufactory, and his capital embarked in it for the purpose of producing articles . . . if persons conspire together to take away all his workmen, that would necessarily be an obstruction to him that would necessarily be a molestation of him in his manufactory.[26]

Thus, nineteenth-century labour law remained basically consistent with that of the eighteenth century. Its central theme, the restriction of combinations, remained the same; its central purpose, the specific legitimation of the industrial hierarchy remained unchanged; and its major weapon, the law of conspiracy, was extended and refined. In 1875, of course, a major reversal of the assumptions of statute law occurred. The Conspiracy and Protection of Property Act inverted the negative tradition of the statutes on trade unions by permissively defining their actions as legal unless they contravened the existing codes of criminal conduct. This by no means marked the end of the trade unions' legal problems, but it did mark the decisive break with the prior tradition of the law because trade-union activity was now assumed to be legal unless its actions would have been criminal if committed by one person.

In the same year, the curtain was finally dropped on the long history of master and servant law, and equality in the labour contract was recognised in the Employers' and Workmen Act. Master and servant law stretched back to 1349 and had been progressively restated in a string of statutes over the eighteenth and early nineteenth centuries. This body of law constituted a major weapon of industrial discipline; indeed, trade unionists credibly claimed that its use had increased during the mid-nineteenth century. Between 1858 and 1867 there were an average of 9,000 prosecutions per year under the law. This figure doubled between 1872 and 1875. Only 13 per cent of these cases were brought against employers. The law provided a convenient instrument for quick punishment or intimidation over a wide variety of offences ranging from neglecting work to refusing overtime. It was particularly useful for enforcing the employment contract in the still numerous trades where long-term hiring remained common. Coal-mining employers fiercely resisted its repeal because it was regarded as essential to ensuring reliable work attendance by hewers and enginemen. Thus, even where the Act was seldom used, as in Lancashire coal mining, 'the moral effect of having the power is often sufficient' to put an end to strikes. And, in fact, employers frequently requested that their prosecution result in fines rather than jail because their purpose was merely to use the law as an intimidation to restart production. As this would suggest, the master and servant law was not confined to small manufacturers who possessed limited resources to handle refractory workers. It was widely used in ironworks as well as on building sites. In the cotton mills, it was used to punish individual acts of ill-discipline on the factory floor. And its breach of contract clauses were used to order the twisters and rovers back to work in the Preston strike of 1853-4.[27]

The master and servant law in particular was a key component in the armoury of social authority. But the creation of a social discipline depended most crucially upon reforming the habits of 'listless independence' that were staunchly resistant to the imperatives of a capitalist definition of time. The problem was not new; Puritan divines had proclaimed the sanctity of regular work habits. But a rising crescendo of complaints in the eighteenth century about the cultural lawlessness of the labouring classes reflected the voids of authority that were produced by urbanisation and the expansion of production beyond the reach of the traditional institutions of hierarchy. Thus, there was a close connection between industrial progress and the central aim of evangelising social reform to restore or safeguard a stable social discipline.[28] And the prime source of industrial discipline was seen to derive from the viability and strength of the more general structure of social discipline. When discipline in industry broke down, it pointed to the failure of those structures to maintain the 'chains of connection' that mediated in social relations. This is why throughout the first two-thirds of the nineteenth century, the collapse of discipline was treated by employers as a pathological syndrome rather than a functional disorder. Industrial conflict in the coal industry of Scotland and north-east England in the 1840s, for example, revealed the decay of those structures. Coal-mine owners understood that smashing the Miners' Association was not enough. Thus, they immediately acquired an interest in social reform they had not revealed before and set about creating a network of pit-houses, schools and libraries that would re-cement ' "those old ties of attachment." ' Re-establishing control over the production process meant restoring the ties of dependence to the social hierarchy in the villages above ground.[29]

Large-scale organisation did little to solve the problem of 'listless independence'. Ambrose Crowley's notebooks are full of complaints about the obstinate independence of his workers in the 1680s. Similarly, when Jedediah Strutt moved virtually an entire village of depressed stockingers to his Belper spinning mill, offering them regular employment at good wages, it took but a few weeks for 'their irregular habits of work . . . to break out, proving both to their own conviction and that of their patrons, their unfitness for power-going punctuality'. Josiah Wedgwood's greatest concern was to root out the irregular attendance of his workers and he devoted about a decade of concentrated struggle to modifying their general social behaviour.[30]

Factory production demanded a highly developed social discipline but the close contact it fostered between workers and masters also provided the best environment for the revitalisation of the chains of social connection that industrialisation itself threatened to undermine. It was for this reason that managerial authority came to be expressed by the re-creation of structures of paternal dependence and reciprocity. Again, there was little that was new in this. But the difference between the early experiments in factory production by Ambrose Crowley, Wyatt and Paul and the later successes of Richard Arkwright or Robert Owen was the failure of the former to impose effectively their will upon the labour force. It was believed that personality played an important role in this success. Arkwright's towering character, it was claimed, bent the most refractory wills. Certainly, the cultivation of a charismatic presence was an essential component of the armoury of a paternally based authority. Josiah Wedgwood, for example, took a secret delight in recounting how ' "my name has been made such a scarecrow to them [the potters], that the poor fellows are frighten'd out of their wits when they hear Mr W. is coming to town, and I perceive upon our first meeting they look as if they saw the Devil" '.[31]

Management by personality demanded a strange mixture of intimacy and aloofness. A tyrannical persona was one side of the coin, but the other was the creation of ties of dependence, obligation and reward. Jacob Bright, whose Rochdale mill was opened in 1809, made it his business to interest himself in his employees' family matters, often serving as an arbiter in private quarrels, helping them out in bad times, and supervising their care of their children. More formal structures were also common. Robert Owen was appalled by the moral degeneracy he encountered at New Lanark and his celebrated system of environmental reform and industrial monitors brought him visitors from all over Europe. But his efforts were unique only in the thoroughness of their application. Similar strategies had been prefigured in the Crowley iron-works of the 1680s and were part of the readily available historical experience from which employers could draw. Thus, just as the truck system was carried over from domestic production, an employer like Strutt held back a portion of earnings each quarter to retain his labour force and to levy as fines upon those guilty of misconduct outside working hours. More benevolently, factory-master Samuel Oldknow kept herds of cattle to supply his employees with milk and meat, being sure to deduct the cost of purchase from wages. Various rituals of reciprocity and social inversion were created to express the ties of dependence. When Matthew Boulton's son came of age, a day of festivities was decreed at Soho which culminated in a banquet for 700 people. Similarly, Richard Arkwright devised a series of customs such as parades, dancing and feasts that marked the first lighting of the factory in the shortened days of autumn. At other times, roles were reversed and workers were treated to entertainment by the management whose repertoire included 'a song celebrating the bountiful benevolence' of the master himself. Wyatt and Paul had vainly tried to secure loyalty by awarding prizes to their best workmen. Arkwright continued this tradition: his practice of giving cows to his superior workmen stands as an appropriate vignette of the interpenetration of old and new economic and social structures during the period of industrialisation.[32] The succeeding generation of factory employers were to extend vastly such structures of paternalism by providing a plethora of treats, trips, schools, institutes, libraries and cottages.

The significance of industrialisation for labour then was that it threatened to extend the market logic of capitalism into every nook and cranny of social relations. That is what Carlyle meant when he spoke of 'cash payment as the sole nexus' of social relations. The effort to secure compliance with this nexus by the re-creation of traditional social relations could not disguise the widespread recognition that the character of capitalist exploitation had changed. The following were just the beginning of a list of grievances a journeyman cotton-spinner articulated in 1818:

> the rise of a master class without traditional authority of obligagations; the growing distance between master and man; the transparency of exploitation . . . the loss of status and above all of independence for the worker, his reduction to total dependence on the masters' instruments of production.

The traditions that industrialisation undermined were the tattered but intact protections of 'independence' against the vagaries of market forces. Thus, as E.P. Thompson has pointed out, the conflicts of the period revolved around the values of customs, justice, independence, security, or the family economy.[33] These were all well-established themes in social and political protest, but the strength of the forces that threatened to create dependence during this period caused them to swell far beyond the prior limits of popular action. Underlying the political and social instability of the early nineteenth century was the effort to control or escape from the clutches of a dependence upon free market relations.

Notes

1. E.P. Thompson, 'The Moral Economy of the English Crowd in the Eighteenth Century', *Past and Present*, no. 50 (1971); Thompson, *Whigs and Hunters* (London, 1974); John Bohstedt, *Riots and Community Politics in England and Wales 1790-1810* (Cambridge, Mass., 1983).
2. W.E. Minchinton, *Wage Regulation in Pre-industrial England* (New York, 1972), pp. 22-3; John Rule, *The Experience of Labour in the Eighteenth Century* (London, 1980), p. 161. The Act of 1726 was repealed in 1756.
3. J.R. Prest, *The Industrial Revolution in Coventry* (Oxford, 1965), pp. 56-61, 90; E.P. Thompson, *The Making of the English Working Class* (New York, 1964), pp. 300-1, 536-8; F.A. Wells, *The British Hosiery Industry* (London 1935), pp. 100-1, 69-85; Gravenor Henson, *History of the Framework Knitters* (Newton Abbott, 1970), pp. 230-2, 357-8, 361-2, 395-412.
4. Paul Mantoux, *The Industrial Revolution of the Eighteenth Century* (New York, 1962), pp. 442-3, 439-60, 462; Thompson, *Making of the English Working Class*, pp. 541-2, 544-5.

5. Rule, *The Experience of Labour*, pp. 97, 100, 107-14.

6. Mantoux, *The Industrial Revolution*, p. 455; Wells, *The British Hosiery Industry*, pp. 81-95; Rule, *The Experience of Labour*, pp. 115-16.

7. Rule, *The Experience of Labour*, pp. 14-19; Ioworth Prothero, *Artisans and Politics in Early Nineteenth Century London* (Folkestone, 1979), pp. 55-8; T.K. Derry, 'The Repeal of the Apprenticeship Clauses of the Statute of Apprentices', *Ec. Hist. Rev.*, 1st series, vol. 3 (1931-2), pp. 68-86.

8. Paul Richard, 'The State and Early Industrial Capitalism: The Case of the Handloom Weavers', *Past and Present*, no. 83 (1979).

9. Thompson, *Making of the English Workign Class*, pp. 245-6; Charles More, *Skill and the English Working Class 1870-1914* (London, 1980).

10. Dennis Chapman, 'The New Shipwrights Building Company of Dundee 1826-1831', *Ec. Hist. Rev.*, 1st series, vol. 10 (1939-40); *Select Committee on the Combination Laws*, 1825, IV (437), pp. 24, 42-3, 254, 261, 267, 295; Prothero, *Artisans and Politics*, pp. 163-4, 170; G.B. Hodgson, *The Borough of South Shields* (Newcastle, 1903), pp. 323, 324; *Newcastle Courant*, 7 February 1851, p. 4; J.F. Clarke, 'The Shipwrights', *North East Group for the Study of Labour History, Bulletin*, no. 1 (October 1967); National Association for the Promotion of Social Science, *Trades Societies* (London, 1860), pp. 510-11.

11. Clive Behagg, 'The Transformation of the Small Producer', unpublished paper, West Sussex Institute of Higher Education, 1984, pp. 60-65; Patrick Joyce, *Work, Society and Politics. The Culture of the Factory in Later Victorian England* (Brighton, 1980), pp. 159-68.

12. Maxine Berg, *The Machinery Question and the Making of Political Economy 1815-48* (Cambridge, 1980), p. 144.

13. Eric Roll, *An Early Experiment in Industrial Organization* (New York, 1968), pp. 179, 197.

14. Sydney Pollard, *The Genesis of Modern Management* (Harmondsworth, 1965), pp. 24, 291-2.

15. Joyce, *Work, Society and Politics*, pp. 101-3; see Jurgen Kocka, 'Capitalism and Bureaucracy in German Industry before 1914', *Ec. Hist Rev.*, vol. 34, (1981); and J. Kocka, 'Family and Bureaucracy in German Industrial Management, 1850-1914', *Business History Review*, vol. 45, no. 2 (1971) for the combined use of family members in management and 'a system of written and generalised instructions which provided fixed lines of communication within and between the officers'.

16. Dennis Chapman, 'William Brown of Dundee 1791-1864: Management in a Scottish Flax Mill', *Explorations in Entrepreneurial History*, vol. 6 (1952), p. 178; Maxine Berg, *Technology and Toil* (London, 1979), p. 61; Pollard, *The Genesis of Modern Management*, pp. 308-13.

17. R.A. Morris, 'Samuel Bentham and the Management of the Royal Dockyards 1796-1807', *Bulletin of the Institute of Historical Research*, vol. 54, no. 130 (1981), pp. 229-38.

18. Chapman, 'William Brown', pp. 124-5; Reinhard Bendix, *Work and Authority in Industry* (Berkeley, Calif., 1956), p. 51; A.E. Musson, 'Joseph Whitworth and the Growth of Mass Production Engineering,' *Business History*, vol. 17, no. 2 (1975), pp. 136-7. A similar absence of managerial initiative can be seen on the railways; see T.R. Gourvish, *Mark Huish and the London and North-western Railway* (Leicester, 1972), pp. 92-6, 168-73.

19. Sydney Pollard, 'Factory Discipline in the Industrial Revolution', *Ec. Hist. Rev.* vol. 16 (1967).

20. Neil McKendrick, 'Josiah Wedgewood and Factory Discipline,' *Historical Journal*, vol. 4, no. 2 (1961), pp. 31, 34.

21. Holbrook-Jones, *Supremacy and the Subordination of Labour* (London, 1982), p. 43; Roll, *An Early Experiment*, pp. 192, 221. It is interesting to note

that Henry Ford experienced a labour turnover of 370 per cent in 1913; see Stephen Meyer, *The Five Dollar Day: Labor Management and Social Control in the Ford Motor Company 1908-21* (Albany, NY, 1981), pp. 80-1.

22. P.W. Kingsford, 'Labour Relations on the Railways 1835-75', *Journal of Transport History*, vol. 1, no. 2 (1953); Harold Owen, *The Staffordshire Potter* (Bath, 1970), pp. 33-6, 44; McKendrick, 'Josiah Wedgwood', pp. 35-6; H.I. Dutton and J.E. King, *'Ten Percent and No Surrender', The Preston Strike 1853-54* (Cambridge, 1981), p. 84; Paul Sweezy, *Monopoly and Competition in the English Coal Trade 1550-1850* (Cambridge, Mass., 1938), pp. 33-4. S.J. Chapman and W. Abbott, 'The Tendency of Children to Enter their Fathers' Trades', *Royal Statistical Society Journal*, vol. 74 (May 1913), pp. 599-604.

23. S. and B. Webb, *The History of Trade Unionism* (London, 1920) pp. 58-60; Rule, *The Experience of Labour*, pp. 130-3, 174-6; Craig Becker, 'Property in the Workplace: Labor, Capital and Crime in the Eighteenth Century British Woollen and Worsted Industry,' *Virginia Law Review*, vol. 69, no. 8 (1983), pp. 1487-1515.

24. Barry Gordon, *Economic Doctrine and Tory Liberalism 1824-1830* (London, 1979), pp. 26-38; *Select Committee on Combination Laws*, pp. 10-11; Webb and Webb, *History of Trade Unionism* p. 93; Alan Campbell, *The Lanarkshire Miners 1775-1874* (Edinburgh, 1979), pp. 63-4, 70-1.

25. *Select Committee on Combination Laws*, p. 8; Sir James Fitzjames Stephen, *A History of the Criminal Laws in England*, Vol. III (London, 1881), pp. 208, 212-15; John V. Orth, 'The British Trade Union Acts of 1824 and 1825; Dicey and the Relation Between Law and Opinion', *Anglo-American Law Review*, vol. 5 (1976).

26. R.S. Wright, *The Law of Criminal Conspiracies and Agreements* (London, 1873), pp. 6-7, 11-12, 48; Stephen, *Criminal Laws*, pp. 209, 221-3; Sir William Erle, 'Memorandum on the Law Relating to Trade Unions', *Royal Commission on Trade Unions*, Eleventh Report, 1868-69, Vol. XXXI (4123). The 1859 Masters and Workmen Act legitimised peaceful picketing but was ineffective because it did not alter the definition of intimidation and molestation and thus allowed the essentially negative bias of 1825 to remain. Erle's language was almost exactly the same as cotton master Henry Ashworth in *The Preston Strike* (Manchester, 1854), p. 15.

27. Daphne Simon, 'Master and Servant' in John Saville, *Democracy and the Labour Movement* (London, 1954), pp. 164-7, 198; John V. Orth, 'Striking Workmen before the Courts', unpublished paper, University of North Carolina, p. 3; *Select Committee on Master and Servant*, 1866; Vol. XIII (449), 1087, 1246, 1370, 1380, 1358-66, 1441, 1323, 1451, 1335-44; D.C. Woods, 'The Operation of the Master and Servant Act in the Black Country 1858-75', *Midland History*, vol. 7 (1982), pp. 97, 106; Dutton and King, *'Ten Percent and No Surrender'*, p. 39; Dutton and King, 'The Limits of Paternalism: The Cotton Tyrants of North Lancashire, 1836-54,' *Social History*, vol. 7, no. 1 (1982), pp. 62-4.

28. The phrase 'listless independence' is in Andrew Ure, *The Philosophy of Manufactures* (New York, 1967), p. 334; R.W. Malcolmson, *Popular Recreations in English Society 1700-1850* (Cambridge, 1973); Richard Johnson, 'Education Policy and Social Control in Early Victorian England,' *Past and Present*, no. 49 (1970).

29. See Ure, *Philosophy of Manufactures*, pp. 407-23 on the necessity for religious and moral influences; Campbell, *The Lanarkshire Miners*, pp. 222-4; Robert Colls, ' "Oh Happy Children!" Coal, Class and Education in the North East', *Past and Present*, no. 73 (1976), p. 99.

30. Stephen Marglin, 'What Do Bosses Do? The Origins and Functions of Hier-

archy in Capitalist Production', *Review of Radical Political Economics*, vol. 6, no. 2 (1974); Ure, *Philosophy of Manufactures*, pp. 333-4; McKendrick, 'Josiah Wedgwood', pp. 38, 51.

31. Mantoux, *The Industrial Revolution*, pp. 24-5, 375-6; Ure, *Philosophy of Manufactures*, p. 15; McKendrick, 'Josiah Wedgwood', p. 39.

32. Bendix, *Work and Authority*, pp. 49-51; Mantoux, *The Industrial Revolution*, p. 381; R.S. Fitton and A.P. Wadsworth, *The Strutts and the Arkwrights 1758-1830* (Manchester, 1958), pp. 99, 100, 101, 233-6; A.P. Wadsworth and Julia de L. Mann, *The Cotton Trade in Industrial Lancashire 1600-1780* (New York, reprinted 1968), p. 437.

33. Thompson, *Making of the English Working Class*, pp. 199-203.

3 THE CHALLENGE OF RADICALISM: THE ORIGINS OF THE MID-VICTORIAN COMPROMISE 1820-1850

Class Formation

Industrialisation threatened the stability of society. The vast expansion of old modes of production, the dissolution of the legal basis of regulating conditions of production, and the appearance of new modes like the factory, threatened to dissolve the delicate balance of those 'fields of force' that had preserved the curious social stability of eighteenth-century society. It was a common perception of people like Robert Owen and William Cobbett that the 'chains of connection' in society were in danger of rupture. This was seen very much as a socio-political process, an 'abdication on the part of the governors'. At the local level, the asserveration through popular riots of duty and reciprocity from the élite was increasingly devoid of results, and increasingly regarded as illegitimate.[1] Indeed, in places like Manchester by 1810, they had already been replaced by something closer to the politics of class. Naturally, this process had been in progress for a long time; it certainly gathered momentum, however, after about 1760. Eighteenth-century England was far from being a placid, Augustan society. The boisterous rowdyism of plebeian crowds and the prickly independence of the gentry shocked foreigners. But the character of plebeian intervention in politics had changed dramatically by the early nineteenth century. In comparison to the interventions of the 1760s, for example, those of 1816-19 were highly politicised illustrations of the extent to which élite hegemony had eroded and could no longer be taken for granted.[2] The mass radicalism that followed the Napoleonic Wars was the first of a series of great social movements that climaxed in Chartism in the 1840s. These movements exposed the social and political tensions that were associated with industrialisation. But, of course, they did more than that. Historians have long argued that they revealed the alterations that industrialisation forced in class relations and, in particular, that they forged the making of the English working class.

It is clearly true that a distinctive phase in social relations was passed through during this period. But in thinking about the process of class formation it is necessary to balance the search for the embryos of modernity with a sufficient emphasis upon the elements of continuity.[3] This is a particular problem at this period when the ideologies and imagery of the past occupied a vital part in the lexicon of radicalism. Indeed, a more accurate conception of the nature of early nineteenth-century radical movements might be to see them as the vast expansion of themes common to customary consciousness and moral economy into one last, magnificent, bellowing of the popular culture and radicalism of the eighteenth century. This is not to suggest the irrelevance of a class analysis of the social movements of this period; but it is to suggest that they revealed a different kind of class formation than that of an embryonic modern working class.

Class formation is commonly misconceived as a linear progression. In fact, it is better understood as a process of composition, decomposition, and restructuring. Class is 'made' only in the sense that at a particular time, a particular set of structures, actions and attitudes are formed by the impact of present experience upon past culture to characterise the relationship of the working class to society. That relationship will alter as the stage of decomposition is set in train by a complex process of social, political and economic change and ultimately a new confection will be produced which follows from (but cannot be read from) the prior stage. Thus, class formation is a process of continual transition, it does not end when the working class is 'made', whatever form that making takes. From this perspective, we are better able to understand the process of class formation in the nineteenth century.

The stage that Thompson so powerfully chronicled in *The Making of the English Working Class* certainly contained elements of 'making.' But perhaps more significant for understanding the response to industrialisation were the elements of decomposition. Industrialisation dissolved a prior state of social relations that stretched back, perhaps, to the late seventeenth century. The sparseness of economic modernity in the process accentuated the appeal to a real or imagined 'traditional' past that underlay the consciousness of the working class in the early nineteenth century. For the past that was crumbling before their eyes was being eroded with techniques and instruments that were familiar to that past. The response of radicalism was to reassert a traditional analysis of society's ills and refine their prescriptions to take account of changing circumstances. Its failure to offer an effective answer to those ills was in large part due to an inability to combat the elements of the restructuring of class relations that were set in train by the 1840s. These elements were largely social and political but their compatibility with the economic structures of class relations provided the basis for the distinctive class formation of the mid-nineteenth century.

Artisan Ideology

The social tensions that accompanied industrialisation reflected the way it exposed the conditions of life and work to the pure logic of expanded market relations. Historians have rightly emphasised how the core of opposition to this process lay amongst artisans and the ideology of opposition grew precisely from their historical consciousness.[4] Economically, artisans were able to conceive of a productive sphere free from the distortions of unrestrained market competition. Stability would be ensured by regulation of the labour and product markets either by the state or by the trade. Politically, as Gareth Stedman Jones has pointed out in a particularly astute analysis of Chartism, artisan ideology was rooted in a radical critique which had begun to crystallise in the 1760s and whose immediate intellectual godfather was Thomas Paine. This critique, whose origins may perhaps be traced back to the Commonwealthmen, rested on the notion that the natural rights of the people had been perverted by the appropriation of land and labour (the Norman yoke) and by the monopolisation of power through 'old corruption'. By the early nineteenth century, its most notable exponents were William Cobbett and Henry Hunt, who envisaged an egalitarian, industrious, society where the wide dispersal of property ownership and minimal government ensured independence and freedom.[5]

Artisan ideology attained a coherence and mass base with the radical explosion at the end of the Napoleonic Wars. The lone dissenting voice of Cobbett was joined by a group of other spokesmen, debating and discussing through the medium of the 'unstamped' press. The major themes that emerged from this critique – priests, taxes, old corruption, access to land, competition – remained the common vocabulary of radicalism throughout the Chartist period. Under the stimulus of Ricardian economics during the 1820s, the labour theory of value, the distinction between productive and unproductive labour, and the relations wages and profits also began to receive attention. But it is difficult to draw a clear distinction between the 'old' analysis, epitomised by Richard Carlile who continued to denounce the priesthood in the 1830s, and O'Brien or Hetherington, who focused more precisely upon the exploitation of labour by capital: 'The working class debate in the 1830s was a debate not between current alternative theories of society, but between those who invoked the older rhetoric of 1819, and those who innovated on it.' Thus the pre-Marxian labour theory of value oscillated between arguing that the structure of capitalism was the cause of labour's failure to receive its full value, or that the monopolies of old corruption were the root of the problem.[6]

The gradual accretion of new elements of criticism and their uncertain integration into the wider body of ideology reflected the character of economic change and the absence of thoroughly new social relations. Thus, the general lack of focus upon the *production* relations of industrial capitalism (as revealed by the labour theory of value) does not demonstrate the inadequacies of lower-class theorists. Rather, it reveals the way those relations did not compose a central problem for artisan, handicraft labour. The problem was not control over execution, it was how to combat the depredations market forces wrought upon the conditions under which the work should be carried on. Thus, the definition of the unproductive classes could be expanded to include monopolising capitalists middlemen as well as priests. But it did not necessarily encompass manufacturers who employed their capital to assure fair standards of production. The parasite groups were those who bought cheap and sold dear, who wished to reduce artisan production to degraded levels, who 'monopolised' markets and power to create, in O'Brien's words, 'the cannibalism of artificial society'.[7]

The focus of artisan ideology was directed primarily to the inequality of exchange relations and to the social and political structures that sustained them. It was a commonplace belief that the distortions produced by competition between labourers were responsible for the degraded and exploitative production relations that reduced the artisan 'from a condition of comparative comfort to a condition of distress'. And competition between capitalists created inefficiencies in trade flows and depressions to provide the conditions for the downward pressure on standards. The presence of the factory and machinery served as a stimulant to competitive degradation, not as its main cause. But a consideration of exchange relations was inseparable from questions of how these were aided and reinforced by the political power structures. The diversion of wealth into the non-producing classes was consequential upon their control of politics. Political reform was essential to the restoration of equitable exchange relations and, thus, the suffrage formed a central part of radical demands from the end of the French wars.[8]

It is worth stressing how closely politics and economics were integrated in artisan ideology. Economic ills could only be resolved by political remedies, and the persistent vitality of the language and notion of 'old corruption' reflected this recognition. This emphasis was confirmed through the 1820s as the debate between the centrality of the home or foreign market raged in political economy. Free trade and the exploitation of the world market was seen as yet another source of competitive degradation of wages and conditions, whilst a protected home market was consistent with the maintenance of artisan standards:

> Were we, at once, to leave off some of our machinery, and lose some (nay almost all) of our foreign trade, and give working men the necessaries of life for a day's labour, our home trade would increase, quite as much, or more, than our foreign trade decreased. At all events, we should not then be living in the midst of starvation in a land of plenty.[9]

This perception, of course, formed the basis for the alliance at the end of the 1820s between political radicals and Thomas Attwood and the currency reformers whose analysis emphasised underconsumption as a cause of distress. Attwood argued that a full employment and full production economy could be secured by matching the supply of circulating money with the productive capacity of the country. This was essentially a problem of government policy which was restricting currency issue and demanded, therefore, political intervention.

Artisan ideology, thus, stood squarely opposed to the developing classical political economy. Francis Place was in despair at the failure, in the 1820s, of the artisans to accept the separations orthodox political economy imposed upon the spheres of political and economic existence. The objection was well expressed in Gast's *Trades Newspaper* in the 1820s:

> The great evil with men who have written on what they term political economy is, that they never take into consideration the habits and customs, and all the natural passions and propensities belonging to human nature. They overlook the immense power which the capitalist has over the labourer, and the manner in which the conduct of the former influences the fate of the latter. They also have in general this radical evil at the bottom of all their systems. They consider men as a machine, and the labourer as a commodity.[10]

Artisan ideology counterposed a 'moral' economy to the 'freedoms' extolled by political economy. The interests of labour could no longer be left to the care of 'paternal' reciprocity or the protection of the state. Both were progressively being abandoned to allow labour to face the uncontrolled effects of mechanisation, free trade, and free market competition. Only political intervention could redress these problems. But the truly significant thing about this artisan ideology was its ability to generate a social and political challenge that extended beyond the purely craft artisans facing the destruction of honourable standards.

The desire to break free of the effects of competition or to control its 'evil' aspects was as common to degraded hand-loom weavers and cotton spinners as it was to shoemakers or tailors. All were victims of the same kind of pressures. Thus in every major movement of the period there was a strong tendency to united action between trades. The Philanthropic Hercules of 1818, for example, consisted of hatters, sawyers, brick-makers, weavers, calico-printers, shoemakers and spinners. And the common thread that runs through both general and sectional movements remained that expressed by the articles of the Hercules: 'maintaining their reputation in society, and supporting their own independence by a just, equitable, and legal demand for their labour'. Thus, the various unions and actions of cotton-spinners in the 1830s aimed at controlling the labour market and reducing hours as a way of stabilising the violent fluctuations in the industry. In addition, the traditions of 'the trade' remained the basis for cross-class alliances with the small masters – who were, in any case, often hard to distinguish from artisans. The stockingers of Leicester formed a union in 1830 and invited the employers to join in an effort to control 'that spirit of competition – that monster which has injured you and ruined us'.[11] Similarly, building workers and small masters joined together in 1833 to regulate the nature of contracts and thus protect the trade from a competitive bidding that naturally favoured the larger general contractors.

This desire to escape from dependence upon unrestrained market relations explains the enthusiasm that greeted the various schemes for co-operative production that appeared from the late 1820s. In the London trades, for example, there were constant references to the need for co-operation. And it was the London trades' experience of an expanded dishonourable division of labour that launched the Owenite schemes for Labour Exchanges and a Grand National Trade Union in the early 1830s. In spite of their short-lived existence, these efforts were notable because they were attempts to create a different structure of labour and product markets from those of industrial capitalism. Middlemen distributors would be eliminated and co-operative production would restore artisan autonomy. But here, as elsewhere in this period, artisan ideology threatened to overflow its limits. Industrial syndicalism was implicit in the building workers' efforts to control the contracting system and for some it contained the vision of a restructured political system capped by a House of Trades that would 'direct the commercial affairs of the country'.[12]

Owenism's appeal lay in the way it provided a coherent analysis of social trends which confirmed the focus on competition as disruptive to decent standards and social peace. But it also offered a means of escape by postulating the reconstruction of community through co-operation. As such, it provided an alternative framework of organising social relationships that spoke directly to the collectivist, co-operative themes of lower-class experience such as the local friendly society. It offered an analysis of economic development that integrated notions of justice and morality. Owenism's indictment of competitive capitalism was as much moral as it was economic. Working-class Owenites were as eager as Robert Owen himself to encourage the moral and inellectual dimensions of life – though they were concerned to do this in a democratic context that the 'social father' found distasteful. Thus, in its social and recreational aspects, Owenism endeavoured to erect a community that would embody an area of cultural independence within which the fellowship of co-operation and morality could thrive.[13]

The movement, however, contained fatal flaws. Most central was its failure to envisage how the co-operative economy would displace the competitive society. As Edward Thompson has remarked, there was an 'inadequate attention to the means' by which this could be secured. Owen himself possessed an essentially Fabian strategy of convincing the ruling classes of the irrationality of present arrangements. His working-class followers relied upon the possibility of implanting islands of co-operation within the sea of competition. But once Owenite unionism was routed in a disastrous series of strikes in 1834, the incipient vision of a restructured industrial and political system to secure independence was truncated. It was precisely at this point that Owenism began to disintegrate. When the movement revived again in the late 1830s, its energies were directed towards experimentation with alternative life-styles. The link between the artisan strivings for independence and Owenite ideology had been broken. And when the Rochdale pioneers opened their co-operative store in 1844, the vision of modifying market relations rather than transcending them was already implicit.[14]

By the mid-1830s, however, it was increasingly obvious that the question of political power could no longer be evaded. Following the Reform Act of 1832, a major reconstruction of state structures was effected. There is a serious need for historians to remove this whole process from Whiggish conceptions of the 'decade of reform'. At the time, it seemed to many as if 'The Thing' of old corruption was about to be revitalised. Indeed, it is undeniably the case that these reforms increased the political, cultural and economic vulnerabilities of the lower classes. The Reform Act saw no gains for those with little or no property. Indeed, in many towns franchises had actually been reduced. On the other hand, the door had undoubtedly been opened to Benthamite reformers. The most obvious consequence of this was the New Poor Law which undermined the last ties of 'community' in social welfare and endorsed free labour-market competition. Similarly, the spread of the new police forces – the 'plague of blue locusts' as it was called in Huddersfield – in the 1830s was intimately connected with the efforts of social reformers to root out lower-class culture and implant the control of evangelical morality in the urban working-class neighbourhoods.[15]

At the local level, these developments were impossible to divorce from the structures of political power in the towns. In Oldham, John Foster has suggested, they were closely related to the effort to reduce the influence the labour community had established over the institutions of local government. The New Poor Law removed poor relief from the select vestry where it was open to popular influence and into the hands of the guardians secretly elected by the ratepayers. Similarly, the professionalisation of the police force in the late 1830s removed it from popular control into the responsible hands of the magistracy.[16] These tendencies only gradually gathered momentum and it should not be assumed that Oldham was typical. But the institutional reforms of the 1830s and 1840s was not viewed as an undisguised blessing by those on the receiving end. In any case, this context is central to understanding the development of radical politics once Owenism declined. The anti-Poor Law movement was the first manifestation of this renewed attention to the politics of the state. But by 1838 its organisation and energies had flowed into Chartism.

In spite of all that has been written about Chartism, there remains an indeterminacy about where the movement should be placed historically. Three lines of argument run through the historiography. First, that derived from Mark Hovell, the first modern historian of the movement, who tended to treat it as the precursor to mid-century working-class liberalism, contaminated by O'Connor's demagoguery. Second, the localist orientation epitomised by the seminal essays in *Chartist Studies* where Chartism is seen as a collection of local movements uneasily bound together by the personality of O'Connor and the agency of the *Northern Star*. And, third, the view orginally adopted by Engels in *The Condition of the Working Class in England*, that Chartism was the first genuinely proletarian social movement. Most of the confusions about Chartism derive from the nature of its ideology.

The traditional elements in Chartist ideology have long been recognised. Thus, the wide appeal of the Land Plan lay partly in the central role the independent cultivator occupied in the radical tradition from the Levellers to Cobbett. Like Owenism, the Land Plan offered a way to restore artisan independence and self-reliance. Similarly, the famous six points of the charter were merely restatements of a radical agenda of 80 years' standing. But it is a constant mistake of the historiography to suggest a dichotomous tension between 'backward looking' and 'progressive' elements. Engels is probably to blame for starting this Whiggish hare. He clearly regarded Chartism as a prefigurative socialist movement. But he saw the economic attitudes of Chartism in contradiction to the progressive, political side of the movement.[17] In fact, it is singularly misleading to treat Chartism as an ideological hybrid unable to thoroughly escape from the chains of the past.

Chartism may best be seen as the climax to an increasingly politicised artisan ideology. As early as the 1820s, artisan radicals in Birmingham had developed a political programme with universal suffrage at its core. Following the disappointment of 1832, a committee of unemployed artisans issued a manifesto that included all the eventual six points. Similarly, Liverpool artisans in the 1840s launched a scheme for co-operative house purchases in order to secure the property that would give them independent political rights. Chartism maintained the integral relationship between politics and economics that was characteristic of artisan ideology – it was never purely a political movement. Indeed, its central theme was to capture the organ of political power in order to redress economic and social ills, and the vocabulary of Chartism encompassed the artisan critique of industrial capitalism.[18]

What made Chartism so potent was that it was not simply the property of those decaying trades most exposed to marauding economic change; its pull was equally strong in the new or expanding urban centres. Contrary to what used to be assumed, for example, it possessed close connections with new and old craft trade unionism. Indeed, this attachment expressed the way trade-union action had not yet been defined as purely an 'economic' matter but was seen as a direct consequence of the 'Baseness of our political system, and the consequent tyranny of capitalists, whom the law allows to ride roughshod over prostrate labour'. Trade-union adherence to Chartism had less to do with divisions between upper and lower trades and more to do with the exposure to the pressures expanded market determination placed upon custom and standards. Only the most aristocratic crafts relatively unaffected by these pressures consistently held themselves aloof. In London, for example, the proletarianising impact of an uncontrollable labour and product market was affecting all the major trades by the 1830s and, as it did so, the artisans turned to Chartism. When masons at the Houses of Parliament struck in 1841 against the attacks on customary modes of working by their foremen, they instinctively responded by conceptualising the conflict as symptomatic of the 'avarice and despotism [that] . . . in these days of competition and rivalry . . . enable the distributors of our produce to wring from working men the means of superfluity and wealth'. Thus, there was a constant series of fluctuating, often informal, contacts and attachments between Chartism and trade unions. The problem was that Chartist support could only be mobilised at certain crucial moments of tension.[19]

Although Chartism was a quite remarkable high point to the instability that accompanied industrialisation, it is not particularly helpful to see it as a failed proletarian movement. Its ability to mobilise across the social spectrum reflected, paradoxically, the absence of a proletarian working class either in its structure or its consciousness. On the contrary, the fractured nature of economic change allowed all groups to unify under the aegis of artisan ideology because the threat to the workshop artisan was paralleled in the experience of those such as cotton-spinners who behaved like artisans in the factory. Controlling the forces of market competition was relevant to both as the means to securing a certain quality of 'independence'. Thus, to judge Chartism from a perspective that assumes it was struggling to become a modern working-class movement is to fundamentally misjudge its coherence with the perceived nature of economic change. The failure of Chartism did not reflect the 'confusions' or inadequacies of its ideology, whose assumptions were perfectly appropriate given past and present experience; nor was its failure due to an incomplete understanding of the course of historical change – no one in the 1840s foresaw the stabilisation of industrial capitalism. Similarly, the collapse of Chartism was not a function of the divisions that existed within the movement – although they played a contributing role. Chartism's demise was the product of the political inability of artisan radicalism to transcend the disintegrative elements that combined in the 1840s to erode its assumptions.

The Revitalisation of Paternalism

There were, perhaps, five elements that may be distinguished as central to the demise of Chartism. In the first place, the strategic presuppositions of radicalism rested upon the possibility of a popular alliance that would include significant sections of the middle class. In particular, the interests of small masters were seen to converge with those of the artisans. Large employers were more problematic, but they, too, were regarded as possessing interests at odds with the expansion of the state in the 1830s which (if history was any guide) promised to extend the political monopolies of the debt-holding, 'moneyed' classes. Indeed, it is important to appreciate that the viability of this analysis crumbled only gradually and throughout the 1830s and 1840s there were constant reminders of its potential. Large employers, like John Fielden, who supported minimum-wage and factory legislation, demonstrated the presence of an 'uncorrupted' middle class with whom cooperation was possible. But there was also growing evidence that industry's interest in competition outweighed its opposition to privilege. The small-master class was increasingly divided between those who identified with the community of the trade and those who accepted the political economy of the competitive system. These latter allied themselves with the values of middle-class discipline, led the assault upon customary standards and were the 'grasping monopolisers' of artisan rhetoric. In Birmingham, it was this petty bourgeois segment which gained control of the organs of municipal government following the reforms of the 1830s. Similarly in Oldham, the political alliance between the working class and the petty bourgeoisie was fractured in the mid-1840s.[20] At the same moment that artisan ideology attained its fullest programmatic expression and presence as a mass movement, the sociological assumptions upon which it rested were decomposing.

In the second place was the nature and direction of the state policy. The radical analysis tended to assume that the policies of the new state would follow the repressive policies that had characterised the Pitt and Liverpool governments' responses to an earlier phase of radicalism. This expectation remained unfulfilled. Although over 500 Chartists were arrested in 1840, the technocratic policies of Sir Robert Peel's second administration, from 1841 to 1846, transcended sectional interests and gave the lie to 'old corruption'. Social and economic stabilisation was Peel's objective and each of the major interests in the country were addressed in turn. The Bank Act of 1844 reformed the 'moneyed' interest and stabilised currency and capital flows. Extended factory legislation appropriated working-class demands as against those of industrial capital. And, finally, the agricultural interest was confronted and diminished by the repeal of the Corn Laws in 1846. By the time 1848 arrived, Chartism was struggling against a state which seemed to embody the national interest.[21]

In the third place, Chartism was increasingly rent by internal divisions. These differences were less a matter of political personalities and more a function of alternative responses to changing political possibilities. The experience of defeat in 1839-40 appears to have been crucial in this process. The Bull Ring riots in Birmingham had been crushed by the combined force of the London police and middle-class magistrates who a few years before had been fervent supporters of reform. The Newport uprising discredited the strategy of physical force. It was at this point – often reinforced by the sobering experience of prison – that the Chartist leadership decisively fractured. Some, most notably O'Brien, tried to shift the focus more towards industrial capital. But the most significant development was the articulation of a moral-force Chartism which explicitly sought alliance with the middle class on the basis of common social and moral principles. This was the kind of opening sympathetic liberals had long been seeking, and they immediately reached out to chartists like Henry Vincent and Robert Lowery to form the Complete Suffrage Union. Feargus O'Connor, struggling to maintain the viability of an independent radicalism, did not have this kind of co-operation in mind when he made his frequent declaration of support for affiliation with the middle class.

The 'New Move' leadership focused around Lovett, Vincent and Birmingham Chartist Arthur O'Neill and each had his favorite panacea that pulled against a national policy. O'Neill set up Chartist churches, Vincent was a temperance supporter, and Lovett was an advocate of education. In the short term, these factions, whose leaders were isolated as naive and impractical, were largely irrelevant to the Chartist presence. O'Connor's abuse of 'knowledge Chartism, Christian Chartism and Temperance Chartism' received widespread support, but the New Move was important because it marked a definitional shift within working-class politics and culture. Lovett provided the most coherent statement of the New Move when he argued that political rights should be delayed until emancipation from social and moral vice had demonstrated working-class competence for political responsibility. The specific parts of Lovett's programme were not in contradiction to Chartism. Indeed, education and self-improvement were commonplace ends in working-class culture. But Lovett's arguments for individual moral self-betterment as a prior condition for the acquisition of political rights stood in direct contrast to the Chartist purpose of improvement through the collective control of the organs of power.[22] The prior premises of working-class radicalism were completely inverted by the acceptance of the assumptions of middle-class ideology that working-class culture was something to be reformed through individualist self-improvement.

In the fourth place, Lovett's formulations also suggest how what Perkin has called 'the struggle between the ideals' as to how society should be organised was fast crowding out any alternative to the entrepreneurial ideal. In the 1840s, it became increasingly difficult to sustain a coherent opposition to the values and assumptions of middle-class political economy or social policy. The range of opinion and intellectual effort committed to political economy far outdid attempts to formulate alternative approaches. Indeed, by the 1840s, the efforts of people like Attwood to build an alternative programme on the basis of a convergence between Tory democracy and artisan ideology had already been recognised failures. In 1837, for example, it was still possible to hope that the New Poor Law could be reversed or obstructed by massive local resistance. By the 1840s it was no longer possible to sustain that faith. In addition, political circumstances worked in the same direction. The success of single-issue campaigns around the Corn Laws or hours legislation and the easing of the depression after 1842 encouraged the very separations between politics and economics that artisan ideology had traditionally resisted. Thus, within trade unionism, there was a growing tendency to assume an opposition between their economic purpose and political action. By 1846, for example, carpenters and joiners in Manchester had abandoned their traditional leadership of united trades action and support for co-operative politics. They were deeply divided between those who identified with the earlier radical positions and those who wished to pursue a policy of pure and simple unionism in separation from politics or the other trades. Thus, Gareth Stedman Jones is quite right to remark that

> there was a greater acceptance of determination by market forces and increasing usage of the term 'labour' and 'capital' without refer-

ence to the political system in which, in the radicalism of the 1830s, these terms were inextricably inscribed.[23]

But this process was grounded in the fifth element of decomposition – the liberalisation of middle-class attitudes towards the working class. In material terms, this occurred largely at the local level, but it may best be initially approached through what has been called the 'mellowing of middle-class liberalism'. There had always been a vocal segment of liberal opinion which objected to the hostile face middle-class ideology presented to the working class in the 1820s and 1830s. Samuel Smiles argued against Edward Baines, in the late 1830s, that it was politically foolish and morally unjust to offer only the hopelessness of Malthusianism or classical political economy to the working class. Co-operation between the classes was impossible on those terms, but it could be attained by accentuating the coherence that existed between working-class aspirations for improvement and liberal notions of progress. This argument was given a considerable boost by the vision of social improvement contained in the authoritative *Principles of Political Economy* published by John Stuart Mill in 1848. And throughout the late 1840s, a political and social perspective which sought the harmonisation of interests increasingly became the liberal orthodoxy. People like Baines were gradually purged of their pessimism about the lower classes and converted to 'an increasingly positive and optimistic view of the working classes'. By 1865, Baines, for example, had moved as far from his earlier hostility to working-class politics as to rejoice at the franchise demand as being 'what was their reasonable right'. The same transformation could be seen in a factory-owner like Hugh Mason. In the 1840s, he 'was the kind of employer anathema to the Chartists, opposing trade unions and factory legislation alike'. But by the 1850s relations had markedly improved; he felt himself to be more like a 'father' than a 'mere capitalist' to his 'brothers and sisters' who worked at his mill so that 'the bond that united them was not the cold bond of buyer and seller'.[24]

There were two central elements to this mellowing of middle-class liberalism. Both were reflected in the ideology and practice of social relations. First, as the above would suggest, the language and strategies of social coercion and intellectual indoctrination were replaced by an emphasis upon the cultivation of paternal sympathy and respect. As William Felkin explained ' "the advisor, protector, and friend have too frequently been replaced by the severe, harsh and haughty master" ' addressing his men as if they were ' "slaves rather than free men" '.

Arthur Helps, one of the earliest exponents of this revitalised paternalism, pointed out that large employers were the 'successors of the feudal barons' whose duty it was to go beyond the cash-nexus relationship and provide guidance and leadership in all respects of their workers' lives. The imagery of the family replaced the language of political economy in middle-class representations of social relations. Helps again expressed this in particularly cloying form:

> I believe that the parental relation will be found the best model on which to form the duties of the employer to the employed; calling, as it does, for active exertion, requiring the most watchful tenderness, and yet limited by the strictest rules of prudence from intrenching on that freedom of thought and action which is necessary for all spontaneous development.[25]

The paternal and parental model had always lain at the basis of factory relations; mid-Victorian factory-owners continued to practice it as their forefathers had done. The owners of the Butterly Coal Company inculcated religion amongst their employees. The building of Saltaire between 1851 and 1871 replicated on a vastly expanded scale the efforts or early industrial pioneers to provide a healthy and moral environment. But in the 1840s the language and style of paternalism expanded from the owner class to become the dominant ideology of the urban bourgeoisie. Indeed, the growing instability of the 1830s and 1840s and the sociological investigations of working-class conditions occasioned the development of this model as the solution not just to factory relations but also the social problems of urban and class society generally. The truly explosive growth of charities and social-reforming institutions from the 1840s was the main expression of this new paternalism. These efforts were characterised by their prying inquisitiveness about working-class life and their desire to restructure it from the inside. They propagated an explicitly paternal basis of dependency.

> The county police had come; penny readings, clothing clubs and missionary meetings. . . . The shadow of the big house loomed . . . yet it was, almost certainly, a misfortune for the labouring man if there was no Big House in the parish.

While this was perhaps more visible in the countryside than the urban areas, charity activism was all pervasive. Domestic missionaries were everywhere by the 1850s, they could be seen at factory gates, in dockyard dining rooms, needlewomen's sweatshops, navvies' encampments, at pubs, in barracks, at railway stations and in lodging houses. A few hardy souls even ventured into brothels. Whether such intrusions were welcome or unwelcome, effective or ineffective, their significance lay in their representation of social relations as ' "that beautiful feeling which connects the superior with the inferior, and binds the interests and pleasures of both into one' ".[26]

The generalisation of class relations as governed by the rules of paternal care, however, demanded that working-class aspirations to independence also be taken into account. The ironic truth was that the paternal style could only be compatible with liberal individualism if it directed its purpose towards stimulating and encouraging self-help and independent action. That is, paternal feelings could only be aroused voluntarily; to coerce would be counterproductive. Thus, the 'independence' of working men had to be recognised and respected. As Tholfsen has correctly noted, a recurrent theme of mid-Victorian ideology was the 'upright and independent working man freely assenting to the view of benevolent employers'.[27] In addition, this reformulation of social relations was a 'negotiated' response to a working-class presence that in the 1830s and 1840s had searched for ways to realise its own notion of independence. To combat this challenge, the main focus of the working-class analysis of class relations had to be shifted away from its emphasis upon competitive market relations as the despoiler of independence. It had to be moved more towards a definition that emphasised the primacy of moral and individual self-improvement as the motors of progressive betterment.

Active efforts on the part of certain elements of the middle class to construct an alliance with segments of the working class pre-dated 1848. Until the late 1840s, these efforts were not very successful. In Oldham, for example, the breakthrough came in 1846 and 1847 when versions of the working-class programme were embraced by the Tory and Liberal bourgeoisie in a seemingly deliberate effort to split the radical alliance.[28] But the process could only blossom once the failure of Chartism had closed off the possibility of any alternative ideological or programmatic alliance. Liberalisation was not a conspiracy; it was the convergence of themes common to both working-class and middle-class culture in the space created by the demise of artisan radicalism. Both cultures possessed certain common historical roots and tendencies.

Radical and middle-class ideology alike were suspicious of government, defined liberty against the state, were in favour of a minimal governmental presence and favoured the reduction of taxes. If the state was no longer seen as the centre of a parasitic old corruption, it was hard to maintain the distinction between the radical and liberal approaches to social change. Similarly, a belief in self-improvement, education, and the integrity that came from self-discipline were deeply engrained in working-class culture. Those values were essential to a self-conscious radical movement: they were, perhaps, epitomised by those Methodists who stewarded the great reform demonstrations of 1816-19. But in a context where they were celebrated by middle-class ideology as the very dynamic of progress, independence and social mobility, they became the basis for a cross-class consensus.[29] From the 1840s until the 1860s, tendencies towards convergence with the values of the liberal middle class relentlessly burrowed their way through working-class culture. The precise details of this accommodation varied and we will not attempt to develop a typology that captures its complexity. Some idea of the process may be conveyed by briefly noting three representative examples of how the balance of consensus and co-operation was achieved.

Saint Monday provides a particularly interesting example because the custom stood clearly at odds with the values of the dominant culture. Douglas Reid's investigation of the tradition in Birmingham showed that its demise did not occur until the 1860s when a series of forces combined to erode its legitimacy. Mechanisation of the hardware trades gradually increased the importance of a regularly ordered working week. Thus, employers pressed to establish recognised hours of work in place of an earlier arbitrariness. In return for the surrender of a flexible definition of time, they granted the half-day Saturday which created a rational division between work and leisure time. Saint Monday came to represent a disreputable anomaly, rejected by the 'respectable' working class. In addition, in trades like button-making, the availability of small machines for purchase or rent allowed artisans new opportunities to set up in business for themselves. To these groups, a new sense of time discipline reflected a new self-interest as they joined the independent master class. Saint Monday was increasingly associated with declining or decaying trades where its persistence merely reinforced its identification as contrary both to progress and to the definition of the respectable working classes.[30]

Convergence could not wait, however, on the development of appropriate self-interest amongst segments of the working class. It had to be actively pursued to strengthen the division between the respectable and non-respectable working class. Paternal middle-class ideology assumed this segmentation and required the creation of different kinds of structures for each group. For the respectable working class, convergence was most obviously located in the voluntary assoiations that came to riddle mid-Victorian society from the late 1840s. John Foster has noted how the expansion of social-reform institutions in Oldham was coincident with the political fracturing of the radical alliance and strengthened the attachment of the respectable working class to the emergent liberal consensus. But the basis for this differentiation was also implicit in aspects of radical activity that were genuinely rooted in the working class.

The teetotal temperance movement provides one such example. The origins of teetotalism lay within the radical culture of Preston in the 1830s. It was formed by a group of artisans and small tradesmen who had close ties with radical politics. Only a few years before, Henry Hunt's election as Member of Parliament had broken the domination of the aristocratic Stanley family over the politics of the town. And the group that formed the teetotal society did so in conscious rejection of the patrician domination of the moderationist wing of the temperance movement. In this context, teetotalism expressed a distinctly radical declaration of independence. The range of causes its leaders supported included the ballot, universal suffrage and opposition to the Poor Law. Initially, its members had no desire to separate themselves from the rest of the working class. But their commitment to individual moral reform and education as the means of self-improvement made growing contacts with middle-class reformers inevitable once the original association with radical culture had weakened. By the 1850s, these convergences became dominant as the drink problem came to be identified as a central drag on lower-class progress. Thus, as the movement came to represent a prime example of the fusing of middle- and working-class definitions of progress, it evolved into an exclusive sub-culture sharply demarcated from the rest of the working class.[31]

The central importance of voluntary association between the classes lay in the way it offered the opportunity to foster paternal 'good feeling' whilst, at the same time, providing an environment for the virtues of independent self-improvement. Achieving this balance required delicate negotiation, and the past history of efforts to provide institutions for the working class was replete with examples of the failure properly to respect the necessary compromises. But the opportunities for avoiding this fate in the mid-nineteenth century were never greater and the working-men's clubs provide a particularly good example of the successful negotiation of this balance.

The clubs were formed in the 1860s to provide a respectable alternative to the pubs. Initially, they were under the patronage of the middle and upper classes who saw them as agencies of self-improvement where 'sympathy' and 'good feeling' between the classes could be forged. But the movement was threatened with destruction almost before it began by the attempt to prohibit alcoholic drinks in the clubs. This was resisted by the working-class members and a pattern reminiscent of the crippling of the Mechanics' Institutes seemed about to erupt. In the end, a compromise was reached which allowed the movement to thrive. The patrons, recognising that the paternal style could only be effective if it accepted the legitimacy of working-class priorities, abandoned their opposition to the sale of drink. Equally, the working men defined their respectable independence by imposing strict sanction against those who abused the privilege. This balance between paternalism and independence remained fairly stable until a revolt against 'patronage' in the mid-1880s removed the middle and upper classes from the governance of the movement's co-ordinating body.[32]

By the 1860s, then, class relations had been restructured through a negotiated reconstitution of the basis for social hierarchy. The internal composition of this balance was a peculiar and in some ways contradictory compromise, but its successful operation lay at the root of the stability of mid-century class and social relations. Elite authority was represented through the language and practice of a revitalised paternalism which allowed for the demarcation of spheres within which the working class could realise an independence prized and articulated by Liberal ideology. Much of the suspicion of trade unionism in the period derived from the implicit threat it posed to that compromise by its imperviousness to paternal intervention and its code of collectivist and exclusionary loyalty. As W.L. Burn pointed out in his anatomy of the period, social and voluntarist ties of association were seen as the key to the reconciliation of liberty and freedom with order. There was a general suspicion of efforts to create formal and permanent bonds of collective representation by groups. Even employers were unable to create lasting associations to represent their interests, preferring to rely upon *ad hoc* voluntarism when confronted by a common threat. And the idea that outside bodies should intervene in industrial relation contravened the notion of social relations as bound by the myriad ties of association between independent beings for mutual good.[33] The presence of labour organisations certainly marked the outermost limits of the compromise that underlay the renowned stability of the mid-century years. But mid-Victorian equipoise was a negotiated formation and nowhere was this more true than in the nature of production relations.

Notes

1. Harold Perkin, *Origins of Modern English Society* (London, 1968), pp. 183-95; Bohstedt, *Riots and Community Politics in England and Wales 1790-1810* (Cambridge, Mass., 1983); Thompson, 'The Moral Economy of the English Crowd in the Eighteenth Century', *Past and Present*, no. 50 (1971).

2. Philip Jenkins, *The Making of a Ruling Class. The Glamorgan Gentry 1640-1780* (Cambridge, 1984), p. xxvi; George Rude, *Wilkes and Liberty* (Oxford, 1963); Perkin, *Modern English Society*, pp. 208-17.

3. See Thompson, *The Making of the English Working Class* (New York, 1964), pp. 193-4, where he begins to approach this problem only to shy away with the assertion that 'nevertheless, when every caution has been made, the outstanding fact of the period between 1790 and 1830 is the formation of the "working class" '.

4. Craig Calhoun, *The Question of Class Struggle* (Chicago, 1982), pp. 119-26; Thompson, *The Making of the English Working Class*.

5. Gareth Stedman Jones, 'The Language of Chartism' in James Epstein and Dorothy Thompson, *The Chartist Experience* (London, 1982), pp. 30-3, 44.

6. Patricia Hollis, *The Pauper Press* (Oxford, 1970), pp. 204, 222-5 and Chapters 6 and 7 generally.

7. Ibid., p. 228.

8. Ibid., pp. 214-17, 203-5, 206-9, 226-7; Prothero, *Artisans and Politics in Early Nineteenth Century London* (Folkestone 1979), p. 336; *The Pioneer*, 9 November 1833, p. 34; David Goodway, *London Chartism 1838-1848* (Cambridge, 1982), pp. 153-4, 160, 173, 207.

9. Quoted in Prothero, *Artisans and Politics*, p. 228; W.D. Rubenstein, 'The End of "Old Corruption" in Britain', *Past and Present*, no. 101 (1983).

10. Quoted in Prothero, *Artisans and Politics*, pp. 229, 225-6; Asa Briggs, 'Thomas Atwood and the Economic Background of the Birmingham Political Union', *Cambridge Historical Journal*, vol. 9, no. 2 (1948), pp. 204-8; Clive Behagg, 'An Alliance with the Middle Class; the Birmingham Political Union and Early Chartism' in Epstein and Thompson, *The Chartist Experience*, p. 67.

11. G.D.H. Cole, *Attempts at General Unionism* (London, 1953), pp. 7-11, 164; John Foster, *Class Struggle and the Industrial Revolution* (London 1974), pp. 108, 110-11; F.A . Wells, *The British Hosiery Industry* (London, 1935), pp. 138-9.

12. Goodway, *London Chartism*, p. 155; Prothero, *Artisans and Politics*, pp. 246-52, 255-6, 300-2; Thompson, *Making of the English Working Class*, pp. 791, 829-30; W.H. Oliver, 'The Labour Exchange Phase of the Cooperative Movement', *Oxford Economic Papers*, vol. 10, no. 3 (1957), pp. 359-60; Oliver, 'The Consolidated Trades Union of 1834', *Ec. Hist. Rev*., vol. 17 no. 1 (1964).

13. J.F.C. Harrison, *Robert Owen and the Owenites in Britain and America* (London, 1971), pp. 67-8, 74. On the integrated nature of Owenism's political, social and cultural aspects and its effort to retain an autonomous notion of lower-class community, see Eileen Yeo, 'Robert Owen and Radical Culture' in S. Pollard and J. Salt (eds), *Robert Owen: Prophet of the Poor* (Cranbery, NJ, 1971); and Yeo, 'Culture and Constraint in Working-Class Movements' in Stephen and Eileen Yeo (eds), *Popular Culture and Class Conflict 1590-1914* (Hassocks, 1981).

14. Thompson, *Making of the English Working Class*, pp. 805-6. Harrison, *Robert Owen and the Owenites*, pp. 56-7; Barbara Taylor, *Eve and the New Jerusalem* (London, 1983), Chapter 5, for a slightly different interpretation of the nature of Owenism after this period. Sydney Pollard, 'Nineteenth Century Cooperation: From Community Building to Shopkeeping' in Asa Briggs and John Saville, *Essays in Labour History* (London, 1960).

15. Robert Storch, 'The Plague of the Blue Locusts: Police Reform and Popular Resistance in Northern England, 1840-1857', *International Review of Social History*, vol. 20, no. 1 (1975).

16. Foster, *Class Struggle*, pp. 60-3.

17. Friedrich Engels, *The Condition of the Working Class in England* (Oxford, 1958), pp. 258-68.

18. This account of Chartism follows Jones, 'The Language of Chartism'; Behagg, 'An Alliance with the Middle Class', pp. 62-3; *Liverpool Mercury*, 27 February 1846, p. 106, and 22 March 1846, p. 247.

19. Asa Briggs (ed.), *Chartist Studies* (London, 1959), pp. 3-4; Robert Sykes, 'Early Chartism and Trade Unions in South-East Lancashire', in Epstein and Thompson, *The Chartist Experience*, pp. 170-72; Robert Fyson, 'The Crisis of 1842: Chartism, the Colliers' Strike and the Outbreak in the Potteries', in Epstein and Thompson, *The Chartist Experience* pp. 194-200; Goodway, *London Chartism*, pp. 208, 224-5; Operative Stonemasons, *Fortnightly Review*, 2 March 1842; Operative Society of Stonemasons, *Narrative of the 1841-42 Parliament Strike* (London, 1842).

20. Jones, 'The Language of Chartism', pp. 38-9, 45, 35, 46-7; Clive Behagg, 'The Transformation of the Small Producer', pp. 35-43, soon to be published as *Politics and Production in Early Industrial Society*; Foster, *Class Struggle*, pp. 205-210.

21. Jones, 'The Language of Chartism' pp. 38-9, 42.

22. B.H. Harrison and Patricia Hollis, 'Chartism, Liberalism and the Life of Robert Lowery', *English Historical Review*, vol. 82, no. 324 (1967); Dorothy Thompson, *The Chartists* (New York 1984), pp. 260-1; William Lovett, *The Life and Struggles of William Lovett* (London, 1967), pp. 205-6, 212-13.

23. Perkin, *Modern English Society*, Chapter 7; Jones, 'The Language of Chartism', p. 42; *Manchester Guardian*, 21 March 1846, p. 10, and 23 March 1846, p. 1.

24. Trygve Tholfsen, *Working Class Radicalism in Mid-Victorian Britain* (London, 1976), pp. 126-8, 128-9, 208, 214-15, 199-200, 317; J.S. Mill, *Autobiography* (London, Longmans, Green new edition, n.d.), pp. 133-4; Joyce, *Work, Society and Politics: The Culture of the Factory in Later Victorian England* (Brighton, 1980) 134, 148.

25. Tholfsen, *Working Class Radicalism*, pp. 136-40; Arthur Helps, *The Claims of Labour* (London, 1846), pp. 9, 24, 33, 36, 68, 79, 118, 157; Foster, *Class Struggle*, pp. 188-9.

26. John Seed, 'Unitarianism, Political Economy and the Antinomies of Liberal Culture in Manchester, 1830-50', *Social History*, vol. 7, no. 1 (1982); F.K. Prochaska, *Women and Philanthropy* (Oxford, 1979), pp. 29-32, 113-14, 182-3; W.L. Burn, *The Age of Equipoise* (New York, 1965), pp. 39-43.

27. Tholfsen, *Working Class Radicalism*, pp. 210; Burn, *Age of Equipoise*, p. 232.

28. Foster, *Class Struggle*, pp. 206-7, 220-2.

29. Tholfsen, *Working Class Radicalism*, pp. 26-34, 61, 64-8; Harrison and Hollis, 'Chartism, Liberalism', pp. 523-6.

30. Douglas Reid, 'The Decline of St. Monday 1766-1876', *Past and Present*, no. 71 (1976); see Dennis Smith, *Conflict and Compromise: Class Formation in*

English Society 1830-1914 (London, 1982), p. 51, on a similar process in Sheffield.

31. Brian Harrison, *Drink and the Victorians* (London, 1970), pp. 113-25; Tholfsen, *Working Class Radicalism*, pp. 68-72.

32. Richard Price, 'The Working Men's Club Movement and Victorian Social Reform Ideology', *Victorian Studies*, vol. 15, no. 2 (1971).

33. Clive Behagg, 'Secrecy, Ritual and Folk Violence: The Opacity of the Workplace in the First Half of the Nineteenth Century' in Robert Storch (ed.), *Popular Culture and Custom in Nineteenth Century England* (London, 1982), pp. 69-70; Burn, *Age of Equipoise*, pp. 232.

4 THE MID-VICTORIAN COMPROMISE IN PRODUCTION RELATIONS 1850-1880

Introduction

Mid-nineteenth century England was the workshop of the world. But it remained a workshop and not a factory. Labour power continued to be 'more important than capital equipment', and although steam power and machinery had left few areas of the economy completely untouched, there were 'fewer still where it ruled unchallenged'.[1] After the crisis of the 1830s and the 1840s had been overcome the continuities bequeathed by industrialisation were reinforced to usher in a long period of stability. Even within those sectors where considerable technical change had occurred, the structure and organisation of labour processes remained basically unaltered until the 1880s and 1890s. These economic continuities were paralleled in other spheres of society. Traditional popular culture was, paradoxically, strengthened even as it was driven to the cultural margins by evangelising reform. Not until the 1870s does this 'pre-industrial' culture crumble under the rise of a mass culture epitomised by the chains of music halls.[2] In politics, too, the continuities of parliamentary politics are well-known: especially in the 1850s and 1860s political loyalty continued to centre around personality and patronage. In the provinces, the patrician mainsprings of political mobilisation, greased by patronage and deference, were adopted wholesale even by the most *nouveau riche* of the age. Like feudal lords, the coal and iron magnates of the North-east marched their men to the polls in 1868. Indeed, Lawrence and Jeanne Fawtier Stone have recently reminded us that the structures of aristocratic life remained virtually intact until the 1880s. The language of class did not come to dominate the language of politics until the 1870s at which time, also, political groupings and loyalties began to shift from their essentially local bias to a national focus.[3]

We have noted these cultural and political continuities because they make the point that whilst mid-century social relationships were distinctive, they can only be understood by recognising their greater coherence with the past than with the future. The same was true of production relations which revealed a balance between capital and labour similar to that we have identified in social relations generally. Three salient features governed the relations between capital and labour in production.

In the first place, the dependence of labour upon capital was primarily a dependence that rested on capitalist market relations for work. Once Chartism and Owenism had failed to find ways of escaping from this dependence, the reliance of even skilled workers upon employers' provision of work was implicit. This was reflected in the way the mutuality between capital and labour (a mutuality that was frequently expressed in artisan radicalism) was articulated as resting upon the respective duties of each side in the production process. Labour was responsible for production and capital for making production possible by its provision of resources and engagement within the market.[4] And this implied a second feature of mid-century production relations: the indeterminancy of the authority relationship at work.

It is common for labour historians to assume that in the 1840s production relations were fractured by the demise of craft autonomy and the construction of new authority relations.[5] But, in fact, the discontinuities of the period were far less marked in production relations than they were, for example, in working-class politics. The progress of industrial capitalism lay in the triumph of capitalist market relations and not in the restructuring of the labour process. The source of capitalist influence over labour at work did not lie in its control over the execution of work. Indeed, as we have seen, large areas of the labour process were quite deliberately evacuated by management. The persistence of archaic features even in large-scale production – such as the hiring of assistants by workers themselves – all made the division between workers and employers ambiguous.[6] The result was that in production there was a sphere of autonomy and independence embedded in the material realities of the relations between workers and employers. The shift in the focus of mid-century labour from the broad challenges of the early century to the localist contests at this 'frontier of control' was a result of the way the triumph of capitalist market relations combined with the persisting independence of labour in the labour process.

Thirdly, it was the presence of this structure that, paradoxically, allowed social relations to be expressed through paternal expressions of the social hierarchy. Indeed, as Patrick Joyce has demonstrated in *Work, Society and Politics*, this representation of production relations became more elaborate and complete in this period than it had been before. Such a representation was appropriate because it could allow for the negotiated balance and compromise as to where the exact boundaries of the relationship should be drawn. In a sense it was the only representation possible given the absence of any alternative ideology upon which the social hierarchy of production should rest. Managerial ideology did not rely upon a claim to technical expertise, for example, as it was later to do. Indeed, it was generally recognised that the source of technical knowledge remained within the sphere of labour. Thus, the relationship of mid-Victorian labour to society was conditioned and shaped by this broad dichotomy between a dependence and subordination that flowed from the triumph of capitalist market relations and the opportunities that existed within the labour process for workers to realise their independence of managerial intrusion. The implications of this dichotomy were far from simple: the resultant reciprocities, conflicts and compromises between capital and labour varied enormously. Nevertheless, this is the cardinal fact of mid-century social relations which enables us more properly to understand the forms and varieties of labour organisation and consciousness.

Labour and Work

In spite of the large amount of scholarship on the Victorian working class, much remains uncertain about the details of its structure and the operation of its various labour markets. But it would seem that social and economic segmentation primarily rested on the extent to which it was possible to erect protections which mitigated or qualified dependence upon the vagaries of the labour market and, thus, give meaning to the sphere of independence in the labour process. In this respect it is possible to distinguish three broad categories within labour, although inevitably there existed considerable overlap between them.

The first was marked by those trades where labour was totally dependent upon the uncontrolled labour market. Very little can be said about the labour market of the unskilled – an area which desperately needs research – but those craft trades which had experienced the full force of structural change in the early nineteenth century were characterised by outworking and varying degrees of degraded sweated conditions of work and life. Although efforts were made from the 1860s to erect trade-union protections in trades like tailoring (the Amalgamated Society of Tailors was formed in 1866, for example), these efforts were generally unsuccessful in most sectors until the state began to regulate selected labour markets through the trade boards in the early twentieth century.[7] These trades illustrate most clearly the key role of the labour market in the structuring of mid-Victorian labour. The autonomy of labour in the labour process was virtually complete. Workers worked in their own homes or in workshops with virtually none of the techniques of capitalist managerial supervision. The lines of authority and demarcation between workers and bosses were rendered meaningless by the layer upon layer of subcontracting that separated the worker from the ultimate provider or recipient of the product. Most immediate supervision was provided by a family member or, in the workshops, by another worker whose subcontracting status and function was hardly distinguishable from that of the actual labourer. In such trades, the factory was a preferable alternative and was to become a central part of the effort to control sweating at the end of the century. But these degraded patterns of independence were, in fact, perverse representations of dependence. Thus, the shedding of artisan labour in recessions resulted in the proliferation of independent producers as the unemployed set up as garret-masters. In a cruel inversion of the traditional artisan progression, the move to independent production marked a step down the social scale to a deeper entanglement in market forces. Henry Mayhew was the pre-eminent chronicler of this structure of industry as it emerged in London out of the early nineteenth century. He told of coopers and cabinet-makers, amongst others, who became small masters when work was short, although they seldom employed anyone, and who were forced to act as a drag upon wages and conditions. This process of degradation was exactly the same as that experienced by framework knitters a century before. By 1850 it was a process that had largely run its course, but it is obvious that this kind of independence within dependence did not permit such workers to become an organised working class.[8]

If one kind of independence led to the garret or sweatshop, the other end of the scale led to the status of the mid-Victorian craftsman. There was a wide variety of trades of this type, from the highly skilled leather-workers or flint-glass workers to the carpenters whose skill status was less secure. But the general characteristic of this category was the continued reliance upon handicraft skill within a labour process that had not been recomposed either by technical change or by drastic changes in market structure. There was a wide variation, too, in the ability to erect protections that preserved a semblance of craft regulation and neither the group nor the trades within it were a unitary, unsegmented whole. Even those like flint-glass workers whose ability to exercise a full craft regulation of the labour process endowed them with truly aristocratic status included semi-skilled groups whose position was a good deal less privileged. Indeed, most of these trades possessed a sector where conditions shaded into the insecurities of the undermass of unskilled workers – a condition that was often a function of different phases of the workers' life cycle. Nevertheless, it was generally possible for trades of this type to take advantage of a labour process that relied upon their autonomy and, as a consequence, it was in this sector that most mid-Victorian trade unionists were to be found.

A third category is provided by those industries where machinery and factories had recomposed the division of labour but where a variety of circumstances combined to allow for craft organisation and control over work execution to persist against the grain of the logic of technical organisation. In large part, this was because the process of change had stimulated a reskilling rather than a deskilling which permitted the artisan to be transformed into the privileged proletarian able to retain certain elements of craft status. The millwright became the engineer by fairly easy stages and in cotton-spinning the massive gender displacement of women was followed by the appropriation of craft positions by the male machine-minders.[9]

The influence of this structure of mid-Victorian production relations was reflected in the main features of labour organisation and action where a premium was placed upon some degree of control over the labour market. The element of continuity was important in this respect. As the prior structures of regulation crumbled in the early nineteenth century, so their purposes were transmitted into union organisation. The weavers of Coventry for example, long used to a collaborative regulation of the trade with the masters, began to turn to union organisation to achieve the same ends only as the masters withdrew from that relationship in the 1840s. The focus on controlling the labour market was the main function of formal labour organisation; regulation of the actual conditions of production could be more effectively achieved by the locality or the specific work group. Thus, whether union organisation took the form of 'new model', old style, or, more commonly, was transient and temporary, a key purpose was to influence the market balance between labour and capital. The national organisation of the new model trade union was one strategy to this end, and was generally adopted by trades whose industries worked to the rhythm of the national or international market. In a trade like that of the shipwrights – which did not see a national organisation until the 1870s – the effort to regulate labour supply was the main business of local unionism, for the actual organisation of work was still very largely the responsibility of the leading men who 'captained' the gangs. Some local unions such as the Wear Shipwrights were able to insist upon apprentice indentures well into the 1860s, and in Liverpool the shipwrights' presence extended even into the product market. It was reported in 1850 that two-thirds of the repair work in the town was done in the public graving docks run by the town council. These contracts were secured by individual shipwrights whose prices undercut those of the private dock masters and it allowed the shipwrights an independent small master status that kept them free from a dependence on the large employers.[10]

This situation was somewhat unusual: Liverpool shipwrights seem to have long held a privileged position in the town and in the eighteenth century posssessed a strong political presence. But if few groups were able to achieve such an extensive control over the operation of the market structure, the stimulus for organisation and conflict frequently flowed from the same source. This was true, for example, in coal-mining where Alan Campbell has shown for the West of Scotland how 'the essential function of trade unionism in the Scots coalfield' throughout the period from the 1790s to the 1870s was the struggle over market relations. When employers spoke, as they did in 1825, of colliers 'endeavouring to place control . . . in the hands of the workmen' they referred to the effort to regulate the market through reducing the darg (that is the workload) and controlling the labour supply. Indeed, between 1827 and 1844 colliers in Lanarkshire successfully reduced the darg from four to two carts of coal per day. Restriction of production, however, depended upon control over the labour market, and the Miners' Association in the 1840s represented the first effort to extend this control to the national level. The reasoning of the Miners' Association drew upon the traditions of regulation that were common to both workers and employers in the industry – most notably in the Northeast with its history of the Vend. They hoped to forge an alliance with the masters on the basis of their mutual interest in high coal prices and higher wages. But competition from new fields and the creation of a national market by the railway were reducing the masters' interest in restriction. Employers were unable to contain competition and their interest lay in a free labour market and the reduction of costs. Thus, a fierce battle was fought in 1844 in the Northeast where these divergent tendencies were strongest when the employers proposed to replace the yearly bond with monthly contracts and the subsequent destruction of the Association settled the fate of mining unionism for nearly 30 years.[11] When stable unionism did re-emerge in the Northeast, it was on a strictly regional basis and associated with an acceptance of the determination of conditions by market relations through the sliding scales. Indeed, the Durham

Miners' Association in the 1870s explicitly abandoned restriction of output as a policy.

After the 1840s, coal-mine owners seem to have taken a deeper interest in the strategies of paternal social control – as noted earlier in Lord Londonderry's efforts in this direction. The truck system, tied housing and schools all expanded during this period. Of course, the end of the bond removed a potent agent of social control, much as the end of the virtual serfdom had done in Scottish mining at the close of the previous century and new channels of social mediation had to be developed. But these were also necessary because labour's dependence upon free market relations did not address the absence of managerial control over the execution of work. In Durham, for example, the cavilling system remained a powerful instrument of worker autonomy at the coal-face. And in the west of Scotland, sporadic attempts in the 1850s and 1860s to gain control over the division of labour were admitted failures.[12] In the coal-mines, then, the structure of the industry allowed for a deep implantation of the tradition and practice of control and autonomy in the labour process which reinforced the importance of the dependencies masters wielded above ground.

This dichotomy was, of course, quite characteristic of mid-Victorian production relations. Autonomous regulation was the main feature of work-place relations and although the extent to which it could be exercised varied widely over time and place its practice was the major legacy of the period to labour organisation and relations. Across those large sectors of industry where the labour process remained unchanged there was no fundamental challenge to the practice of work control. We may note the case of the slate quarriers of North Wales to demonstrate this point; for although their situation was somewhat unusual, they are one of the few groups to be the object of close study in this respect.

Quarriers' work autonomy derived from their technical knowledge of handling rock. They were openly contemptuous of management because most of the managers had never been quarriers and were, in any case, English and Anglican. The work control of the men was institutionalised in the bargain system whereby each caban, or work group, negotiated a monthly contract for the quarrying. Until the 1880s, the cabans conducted genuine negotiations with management not only over price but also over the place of work. Attempts to replace this system with hourly pay were fiercely resisted and in 1876 were the occasion of rioting at Betws Garman. Supervision was frequently non-existent. In 1865 there were at least 25 quarries worked only under the supervision of a quarryman and clerk. A strong sense of job property rights existed; control over time and pace of output lay at the discretion of the men. Over the course of the mid-century this independence tended to increase. A strike at Penrhyn in 1874 against 'unfair' managers forced their dismissal and the creation of a committee elected by the men whose initial power to investigate all letting complaints soon extended to a collective control of all contracts. Through the informal organisation of the caban, the balance of power in the industry swung decisively in favour of the men and 'between 1874 and 1885 it certainly prevented management from having a free rein in the work and from introducing any major new regulations or reorganization'. In this context, it is hardly surprising that Lord Penrhyn, the quarry magnate, used charity donations, sick and pension clubs and later religious and political favouritism to secure a consent that could not rest upon the direction of work organisation. The erosion of this example of the mid-Victorian compromise began in the mid-1880s as the owners faced tightened product markets and reduced profit margins. The bargain system began to be replaced by a new method of individual contracting and a challenge was mounted against the quarriers' control of time. The subsequent 20 years saw a gradual crumbling both of the work-control power of the men and of the cultural solidarities upon which it rested. This process climaxed in the famous Penrhyn strike of 1903-5 which ended in the virtual destruction of the community.[13]

But, as we have suggested, the presence of labour-process autonomy was not confined to those sectors of industry where the technical nature of work left no alternative to surrendering production into the hands of the workers. In the highly mechanised industries, too, the most notable characteristic of production relations was the continuation of a craft style of union organisation and policy. In cotton-spinning and engineering the ability of labour to exercise a high degree of control over labour supply was a significant precondition of this development, but it also rested upon the way industrial organisation had progressed and the active intervention of the workers themselves. In cotton-spinning, the assumption of Ure and Marx that automatic machinery would rapidly convert the unruly independence of the domestic worker into the docile subservience of the machine-minder proved to be false. Not until the 1860s did the self-actor become dominant over the hand-mule and this 50 year gap between factoryisation and complete mechanisation allowed spinners to consolidate their hold over labour recruitment and wage-list bargaining. In addition, the technical basis of skill rested upon the manual interventions that early machinery required and these were carried over to diminish the self-acting properties of the mule. Certain motions – particularly nosing and strapping – demanded constant adjustment to prevent the yarn from snarling. This reinforced the conviction of the operative spinner that

> no two mules could ever be alike. As a consequence he proceeded to tune and adjust each of his own particular pair of mules with little respect for the intentions of the maker or the principles of engineering. Before very long no two mules ever were alike.

Thus, in contrast to the USA where mules were run by unskilled women totally subservient to management, in Britain the active intervention of the spinners had secured them a skilled position in the division of labour. Even as late as the 1920s, the warnings of William Brown and James Montgomery about the delicacy of social arrangements in a mill were being repeated by authorities on mill management: 'the organization of labour is practically in their [the spinners] hands, and the management must organize exactly on the lines laid down in a series of rules as the basis upon which they work'.[14]

But the basis of the independence of the men from detailed managerial intrusion also rested upon a second factor. The industry had developed in a highly competitive environment which made employers reluctant to tamper with the original division of labour. Employers needed a labour stability that could be achieved by transfering the family division of labour into the factory and endowing the male minder with his natural responsibility for discipline, supervision and entry into the trade. Even Ure was willing to admit the necessity of this:

> the spinners, being obviously responsible for the quality of the yarn, must of course have the selection and hiring of their juvenile assistants. In fact, mule spinning could not go on with any degree of prosperity if the assistants were independent of the operative.

Thus, from the beginning, spinners were able to control entry into the trade – as they had in the old hand-mule days. This became the central aim of their 'closed' union policies and the reason for their exclusionist attitude to piecers, card-room workers and others.[15]

The case of the engineers was somewhat different. As the millwright was transformed into the metalworking engineer, capitalisation and mechanisation disrupted the division of labour. Throughout the 1830s and 1840s, recurrent depressions led to a constant search for ways to cheapen the cost of working. The industry saw an expansion of piece-master subcontracting, systematic overtime and the influx of 'illegal' men into areas of skilled work. But the economic upturn at the end of the 1840s and the unification of regional unions into the Amalgamated Society of Engineers provided the opportunity to confront these problems. A series of local trade movements in the Northwest became focused on the large firm of Hibbert and Platt, where cheapening systems were particularly pronounced. The employers were divided and the men met with some initial successes. In May 1851 they managed to regain certain kinds of work that had slipped from their control and to force the dismissal of an obnoxious piece-master. Advances were secured elsewhere in the North and the engineers were emboldened to stake out claims to a wider sphere of autonomy. Overtime, it was argued, properly belonged within the sphere of worker discretion:

> In the settlement of this question, employers can scarcely claim to have a voice . . . or we conceive that a workman who has completed his working day in a satisfactory manner, has no right to bind himself to the performance of extra work, or at all events that such should be entirely optional on his part.

In November the executive committee of the ASE banned all overtime and piece-work, and prohibited the employment of illegal men. This stimulated the employers to join together in the Central Association of Engineering Employers and to declare a lock-out.[16]

The struggle that followed was one of the most famous in the nineteenth century. It opposed the claims of employer paternal authority to those of 'craft' independence. The employers asserted the 'right to do what they wish with their own', and engineers retorted by declaring that 'the right of a working man to dispose of himself is jeopardised, and in its place a power is sought to be established enabling the employer to command the services of his workpeople day and night without intermission'. The subsequent employers' victory, however, was largely formal. Rules restraining overtime, piece-work and the labour supply were deleted from the ASE rule book. Henceforth, the Executive of the Union retreated from the matter of trade policy and the primacy of local initiative in the engineering union was implanted. Over the following 20 years, a combination of workshop action and district committee coordination saw the progressive achievement of the aims of 1851. Many sharp battles were fought in the 1850s and 1860s on such issues as the nature of supervision. More significantly, in the core areas of the North of England, employer prerogatives on overtime and methods of wage payment were rolled back. The spread of piece-masters was mainly confined to Lancashire and its worst abuses halted. By 1876 only 7 per cent of engineering workers were on piece-work, and only 15 per cent worked systematic overtime.[17]

The engineers' experience was not unique. A similar pattern can be traced elsewhere. In printing, for example, the sources suggest a similar expansion of worker influence over a range of issues. Typographers in particular were markedly successful in restricting apprenticeship. An inquiry in the 1860s revealed that the apprenticeship ratio had widened from two to five men in 1840 to two to seven in 1867. And London masters in the late 1860s complained bitterly to the Royal Commission on Trade Unions about the constrant restrictions they faced from 'custom and practice'. The same was true in the building industry where the 1850s and 1860s saw a progressive demise in the area of effective managerial control and a growing ability of the work-groups to influence the details of production.[18]

The significance of the mid-nineteenth century for the history of production relations in Britain lies in the way it saw the implantation and expansion of these structures of work organisation and control. But it is obvious that this was not solely the product of an autonomous labour action. If the structure of industrial organisation tended to create the spaces for this autonomy to exist, it did not necessarily open the opportunity for a given kind of action, organisation or policies. We have already noted how outworkers' labour-process independence was merely a bastardised form of total, degrading dependence. What is more, employers were also an active part of the process that created the structures of production relations. Their opposition or acquiescence helped determine the broad variations in the nature and extent of the sphere of autonomy in production and the many shifts that occurred in the 'frontier of control' between men's responsibility and employers' authority. Elsewhere, I have suggested how negotiation by imposition characterised both sides' ideas of how industrial relations were to be conducted. But, as others have pointed out, the relationship was not always conflictual; it contained important elements of co-operation that were, so to speak, structured in.[19] Employers gained very real advantages from allowing large areas of responsibility for actual output to be devolved onto the men. Handing labour recruitment over to the spinners, for example, not only relieved employers of the trouble of labour-market structuring, it also displaced disciplinary responsibility onto the skilled workers. Apprenticeship rules served similar functions. The elements of craft training were provided to a pool of future recruits at worker expense; the only question was how big the pool should be, but in the mid-nineteenth century uneasy compromises could usually be reached on this question. Similarly, whilst craft pride and responsibility might prove obstinate barriers to improving masters, they served equally as rudimentary quality control devices. Liverpool shipwrights, for example, sent delegates to the docks each day to make sure 'that the proper compliment of men were employed on a job . . . [and that] every ship is caulked in a proper manner, and to tell the men to do their work well'.[20] Like many craft trades, the boilermakers had rules on proper working and fined those who cheated their employers by shoddy work.

Naturally, it was possible for these structures and arrangements to become impediments to industrial organisation and when that happened a new terrain of compromise tended to be negotiated through conflict.[21] The precise boundaries between the sphere of worker independence and employer authority were not predetermined but were a matter of constant negotiation in the everyday life of the workshop or factory. Such 'negotiation', which sometimes led to conflict and ultimately always to compromise, was essential to the stability of mid-century industrial and class relations. But this bargaining was conducted informally and assiduously avoided any permanent institutional mediation. This squeamishness reflected the way class relations as a whole were expressed through paternal representations. Indeed, it should be plain that the articulation and representation of social hierarchy as resting upon paternal dependency was in no sense contradictory to the structures described above. On the contrary, such a representation was quite coherent with an industrial structure dominated by 'archaic' modes which left no room for the bureaucratic manager but did permit the sturdy independence of the respectable working man. This was also a style that was vague and shifting as to where the boundaries of that independence began or ended. In theory those boundaries were infinitely expandable to the point that working-class reliance upon paternal guidance – either social or political – was no longer necessary or appropriate. In practice there was constant tension on this very issue and the reality of production relations was that neither side of the dichotomy decisively dominated the other. Paternalism was not internalised to crowd out the class consciousness of independence within the working class, but neither may the autonomy of the working-class experience be seen outside the context of the paternal model of the social hierarchy. The balance – the negotiated compromise – that was achieved between the economic and social pressures of dependence and independence was reflected in the nature of mid-century working-class consciousness which has proved something of a puzzle to historians of labour.

Mid-nineteenth Century Working-class Consciousness

Working-class consciousness in the mid-nineteenth century was notable for the absence of class solidarities. The earlier tendencies to form broad industrial and political fronts and alliances was replaced by a narrow concentration on limited objectives and alliances with sections of other classes. Trade-union strategies were deliberately sectionalist and exclusionary towards other groups in the working class. Those organisations formed to transcend divisions – such as the National Association of United Trades – never attracted much support and even the Trades Union Congress (TUC), established in 1869, remained of little account to all but a small group of politically oriented leaders until the 1890s. Similarly, national labour politics were almost totally non-existent apart from some single-issue campaigns on trade-union law and the franchise in the 1860s and 1870s.[22]

But it would be a mistake to view this shifting focus as the symptom of a truncated development. This was not the moment when the British working class jumped the rails of its natural, historical destiny to become a grey replication of its bourgeois masters. It was a moment, instead, which reflected the peculiarities of British industrial and economic development, the importance of continuous structures of sociopolitical relations and the failure of artisan radicalism to provide an alternative to the political convergence between working-class politics and mellowed liberalism. The solidarities upon which working-class collective action was based also reflected these realities. Three themes dominated the consciousness of mid-Victorian labour: independence and respectability, sectionalism, and localism. Each was interdependent and frequently ambiguous and they were capable of composing very different forms of collective action and loyalty. Independence and respectability expressed both class pride and social acceptance; sectionalist organisation or attachment was the only sure way of securing the protection for independence; and localism (either of group, neighbourhood or trade) provided the focus for collective identity or solidarity. Not until the end of the century were these collectivities overriden (but not displaced) by a sense of class as the prime (but not the only) category of economic and political collectivity.

The importance of independence and respectability for the mid-Victorian working class reflected an acute sensibility that any protections they might possess against economic and social degradation were inherently fragile. The presence of a vast undermass of degraded, sweated outworkers and others was a constant reminder of the immediacy of an utter dependence upon an uncontrolled labour market and the humiliating exposure to the condescensions of paternal charity or a debasing reliance on the Poor Law. Once consigned to this segment of the working class, all hopes of independence and, therefore, respectability were lost. Those fortunate enough to erect protections against this threat could only do so on the basis of an exclusionist segmentation. It was this group, of course, which composed the labour aristocracy – a term whose value as a sociological description outweighs its weakness as an analytical explanation of the course of the nineteenth-century labour movement.[23] Even within this minority, the dependability of their protections against dependence was always problematic. Aristocratic trades were themselves broadly divided into privileged and less-privileged sections between which there was always the possibility of movement.

This insecurity heightened the significance of expressing differentiation through cultural and social institutions that endowed a respectable status. The importance of this separation strengthened throughout the period, as the growing residential and marriage segregations within the working class and the eager collaboration in middle-class-patronised social institutions both illustrate. But respectability was defined largely by the extent to which independence was secured and, thus, there was always a tension between the limits of patronage and the sphere of autonomy within the structures that mediated class relations. To be patronised was an infringement upon independence and there was a fine line to be drawn between these dichotomies. Both were indices of respectability, but the sanction of one's betters was accepted only so long as it did not intrude upon the sphere of autonomy and independence to threaten overt dependence. In social institutions, as in production relations, this line was drawn at many different points. The friendly societies of Kentish London adamantly rejected patronage without rejecting the honorary attachment of members of the local élite. On the other hand, model artisan dwellings in Woolwich and Plumstead failed to attract respectable tenants because of the infringements upon independence that accompanied middle-class supervision of living quarters. Even in the rural areas, there was always that 'thorny, intractable side' of independence 'which the most benevolent squire or parson could never reach'.[24]

The trade unions, of course, represented the clearest examples of the logic of this side of independence. In their efforts to control the labour market of the trade by fairly strict standards of entry they also epitomised its exclusionary basis. This was indispensable to their own security and it reflected, also, the segmentation of craft labour effected by the industrial revolution. It also meant, however, a closed mentality to the claims of other groups that was difficult to break down later in the century. But this exclusionism was contradicted to some extent by the localist orientation that lay at the basis of trade-union action and organisation. Both the new and the old model unions remained firmly decentralised. The advantages of national linkages lay primarily in the easier transmission of information between regions and in the administration of benefits. Indeed, outside the locality, the conception of trade unionism remained mainly oriented towards that of the friendly society. Trade policy and rules were the product of local initiative. Exhortation was just about the only weapon general secretaries or executive councils (themselves working members) possessed. Strikes were generally the sole responsibility of the district; the mechanisms for co-ordinating and sanctioning strike action were only weakly developed. Not until the 1890s did this local orientation change. As a consequence a high degree of informality characterised trade-union organisation which could be seen in the sharp fluctuations in union membership figures, the emphasis upon 'the trade' as a whole during industrial disputes, and the reliance upon the solidarities of the 'craft', workshop and locality to secure unity. Few unions could have been as informal as the brass cock founders of Birmingham who did not bother to write their rules until 1885. Yet since the 1820s these workmen had possessed an organisational presence and a clear understanding of the conditions under which they would work. Their frequent disputes with masters confidently referred to the sanctifications of custom and practices.[25] This is obviously something of an extreme case, but its tendencies were typical of mid-Victorian unionism. The solidarities of craft and workshop were the key elements of collective action in mid-century industrial relations.

Many rituals and ceremonies expressed the culture of the workshop. This workshop culture flowered during this period precisely because it reflected the autonomous sphere that remained extant in production in contrast to the growing pressures of market dependence. The use of custom and practice to govern the productive activity of the workshop was 'a way of shifting the debate from the context of market considerations, where the employer inevitably held *carte blanche* to institute whatever changes made his business more competitive, to ground held rather more firmly by the workforce'. Thus, the 'education' apprentices received before they began to learn the mysteries of the trade focused around the lessons of workshop solidarity against the intrusions of the foreman or manager. The inner life of the workshop, as the journeyman engineer Thomas Wright called it, was opaque to outside observers at the time and has largely remained uncovered. But what we do know of it suggests that it consisted of a 'highly active form of popular democracy'. There was, for example, a strong tradition of shop meetings to adjudicate disputes between men, sometimes complete with the ritual and procedure of the court-room. In its turn, this reflected a wider tradition of primitive democracy within working-class collective organisation that like the culture of the workshop has also gone largely unrecognised. In late eighteenth- and early nineteenth-century lower-class politics the notion of accountability of delegates to the sovereignty of popular opinion was consistently visible. At the very moment Edmund Burke was giving expression to modern theories of representation, the mandating of MPs' votes on important issues was a point of contention with the craftsmen voters of Norwich. When the National Charter Association was formed in 1841 a similar debate opened within Chartism. The salaried officials responsible for organisation in each locality were required to present themselves for the approval of each quarterly meeting. Frequent elections were scheduled and short terms of office were mandated. A similar concern was directed to controlling the executive of the Association which was supervised by an Annual Delegate Conference. Representatives to this convention were also restrained: the practice of reporting back and of mandating delegates to adopt the posture of their constituents were commonplace. This tradition of local control also existed within trade unionism. Indeed, as I have shown elsewhere, the sovereignty of the workshop was central to the authority structures of collective action and organisation.[26]

The themes of consciousness sketched above most usually produced the archetypal mid-Victorian liberal working man. But they did not always do so and one of the revisionist tasks that remains to be undertaken is to explore the different typologies of class relations that characterised the mid-nineteenth century. The comparison between Birmingham and Sheffield made by Dennis Smith is suggestive in this respect. Both towns were strongholds of small-scale artisan production but their very different social relations produced different structures of politics. In the former an active middle class which sought alliance with the small manufacturers and artisans was present from the onset of the industrialising process. In Sheffield, on the other hand, the bourgeois presence was weak and until the 1860s this vacuum allowed the artisan neighbourhoods to survive undisturbed either by industrial reorganisation or social reforming paternalism. Thus, a style of politics was spawned which represented more closely the continuities of the artisan tradition. A political machine led by the former Chartist Isaac Ironside dominated local politics until the late 1850s; its central theme was the democratisation and devolution of municipal power. Issues of town government were discussed in neighbourhood ward meetings (called motes) where decisions were reached through a form of participatory democracy. This localist structure of decision-making could exist as long as large employers were either absent or had no wish to intervene in municipal affairs. Both conditions crumbled with the expansion of large steel firms following the Crimean War. By the early 1860s steel employers began to dominate municipal government and to press for the centralisation of services and power. This development was not peculiar to Sheffield. In Birmingham, too, the 1860s saw the primacy of small tradesmen on the local council give way to big businessmen who were eager to end parsimonious government and expand municipal services to create a more socially efficient environment. Unlike Birmingham, however, the old artisan communities in Sheffield had not already been subdued by the market relations of industrial capitalism. In the 1860s, tensions mounted as the artisan neighbourhood annd trade solidarities were undermined by the steel companies. This tension climaxed in the notorious violence of the cutlery trades in the late 1860s which marked both the dying protest of these older solidarities and the occasion for their final demise. At the same time the familiar segmentation within the working class was in progress. The Sheffield outrages, as they were called, indicted the trade policies of guild-like regulation practiced by the old artisan crafts. William Broadhead – a leader in the outrages and representaive of this obsolescent view – fled to the United States. Respectable leaders like William Dronfield emerged to represent the policy of alliance with the middle-class industrialists. In 1868 the primacy of this group was marked by their invitation to A.J. Mundella – the champion of paternal conciliation of industrial disputes – to become the parliamentary candidate of liberal radicalism.[27]

At the other end of the spectrum produced by the mid-Victorian structure of social relations was that described by Joyce in the factory towns of the Northwest. Here the paternal closeness of the factory owners to the neighbourhood enabled the notion of the factory community to be so extended that it came to completely define the nature of political solidarities. Thus, 'the factory functioned as a political force because it represented a common life'. Political loyalties were sharply demarcated between neighbourhoods in mirror image of the particular colouration of the local employer. In one case, for example, radical deviants from this political hegemony were ritualistically ejected from the factory and stoned out of the community.[28]

The Fragility of Compromise

An implicit tension existed within mid-Victorian social relations between the limits of paternalism and independence. The negotiation and maintenance of equipoise depended upon a reconciliation between the claims of paternal oversight to social progress and the assertion of an independent sphere of working-class life. The exact point of equipoise was the result of many local circumstances, conditions and events and the maintenance of equipoise was always a delicate balance. Thus, in a larger sense, this structure of social relations was inherently fragile because paternalism had only been negotiated, not internalised. This fragility was revealed particularly in industrial relations where there was a general absence of structures to mediate and compose differences. Thus, when the balance ruptured here it tended to degenerate into mutual contempt. The ferocity of conflict in small trades when the community norms of the trade were violated was paralleled in the larger trades when the paternal bargain was transgressed. In modern Japan elaborate rituals of rejection are played out when this occurs and in mid-nineteenth century Britain similar charivari-type expressions of rejection were not unknown. Thus, even in those areas where factory paternalism was strongest, employers could experience the complete collapse of their authority in the mills. The most celebrated example of this was the Preston strike of 1853-4 during which mill-owners were hooted in their own factory and in one case a band played music while a crowd 'danced and played in ridicule and defiance of their employer'. When social relations had degenerated to this point and the usual appeals to personal loyalty were of no assistance, employers reached for the authority of the law to restore order. In the case of the Preston strike, they also moved to erect structures of collective bargaining.[29]

But spinning was exceptional in the mid-nineteenth century in possessing anything approaching a fully-fledged collective bargaining system. The conciliation craze of the late 1860s and early 1870s saw various systems established in a variety of industries and it is worth asking whether, as I have argued for the building industry, these systems represented a reaction to the growing sphere of 'independence' of the mid-Victorian artisans.[30] The typical conciliation system of the period either attempted to evade managerial intrusion – as in the coal and iron trades' sliding scales that linked wage movements to selling prices – or attempted to give formal expression to the paternal representation of social relations, as in the large role that was assigned to outside arbitrators for the resolution of disputes. But the onset of the great depression in the late 1870s intervened to prevent these systems from fully flowering and by the 1890s they were replaced by more modern structures of collective bargaining. The necessity for these early systems, however, served as a warning signal that the prior reliance was upon informal voluntarist mediation of social relations was beginning to become obsolete.

In the main, of course, the generally unproblematic course of British capitalism in the mid-nineteenth century allowed the inherently fragile balance of social relations to remain untested. By the 1880s, a variety of socio-economic forces combined to undermine this balance and to render it redundant. In social-cultural relations, the co-operation between paternal patronage and respectable independence was replaced by a more explicitly class basis for organisation and activity. In economic relations, a new set of imperatives and a new phase of industrial organisation demanded a more explicit ordering of authority relations at work in which the role of the employer was more intrusive. The prior indeterminacy of where employer authority ended and craft-style independence began could no longer be easily tolerated. As a result, the mid-Victorian compromise crumbled and a new configuration of social and production relations emerged.

Notes

1. Raphael Samuel, 'The Workshop of the World: Steam Power and Hand Technology in Mid-Victorian Britain', *History Workshop Journal*, no. 3 (Spring 1977), pp. 16, 46.

2. See Hugh Cunningham, *Leisure and the Industrial Revolution* (London, 1980); Peter Bailey, *Leisure and Class in Victorian England* (London, 1978);

for the continuing importance of traditional fairs, many of which were formed in the eighteenth century, see Mark Judd, ' "The Oddest Combination of Town and Country" : Popular Culture and London Fairs 1800-60' in John K. Walton and James Walvin (eds), *Leisure in Britain 1780-1939* (Manchester, 1983); for some fascinating studies that demonstrate this continuity in popular culture see Storch (ed.), *Popular Culture and Custom in Nineteenth Century England* (London, 1982), Chapters 1, 4, 5 and 6.

3. Norman Gash, *Politics in the Age of Peel* (London, 1953); D.C. Moore, *The Politics of Deference* (Hassocks, 1978); Lawrence Stone and Jeanne Fawtier Stone, *An Open Elite? England 1540-1880* (Oxford, 1984); T.J. Nossitor, *Influence, Opinion and Political Idiom in Reformed England* (Brighton, 1975), p. 80ff; Asa Briggs, 'The Language of Class' in Asa Briggs and John Saville, *Essays in Labour History* (London, 1960).

4. See the remarks of Patrick Joyce, 'Work' in F.M.L. Thompson (ed.), *The Cambridge Social History of Great Britain 1750-1890* (forthcoming), pp. 87-90; and on reciprocities see Joyce, 'Labour, Capital and Compromise: A Response to Richard Price', *Social History*, vol. 9, no. 1 (1984); Joyce, 'Languages of Reciprocity and Conflict: A Further Response to Richard Price', *Social History*, vol. 9 no 2 (1984). The sense that co-operation rested upon the complementary contributions of capital and labour to trade is well conveyed by the famous poem *Capital and Labour* written in 1872. A few lines convey the message: 'What can Labour do alone?/Grind its nose against the stone, turn a gristless mill?/What can Capital indeed/By itself? But hoard its seed/Eat a golden pill/Labour should cooperate/And to help with all their might/Masters to compete/March we hand in hand/Capital with all its gold/Genius, skill, with arts untold/Labour's horny hand.'

5. See Foster, *Class Struggle and the Industrial Revolution* (London, 1974), pp. 224-38; Joyce, *Work, Society and Politics: The Culture of the Factory in Later Victorian England* (Brighton, 1980), pp. 60-1; G.S. Jones, 'Class Struggle and the Industrial Revolution', *New Left Review*, no. 90 (1975); for a contrasting view, see A.E. Musson, *British Trade Unions 1800-75* (London, 1972) Chap. 6.

6. Joyce, 'Work', pp. 47-63.

7. Schmiechen, *Sweated Industries and Sweated Labor* (Urbana, Ill., 1984), Chapter 4.

8. Clive Behagg, 'The Transformation of the Small Producer', pp. 55-6, soon to be published as *Politics and Production in Early Industrial Society;* Eileen Yeo and E.P. Thompson, *The Unknown Mayhew* (New York, 1971), pp. 111, 195, 203, 211, 218-22, 425.

9. E.P. Thompson, *The Making of the English Working Class* (New York, 1964), p. 263.

10. Prest, *The Industrial Revolution in Coventry*, pp. 80-90; *Royal Commission on Trade Unions, 1867-69*, 1867-68, Vol. XXXIX (3890-V), ques. 16620, 17253-306; Liverpool Town Council, *Shipbuilding in Liverpool* (Liverpool, 1850),pp. 30-1, 51-4, 124-6.

11. Campbell, *The Lanarkshire Miners, 1775-1874* (Edinburgh, 1979) pp. 65, 265-70; A.J. Taylor, 'The Miners Association of Great Britain and Ireland 1842-48: A Study in the Problem of Integration', *Economica*, vol. 22, no. 85 (1955); Raymond Challinor and Brian Ripley, *The Miners' Association: A Trade Union in the Age of the Chartists* (London, 1968), Chapters 6-9.

12. Campbell, *The Lanarkshire Miners*, pp. 106-8, 212-25; Dave Douglass, 'The Durham Pitman' in Raphael Samuel (ed.), *Miners, Quarrymen and Saltworkers* (London, 1977), pp. 218-19, 229-39, 246-7.

13. R. Merfyn Jones, *The North Wales Quarrymen, 1774-1922* (Cardiff, 1981), pp. 76, 81-4, 86-9, 93-8, 143-62, 182-212, 221-2, 300-4.

14. Harold Catling, *The Spinning Mule* (Newton Abbott, 1970), pp. 74-9, 161;

William Scott Taggart, *Cotton Mill Management* (London, 1923), pp. xi-xxix.

15. Andrew Ure, *The Philosophy of Manufactures* (New York, 1969), pp. 289-90; William Lazonick, 'Industrial Relations and Technical Change: The Case of the Self-acting Mule', *Cambridge Journal of Economics*, vol. 3, no. 3 (1979); Lazonick, 'Production Relations, Labour Productivity and Choice of Technique: British and U.S. Cotton Spinning', *Journal of Economic History*, vol. 41 (1981), pp. 501, 506; H. A. Turner, *Trade Union Growth, Structure and Policy* (Toronto, 1962), pp. 128, 141, 149.

16. Keith Burgess, *The Origins of British Industrial Relations* (London, 1975), pp. 18-22; *The Operative*, 12 April 1851, p. 234; 3 May 1851, p. 281; 17 May 1851 pp. 316-19; 24 May 1851, p. 333-4; 28 June 1851, p. 410; 19 July 1851, p. 23; 16 August 1851, p. 37; 30 August 1851, p. 69; 6 September 1851, pp. 76-9; 13 September 1851, p. 84; 11 October 1851, p. 117; 25 October 1851, pp. 132-3; 22 November 1851, p. 167; 6 December 1851, p. 180.

17. *The Operative*, 17 January 1852, p. 233 and 31 January 1852, p. 244; Burgess, *Origins of British Industrial Relations*, pp. 38-42; Burgess, 'New Unionism for Old? The Amalgamated Society of Engineers in Britain 1880-1914,' unpublished manuscript, Roehampton Institute of Higher Education, 1981, p. 2; Holbrook-Jones, *Supremacy and Subordination of Labour* (London 1982), pp. 69-73; J.B. Jeffreys, 'The Wages, Hours and Trade Customs of the Skilled Engineer in 1861', *Ec. Hist. Rev.*, 1st series, vol. 17, no. 1 (1947), pp. 27-44.

18. *Royal Commission on Trade Unions, 1867-69*, ques. 19785, 19802, 19930-943; Sarah C. Gillespie, *A Hundred Years of Progress* (Glasgow, 1953), pp. 37-56, 65, 91, 96; *The Printer's Journal and Typographical Magazine*, 21 October 1867, p. 464 and 12 September 1868, pp. 125-6; John Child, *Industrial Relations in the British Printing Industry* (London, 1967), pp. 112-13; Richard Price, *Masters, Unions and Men: Work Control in Building and the Rise of Labour 1830-1914* (Cambridge, 1980), pp. 79-93.

19. Joyce, 'Work'; 'Labour, Capital and Compromise: A Response to Richard Price', *Social History*, vol. 9, no. 1 (1984); Joyce, 'Languages of Reciprocity and Conflict: A Further Response to Richard Price', *Social History*, vol. 9, no. 2 (1984).

20. *Webb-Collection*, E.A., Vol. 32, f. 405.

21. Thus, for example, the brickmakers of Manchester recounted in Richard Price, 'The Other Face of Respectability: Violence in the Manchester Brickmaking Trades 1859-1870', *Past and Present*, no. 69 (1975).

22. S. and B. Webb, *History of Trade Unionism*, (London, 1902), pp. 168-77, 206.

23. Alastair Reid, 'Intelligent Artisans and Aristocrats of Labour: The Essays of Thomas Wright' in Jay Winter (ed.), *The Working Class in Modern British History* (Cambridge, 1983), H.F. Moorhouse, 'The Marxist Theory of the Labour Aristocracy', *Social History*, vol. 3, no. 1 (1978); Alastair Reid, 'Politics and Economics in the Formation of the British Working Class: A Response to H.F. Moorhouse', *Social History*, vol. 3, no. 3 (1978). See the recent essays in Eric Hobsbawm, *Workers: Worlds of Labor* (New York, 1985), Chapter 13 and 14, for an effective rehabilitation of the notion of the labour aristocracy against its critics.

24. Robert Gray, *The Labour Aristocracy in Victorian Edinburgh* (Oxford, 1975), pp. 95-9 and Chapters 4 and 5 generally; Geoffrey Crossick, *An Artisan Elite in Victorian Society* (London, 1978), pp. 109-10, 117-18, 137-8, 145, 194-7; Crossick, 'The Labour Aristocracy and its Values', *Victorian Studies*, vol. 19, no. 3 (1976); W.L. Burn, *The Age of Equipoise* (New York, 1965), p.240.

25. Price, *Masters, Unions and Men*, pp. 207-35; Turner, *Trade Union Growth*, pp. 85-9; Behagg, 'Secrecy, Ritual and Folk Violence: The Opacity of the Workplace in the First Half of the Nineteenth Century' in Robert Storch

(ed.), *Popular Culture and Custom in Nineteenth Century England* (London), 1982), pp. 163-64.

26. Behagg, 'Secrecy, Ritual and Folk Violence', pp. 159, 164, 170; Thomas Wright, *Some Habits and Customs of the Working Classes* (New York, repr. 1967), pp. 83-108; James Hopkinson, *Memoirs of a Victorian Cabinet Maker* (London, 1968), pp. 23-4; John A. Phillips, *Electoral Behaviour in Unreformed England* (Princeton, NJ, 1982), pp. 148-9; Yeo, 'Some Practices and Problems of Chartist Democracy,' in James Epstein and Dorothy Thompson (eds.), *The Chartist Experience* (London 1982), pp. 354-8, Price, *Masters, Unions and Men*, pp. 212-15.

27. Dennis Smith, *Conflict and Compromise. Class Formation in English Society 1830-1914* (London, 1982), pp. xi, 31-3, 40-3, 68-9, 76-7, 84-6, 164-9; E.P. Hennock, *Fit and Proper Persons* (London, 1973), p. 56ff.

28. Joyce, *Work, Society and Politics*, pp. 181, 204-20.

29. Tadeshi Hanami, *Labour Relations in Japan Today* (Tokyo, 1981), pp. 43, 45, 49-51, 61-3; H.J. Dutton and J.E. King, *Ten Percent and No Surrender* (Cambridge, 1981), pp. 79-81.

30. Price, *Masters, Unions and Men*, Chapter 3.

5 WORK AND AUTHORITY 1880-1914

The Disruption of Equipoise

In the late nineteenth and early twentieth centuries, the cultural, political and social structures that had sustained and represented the balance and equipoise of mid-Victorian society were displaced. This was a social process in the widest sense of the term; its traces were evident in every sphere of society. Although we cannot hope to capture here the full complexities of the process, it may best be regarded as a process of social and political realignment which contained two central elements. The first was the growing importance of class as the major nexus around which social relationships were organised and conceived. In particular, there was a new stage in class formation which marked the making of the classic 'modern' working class. This is apparent at whatever level one looks at labour in society. Sociologically, the networks of class community became more self-contained and combined with a growing national presence of working-class organisation and action. Mid-century institutions of social improvement, for example, ceased to define leisure and cultural patterns; or, where they survived – as in the case of the working men's clubs – they explicitly shed their moral reforming patina and became exclusively defined by the needs of the class they served. A new segmentation within the working class emerged to replace the segmentations of the mid-nineteenth century. The mid-century distinctions between respectable and non-respectable, skilled and unskilled, were essentially status identifications. Those of the late nineteenth century rested upon economic criteria that were linked more explicitly to class identification: skilled and semi-skilled, union and non-union. It was a partial reflection of this that the localist, sectionalist and exclusionary features within working-class organisation and action tended to diminish. They did not always do so, but as a general trend the solidarities of class came to dominate the nature of collective action.

This is, perhaps, most readily illustrated by the new political presence of the working class. A distinctive labour politics replaced the earlier acceptance of liberalism. From the 1880s, the language and alignments of class override the categories that had previously defined political identification such as religion or paternal loyalty. This was, of course, a slow process; it was not complete until the 1920s, and neither was it a phenomenon solely confined to the working class. There was a heightened consciousness within the middle class as it experienced its own particular set of disruptive pressures – such as the falling property values and increased tax burden of the early twentieth century.[1] The suburbanisation of Conservatism (epitomised by the displacement of Balfour by Bonar Law) was one notable manifestation of that process.

The second element of realignment tended to follow from these developments: it lay in the way collective organisation came to be the prime means by which the representation of groups and the mediation of their relationships were achieved in society. In place of the mid-Victorian notion of the individual joined with others in voluntary association, the units of group representation and organisation become more formalised and professionalised. Again, capital-labour relations provide the clearest example with the growth of collective bargaining systems in industry. In 1889 only weaving possessed a national bargaining structure. By 1910, such agreements covered virtually all the major industries in the country including some, like the railways, which possessed no traditions of workshop bargaining. But we should also note that the systematisation of relationships between groups and classes was to be found in virtually every sphere. In the academic world, for example, the man of letters was replaced by the specialised expert, sporting the new-fangled qualification of the PhD and banding together in professional associations for mutual edification and to represent their discipline in the outside world. Historians formed the Historical Association in 1906. Even employers, who, as we have noted, were notoriously difficult to organise for collective representation began to form permanent associations at regional and national levels to mediate their dealings among themselves and with other groups. By the 1890s, for example, all major industries possessed employer associations. In 1898 an Employers' Parliamentary Committee was formed from an alliance between metal working employers and free-labour advocates. As one of its leaders pointed out at the time, employers 'hitherto having no corporate organization, are consequently not listened to' and collective representation was necessary to present their views to government and public. This, of course, was somewhat disingenuous. But the fact that 'corporate organization' was now increasingly considered desirable was, in itself, a major indication that new systems and structures of social relations were developing.[2]

A major historical question of the period, then, is how the prior structures that governed and mediated relationships within and between groups in society were disrupted and displaced. Naturally, to put it like this suggests too much of a disjuncture. The new configurations of social relations were greatly influenced by previous forms and values – the very nature of labourist socialism is one conspicuous illustration of that. Equally, it is plainly clear that the dynamic of this process may not be reduced to a single element, but was a function of a multitude of influences. Nevertheless, it is useful to bring into sharp focus the one particular location of industry both because it provides a good example of the process of disruption and also because it was a major area where the realignment of relationships was experienced. The disruption of prior structures of social relations in industry was broadly a function of changes in the work process. In particular, the changing relationship between work and authority at work was altered, prompting the emergence of new structures to mediate and represent social relations.

The Limits to Change

Looking back from the vantage point of 1915, Alfred Williams, the Swindon railwayman, pondered the general changes that he had experienced in the nature of work in the railway factory:

> A decade and a half ago one could come to the shed fearlessly and with perfect complacence; work was a pleasure in comparison with what it is now . . . The workman was not watched and timed at every little operation, and he knew that as the job was one day so it would be the other.

And at another point, he noted – not entirely with regret – how the old habits and customs of the workshop had also disappeared:

> Sky-larking and horse play are not nearly as common and frequent as they were formerly . . . there is now not the time and opportunities . . . to indulge in [the] practical jokes . . . of All Fool's Day or New Year's Day . . . so striking is the change that has taken place not only in the administration, but in the very life the last decade.[3]

It was surely not the case that workshop customs were destroyed during this period: pressmen are still known to smear ink over the apprentice out of his term. What Williams was describing was the relegation of those customs from a central expression of workshop community to the margins of work-place social relations. Aside from the changes in the social atmosphere of his particular place of work, the other main aspect of Williams's book, *Life in a Railway Factory*, is a chronicle of changes that had occurred in the process of production. The intensification of work, the downward pressure on piece rates, the extent of technological change, and the increased bureaucratisation of supervision are all recorded in detail. These themes are central to the history of labour's social relations during this period. They may be encountered at any point one cares to enter the world of late nineteenth-century work and they were integral to Williams's description of the altered social atmosphere of the work-place. Together, they capture the essentials of a process that displaced the mid-Victorian compromise and installed a new configuration of authority relations at work.

Britain was not peculiar in experiencing a general trend towards the reorganisation of production in this period. It is generally agreed that the late nineteenth century marked a new stage in economic development intimately connected wih a new political economy of the world market. Stimulated by increased competition, technical change, high interest rates and falling profit margins, the imperatives for more efficient ways of working were present in all industrialised countries. The period is marked by a growing sophistication in cost accounting, a new interest in the spatial organisation of the factory, the development of new technologies, the installation of bureaucratised hierarchy and a host of other common features.[4] The problem of labour costs was, of course, at the centre of the experience as the most controllable of all costs and the overriding fact of the period is the avid search for ways to achieve an intensification of labour utilisation. We should emphasise the generality of this theme. It was neither confined to Britain, nor limited to those sectors of her economy that produced exports.[5] The changing cost structure of industries that served the domestic market stimulated an interest in reducing labour costs equally as great as those industries exposed to the cold blast of international competition.[6] But it proved difficult to achieve more economic working without disrupting the existing structures of social relations in industry. The common feature of managerial strategies during this period was that they required an elaboration of direction over the processes of production. It was this, and the related phenomenon of intensified labour, that was largely responsible for the decomposition of the mid-Victorian balance in production relations.

This process did not take place outside of history. The shape and form of new techniques of organising production and the reactions they inspired from workers were determined by the past history of economic and social relations and the extent to which alterations in the production process could be reconciled with the heritage of that history. In addition, there was an enormous variation in the strength of the imperatives to change, both within and between different economies. When Henry Ford declared that history was bunk, he was giving expression to his ability to regard the labour process as a virtual *tabula rasa* and largely disregard past ways of working. Naturally, this created its own problems. The necessity to integrate a raw, immigrant labour force who neither spoke English, understood the American way, nor accepted the necessity for regularity of work, led Ford to construct his notorious Sociological Department. The techniques of the social worker and the police spy were used to acculturate this labour force into a loyal stable supply of labour.[7] But in Britain the opportunities for this degree of labour-process reorganisation and, therefore, the need for Fordist solutions to its problems, were far narrower. The reasons for this lay in the greater presence of the restraints of both history and contemporary circumstances. There were three such factors in the British experience that were of particular importance in conditioning the dynamic of labour-process change.

In the first place, in spite of the expansion of the world market, the market structure for many British goods did not fundamentally change. This was particularly the case with the products of heavy industry. Thus, the traditional techniques both of production and marketing remained viable. The dynamic basis of American engineering production, for example, was the discovery or creation of the standardised mass market. The closest parallel to the production of the Model T in Britain was the bicycle industry, and, significantly a production-line labour process was installed in that industry from the very beginning. British car manufacturers, on the other hand, had no interest in producing for a mass market that hardly existed for their product. Not until the later 1920s did the assembly line come to British car factories. Where the pressure of competition was sharp enough – as into the boot and shoe industry – efforts were made to bring production into line with the needs of the market. But it was more usually the case that the internal restraints on reorganisation were stronger than the imperatives to change. British capitalists – for example, in iron and steel – were quite happy to accept declining product markets and less than optimum returns in exchange for technological, social and market stability.[8] Similarly, the main response by British industry to shifts in world market structures was defensive. Existing markets were protected through horizontal cartels such as those in sewing cotton and tobacco.

The imperatives for change, then, were profoundly sectoral rather than general. The presence of the Empire was of great importance in this respect. Britain's main political response to the emergence of the multilateral world economy was to retreat into an Empire which shielded the erosion of her unique market supremacy. But this development served to reinforce further the restraints upon change. The protected Empire markets demanded the products of traditional sectors like textiles and hardly required an alteration of archaic features. Similarly, the widening gap between rates of return on home and foreign investment tended to starve domestic industry of new capital.[9]

A second group of restraints upon labour-process reorganisation, therefore, lay in the way the circumstances of the period tended to confirm rather than to question the existing organisation of industry. In the main sectors Britain had long before made the initial capital investment in technology and plant. Given the often attenuated nature of the competitive challenges, it was frequently not worthwhile to take full advantage of the new technologies that became available later. The failure to replace the Bessemer process with the Gilchrist-Thomas method of steel-making is one of the best known illustrations of this. But the same was true in the cotton-textile industry where the historical development of separate spinning and weaving sectors discouraged the adoption of ring spinning. Britain's failure to seize the moment of the second industrial revolution was in no way irrational. There was no certainty that the demand justified the kind of upheavals necessary to implant these new systems all the time the market for British goods could be satisfied through 'inefficient' old processes. Much of the debate amongst economic historians about entrepreneurial failure in late Victorian England is misplaced because it tends to ignore the presence of these kinds of restraints.[10]

This debate, however, has also failed to recognise a third set of restraints on reorganisation that lay within the past history of social relations. In both North America and Britain, the new strategies of productivity confronted what Bryan Palmer has called a 'culture of control' which rested upon the way the prior structures of production relations were dominated by the autonomy of the skilled workman and the (often coincident) indirect management of the subcontractor. The extent to which these restraints could be overcome helped determine the nature and degree of reorganisation. There is little doubt that these restraints were more successfully transcended in the United States where the subcontracting basis of small-scale manufacture was rooted out by a managerially dominated hierarchy and the craft organisation of heavy industry was decisively smashed in set-piece industrial warfare.[11] There was nothing to compare in Britain with the breaking of the Amalgamated Association of Ironworkers in the Homestead strike of 1894. It is well known that the appeal of Taylorism as a managerial ideology was considerably attenuated in Britain in this period. And part of the reason for this lay in the conjuncture between the structural economic restraints mentioned earlier and the consciousness that any attempt to confront the spheres of skilled-worker autonomy would encounter serious difficulties. This recognition was acknowledged by Edward Cadbury, for example, and it allowed his traditional Quaker paternalism to be reformulated into a 'human relations' approach to management in opposition to the crass materialism of Taylorism:

> The reduction of the workman to a living tool [he wrote] with differential bonus schemes to induce him to expend his last ounce of energy, while initiative and judgement and freedom of movement are eliminated, in the long run must either demoralize the workman or . . . in England produce great resentment and result in serious difficulties between masters and men.

Precisely the same cautions were to be found in the opinions of the engineering journals. The interest in improved efficiency was matched by a scepticism of the originality or practicality of Taylorist methods. There was a widespread feeling that scientific management was merely a 'high sounding title to an old and well understood' need to lower ceaselessly the cost of labour and a suspicion that the costs of its administration outweighed the benefits to production. More seriously, however, 'we do not believe the latter [Taylorism] would be tolerated by the workmen of England and Scotland. We do not believe they would submit themselves to the route card and we are doubtful if they would accept the teachings of the motion masters.' It was argued that cheaper and less disruptive aids to better working could be found in various environmental improvements such as 'the clean, wholesome, well ventilated and properly lighted shop'. Indeed, where scientific methods of the American type were introduced, care was often taken to provide compensatory benefits for the workmen. When Willans and Robinson reorganised their production process in 1897, the introduction of the premium bonus system was balanced by a series of social welfare provisions which included a sick club, canteen, and bathroom. On the other hand, where scientific methods were simply superimposed upon the existing organisation of production, it almost always occasioned opposition and conflict. Tin-plate workers, for example, successfully resisted the premium bonus system of wage determination until the First World War and there were many other examples of local conflict that centred upon labour-process reorganisation.[12] A particularly appropriate example is provided by the fate of scientific methods introduced in the London engineering firm of Thorneycrofts in the early 1900s.

The techniques of reorganisation employed at Thorneycrofts were a textbook illustration of the needs of British industry to adopt improved methods of production. There was no evidence of entrepreneurial failure here. Feed and speed charts were devised and monitored by special supervisors; the old lax methods of clocking in were replaced by time clocks which allowed a two-minute grace period; 'discipline men marched round' to see that work began as soon as the factory hooter sounded. The sharpening and grinding functions were hived off into specialised jobs within a separate department. Visits to the lavatory were limited to seven minutes and the doors were taken off to discourage malingering. The result was that 'passive resistance and sabotage were rife'. The separation of grinding was violated by continual pressure on the store-keeper to permit access to the emery wheel and once the precedent had been secured 'we were soon walking in and out at will'. Feed and speed men were harassed, bullied and sometimes assaulted; the charts disappeared; work was spoiled when speed-ups were ordered. The result was a compromise that was typical of the nature of reorganised production in British enginering: 'that part of the scheme dealing with the systematizing of production was retained and is in general use today, but the harsh repressive features were withdrawn'.[13]

The typicality or otherwise of what happened at Thorneycrofts is not the crucial point. What this case reveals is the way the historical structuring of social relations was a key agency in determining the outcome of technological and organisational possibilities. Thorneycroft's workers were – or had been – archetypal mid-Victorian artisans. They were living representations of the mid-Victorian compromise in social relations. Strikes were rare and when Tom Mann worked there in the 1870s and 1880s, self-improvement societies flourished. Some of the men had formed a Shakespeare society.[14] Whether these organisational activities survived into the twentieth century is not clear; certainly the attitudes they epitomised did not. Those same structures that had secured the social peace of the mid-Victorian period also served to obstruct managerial freedom once the balance of the mid-Victorian compromise was disrupted by organisational change.

Similar restraints honeycombed the length and breadth of British industry. In cotton-spinning the failure to adopt ring-spinning was conditioned both by the organisational history of the industry and also by the historical development of social relations which had institutionalised the spinners' power at the work-place. Ring-spinning required the use of better-quality cotton, but the employers were denied its productivity benefits because the mutually determined price lists awarded the advantage of increased output to the men in the form of higher piece prices. The answer to lowering labour costs did not, therefore, lie in the adoption of better machinery but in the use of 'bad' cotton which intensified labour and displaced the imperative for increased production on to the workers' wages. Employers could contemplate this strategy partly because the internal subcontracting structure of the industry allowed the skilled minders, in their turn, to pass the higher speed of working down to the less skilled piecers. Unlike in the United States where employers controlled both the division of labour and wage determination, British employers had no particular incentive to switch to machinery as the means of lowering labour costs and increasing output.[15]

A similar set of historical restraints was to be found in the steel industry. Joint arbitration structures had been originally devised in the 1860s as a means of ensuring better worker discipline. By the end of the century, however, they had come to serve as the means by which the unions retained control over manning and wage rates. The employers chose not to confront this entrenched union power because of the weakened market position of the industry at the end of the century. And this stasis – which was actually reinforced by the granting of bargaining rights to the newly formed Steel Smelters' Association – determined the failure to undertake structural change. By contrast, in the United States the reorganisation of the industry followed the destruction of the Amalgamated Association. British employers were unwilling to contemplate such a course for fear of permanently losing their market share from the potential flood of imports.[16]

In the boot and shoe industry the honourable section of the London trade possessed highly restrictive piece lists wich impeded the ability of the industry to respond to the mass-market opportunities of the 1880s. The London Metropolitan Branch, for example, 'retained such a tight hold over their employers that they were able to continue demanding piece rates appropriate to high quality expensive goods on products intended for a lower quality inexpensive market'. This situation encouraged the shift of production to Northampton – which the union quickly followed – and to the expansion of East End sweatshops – which ultimately led to the union demand for factory working where their control could be more effective. It proved impossible for employers to escape the restraints imposed by these traditions of control and not until the lock-out of 1895 did they secure the freedom and flexibility they needed. The ultimate ability of the boot and shoe industry to reorganise its labour process was coincidental with its success in meeting the American intrusion into its traditional markets.[17]

The presence of these structural and social restraints determined the character of the strategies employers used to improve production and output. In the main, these strategies were piecemeal and mobilised both new and old methods to secure intensified work. In the small, unspecialised firms that dominated the engineering industry, for example, the acquisition of a new machine placed alongside the generation of 1840s machines might be the only evidence of modern currents. In Alfred Williams's railway factory, the smithy remained the stronghold of traditional work organisation throughout the period, escaping the intrusions of new bureaucratic methods of discipline. Some interesting illustrations of the interpenetration of old and new methods are provided by an account of early efforts to devise new forms of wage incentives compiled by D.F. Schloss in 1895. In one sheet and pipe lead company, a bonus system was created which gave the men whatever labour costs they saved from better working. But the bonus was distributed only once a year – hardly a pressing incentive – and the main purpose of the scheme was to avoid the necessity for close supervision. The weakness of this effort bargain arrangement was reflected in the sharp decline in the bonus from 10 per cent in the first year to 1.65 per cent in the second. Similarly, in 1891, before Willans and Robinson completely reorganised their plant, a system of premium on results was introduced for foremen and managers only. This replaced the paternal tradition of periodic gifts from the directors, but it was, in fact, a form of driving designed to overcome the 'bad speed of working by the men' by making tighter supervision in the foremen's interest. Once this began to show results a 'reference rate' was established for the cost of each operation. A bonus of 50 per cent of the amount saved was awarded on top of the time wage – the other 50 per cent going to the company. Although by 1895 about half of the work-force was covered by this scheme, the system was not systematically applied because it could be worked only on those operations which had been run long enough to be properly costed. Finally, the Thames Ironworks and Shipbuilding Company at Blackwall tried to devise a scheme that would leave the traditional division of labour undisturbed by offering each work-group a bonus to be divided in fixed proportions on the basis of labour savings. The group was free to accept or reject the offer in which case it would be referred to another group. But the system was inordinately complex and involved extensive book-keeping because each 'fellowship' had its own standard labour cost and bonus.[18]

These efforts may be seen to reflect the wide concern to find ways of increasing productivity through sophisticated incentive systems, but they represented only a partial break with traditional methods. Responsibility for increased production tended to devolve onto the men and new structures of supervisory authority were generally absent. Indeed, the Thames Ironworks scheme was quite consciously designed to reinforce 'paternal' good feeling between employers and men in the wake of the unrest of the late 1880s. Furthermore, the incentive aspects of these experiments resembled the scheme devised by F.A. Halsey in North America which divided the saving equally between masters and men. The drawback to such a division was obvious; it failed to provide a continuous incentive to labour saving and the decision as to how much extra production could be gained lay solely with the initiative of the men. There was no in-built differential incentive to work ever faster and, thus, no dependency upon a scientific organisation of the work. In general, therefore, these schemes remained closer to the profit-sharing schemes of the mid-Victorian era than they did to the systematisation of scientific management.[19]

This would appear to have been quite typical. Throughout the economy, certain traditional forms of industrial organisation attained a new vitality in the 1880s. Various kinds of sweating expanded in building and cabinet-making, as well as in the familiar domestic trades. In pottery, the beginning of a new division of labour which threatened to deskill the hollow-ware pressers was combined with the resumption of traditional pressures against allowances and wages. In engineering, the first decisive breach in the 'terrain of compromise' reached in the 1850s came during the depression of the 1880s which stimulated a renewed expansion of traditional methods of intensification. Worker restraints on piece-work and overtime were broken down under the pressure of the depression. In Coventry, for example, piece-work was unknown in the 1860s but, by 1893, 83 per cent of ASE members were under this form of wage determination. Similarly, the numbers of engineering workers subject to systematic overtime quadrupled between 1876 and 1892.[20]

In the printing industry, the 1880s saw an expansion of the piece-stab combination of wage payment – again, a traditional method of increasing production and depressing conditions. Printers were willing to work on either method but objected to their presence in the same shop because it threatened chapel control over the distribution of 'fat' and 'lean' work. Clickers appointed by the chapel traditionally ensured the fair distribution of hard and easy work amongst members. Under the piece-stab system, however, employers offered high time-wages and security of employment to those on 'fat' work which resulted in cheaper production than under the piece system. In addition, the system implied a speed-up because piece-workers had to work harder to achieve their expected wage from 'lean' copy and their pace then became the standard expected from the stab-workers. Furthermore, apprentices or women could be used to replace male workers on the fat or easy work. These insecurities were heightened by the contemporaneous decisive expansion of machine composing. The successful development of Linotype resolved the failure of earlier machines to distribute the type properly and threatened to increase the displacement of skilled labour at a time when the printers were already experiencing high rates of unemployment. Employers tended to keep the machine-operators in copy at the expense of the hand-workers because of the need to amortise the cost of the machines and the Linotype set type at four times the speed of the hand compositor. The key aim of the printers was to control machine-manning, manipulate wage rates and thus remove the cost advantage of the machine compositor over the hand-compositor.[21]

The techniques that were used to intensify work in the late nineteenth century, therefore, were by no means exclusively those of a wholesale technical reorganisation. But in their potent mix of both old and new methods of production they effectively disrupted the existing relations of production. In looking at the dynamic of this process, it is possible to draw two broad (and not completely separable) distinctions. In the first, the most obvious manifestation of this disruption was the intrusion of a new organisation of production (either of a limited or extensive nature) which inherently demanded a reorientation of authority relations. This kind of change was typically located in the craft sectors of the economy, although there were considerable variations in the degree to which different crafts were affected. In the second, the process of disruption was more a result of the internal decay of prior social relations and was most readily visible in those industries that experienced the growth of the new unionism.

Management and the Crafts

Much of the industrial tension of the period derived from the way the boundaries and responsibilities of craft skill came under siege. New machinery was often the source of this disruption of social relations because it required the intrusion of management into the details of production. In railway-factory stamping sheds, for example, the replacement of small drop hammers by a 'yankee hammer' fired by continuous oil furnaces both sped up production and involved a new supervisory regime:

> Every operation was correctly timed. The manager and overseer stood together, watches in hand. It was so and so a minute; that would amount to so much in an hour, and so much total for the day.

In a similar way, high-speed steels in engineering required that discretion over cut and speed be removed from the men. With the traditional single-edge carbon tools the range of speeds for all practical cuts was very small. But the new steel tools provided a much greater range of speeds for the same cuts, thus a more specialised knowledge was required to determine the most economical speed for a given area of cut:

> In fact, this speed is so largely dependent upon the shape and cutting angle of the tool, section cut, and material operated upon that it is beyond the ability of the workman to predict and recourse must be made to experimentally determined data.

Careful supervision to determine exactly what the machine would do provided the basis for speed tables that were enforced by speed and feed men 'who having nothing else to do but walk around the shop and see that speeds, and feeds, and cuts are kept up to their proper values.'[22]

The development of high-speed tools and the introduction of the new turret and capstan lathes altered the division of labour in engineering. The process was more ambiguous than a simple deskilling and like most of the changes in this period did not result in a thoroughly new division of labour. One main direction of change was to reorder job tasks and shift the discretionary responsibilities. Speed and feed men (who were often recruited from the turners) assumed responsiblity for the speed and depth of cut. But turners and fitters also acquired new skills such as the need to read more complicated designs and blueprints. On the other hand, the widespread fear of deskilling that motivated the many conflicts over machine-manning in the 1890s was quite rational. New classes of men were recruited to work the new machines; boring, chucking, grinding and polishing work was separated into distinct departments. Employers were explicitly announcing the future demise of the fitters and turners; and the percentage of jobs where skill was increasing were a diminishing proportion of total occupations.[23]

Equally as important as these developments in altering production relations, however, were the new payment systems required by the new technologies and organisational principles. The most famous of these was the premium bonus system first devised by James Rowan, a Scottish engineering employer, who introduced it into his works the moment the ASE had been defeated in 1898. His example was quickly followed by others and by 1909 about 9 per cent of ASE members worked on the method, although it was the First World War that saw the real expansion of the system. Premium bonus represented an effort to overcome the hindrances piece- and time-work presented to the intensification of labour. The disadvantage of piece-work was that the rewards of increased productivity went solely to the worker. In the competitive environment of the late nineteenth century this was likely to encourage rate-cutting and lead to conflict. In addition, the traditional hostility of engineering workers to piece-work had forced employers to accept mutuality in wage determination which generally imposed what amounted to a maximum rate of time and a quarter. There was no incentive to perform the job any quicker because it would not be recompensed.[24] On the other hand, with day wages, the value of increased output went solely to the employer but it could only be achieved by personal driving.

Premium bonus promised a way around these difficulties. In place of a constant ratio of the division of benefit between the employer and workman from increased production, the bonus varied on the basis of the time saved on a job. The trick to its incentive aspects and to its effectiveness in lowering the cost of production lay in the way the bonus was calculated as a ratio between time allowed, time taken and time saved. Thus, if the time allowed was 100 hours, and the man did the job in 60 hours, he saved 40% of the time allowed. His bonus would be 40% of the time taken (i.e. 24 hours) and his pay would amount to 84 hours for 60 hours work. At this level the worker was better off under the Rowan system because with the same example under a scheme that divided the bonus equally between employer and workman only 20 hours' extra would be earned. Under Rowan's scheme, however, the more time that was saved the less of it the worker received as a bonus. Thus, it was calculated that if a worker saved two-thirds of the time allowed, under ordinary piece-work his wage would be 300 per cent of the standard rate, under the Halsey scheme (which divided the benefit equally) it would be 200 per cent and under Rowan it would be 165 per cent. Rowan's scheme was particularly appropriate where setting-up time composed the bulk of job-time and, thus, it was probably used to replace time-work rather than piece-work. On pure repetition-work piece payment remained appropriate because constant observation enabled an accurate assessment to be made of the time a particular job should take. But in the general work typical of British engineering it was not possible to calculate time allowances with such precision because setting-up time could occupy as much as five times the actual machine time. Thus, time allowances could afford to err on the generous side because the more time that was saved, the more the employer benefited and the worker retained an incentive free from the fear of rate cutting. In this subtle way, therefore, premium bonus acted to encroach upon the discretionary zone of the worker by displacing his control over time for feed and speed into the tables and charts of the managerially determined premium bonus calculation.[25]

In spite of its internal logic, however, premium bonus was not a self-acting incentive system and by itself was insufficient to raise productivity. The method inevitably implied a reorganisation of production and, in particular, a bureaucratisation of supervision. Rowan spent three or four years reorganising 'our previous methods and appliances . . . until the shop was re-equipped on a modern and up to date footing, after which the process became one of rounding out and filling up the minor requirements, and replacing what had become obsolete'. It was shown that even relatively minor reorganisation – such as the relocation of machines from cramped working spaces – could result in considerable gains in productivity when they were combined with premium bonus. And one of the themes of management literature throughout this period was the benefit to be gained from attention to this kind of detail. The heart of the premium bonus system, however, was that it 'brought management into touch at once with the methods employed in the workshop and their results in detail'. There was general agreement that the efficiency of inspection had to be improved under premium schemes because of the danger of men working too carelessly. Thus, the ASE complained that wherever the system was introduced, time clocks and clerks were natural accompaniments. And the key to the system's effective operation lay, first, in the rate-fixing department which gathered the data upon which rates were calculated and, second, in the proper tracking of each job as it progressed through the works. At Rowan's, for example, each job had a ticket to be signed by the foreman on its completion. In addition, from the 1890s, greater attention began to be paid to improved methods of cost accounting and more systematic record-keeping 'so that the course of material in the shops may be accurately followed step by step by the cost accounting department in a systematic and progressive manner'. As one writer pointed out, 'the real object of modern organization is to strengthen the administrative arm in its control of routine, and to keep it closely informed as the fluctuations in sectional and departmental inefficiencies'. The supervisory corollary of this was obvious: bureaucratic tracking of work-flow meant precise attention to the procedures and orders issued by management and a more exact regulation of time-keeping. It was urged that toilets be placed 'so that anybody from a distance can see into them' to counter illegal smokes and observed that 'many large works have a clerk specially for the purpose of booking the time at which men go into and come out of the w.c.'. Better methods of gate-keeping were discussed along with detailed recommendations as to how to avoid inaccuracies in the booking of time for jobs.[26] Bureaucratisation of management and tighter supervision were thus implicit in the reorganisation of work whether or not it centred around premium bonus or other new methods.

But the consequences of this deeper intrusion by management into the sphere of work execution extended beyond its impact on the craft workmen. The creation of a supervisory hierarchy redefined the traditional role of the foreman as an autonomous figure in his own right. This was a change noted again by Alfred Williams and his description of the 'old' foreman of the frame shed contrasts sharply with the conception of the foreman presented in the management literature.

> He [the old foreman] was clever, intelligent . . . a natural leader . . . [who] often came late and left early, but there was no rigid law then compelling the foreman to be forever at his post . . . a fatherly ruler and the despot, but very proud of his men . . . He hated all inter-

> ference and would not stand patronage even from his superiors, and when argument failed clever manoeuvring saved the day.

Williams may have idealised the case, but the work of Joseph Melling has shown that the qualifications for foremanship were no longer regarded as lying in superior knowledge of the craft or the independent ability to ensure a smooth functioning of production. Organisational knowledge and loyalty to management came to be emphasised as the prime qualities of the supervisor as his independent autonomy was replaced by a precise location in a hierarchy of command and control. In many trades foremen were losing their traditional responsibility for such things as labour recruitment, control over work-flow and distribution of tools. The creation of separate draughting departments under direct managerial control, for example, replaced the earlier practice of 'working with sketches traced upon cloth by the draughtsman or supervisor and carried by the foreman during the completion of the job in hand'.[27]

The separation of the supervisory function from the place of production was emphasised by the provision of offices to enable foremen to view an entire department. It was recommended that freedom of movement around the works be restricted and that care be taken 'that none of the foremen regard their offices as convenient retirement rooms to nap'. The foreman should never do any of the work himself, his job was to walk about 'with his eyes all over the place'. The supervisory division of labour also became more complicated. Many functions previously performed by one man were now distributed amongst several, each with his own sphere of responsibility. White-collar clerks figured large in this new form of supervisory hierarchy; they were described by Williams as the new 'shop disciplinarians'. In addition, the rate-fixing and planning departments possessed a similarly complex white-collar division of labour which took over many of the foremen's traditional responsibilities. There is good reason to suppose that scientific management disrupted the role of foremanship in a similar way as it threatened craft deskilling. Premium bonus, for example, represented an alternative to the kind of personal supervision previously exercised by craft foremen. But foremen did not militantly oppose these changes in large part because employers made determined efforts to ensure that they remained the loyal NCOs of industry.[28]

This pattern of a more detailed managerial intrusion into the spheres of craft autonomy was not peculiar to engineering. It was a trend that could be found in many sectors of most crafts. The boot and shoe industry provides another exmple. This industry had passed through several stages of mechanisation. Fierce conflicts had been fought in the mid-century over the sewing machine. But these earlier stages had generally allowed a sharpened division of labour to be contained within craft work. Machines to close the uppers, for example, had been rented to domestic producers. The development of the lasting machine in the late nineteenth century, however, promised the mechanisation of the final stronghold of craft labour and the introduction of a thoroughly new, Taylorist, division of labour in the factory. Lasters had traditionally performed a variety of jobs that had nothing to do with the actual lasting of the shoe and their wage lists reflected this diversity. The machine permitted these functions to be split away and for each specific job to become a discrete, simplified task within a team system of labour where boys replaced the men. In its turn, this allowed the complicated piece-lists – which were the bastions of craft restrictionism – to be replaced by the adoption of day wages. But under day wages there was no internal incentive for increased production and more elaborate structures of supervision were thus required.[29]

Until 1895, however, the restrictive traditions of work-place unionism impeded the employer's ability to realise fully the benefits from those parts of this system they were able to introduce. Time-keeping, for example, was notoriously lax. In Northampton, piece-workers wandered in and out of the factory at will until employers resorted to locking the doors. In the 1890s the employers launched a campaign to abolish the autumn race-meetings and alter the military training period because they encouraged absenteeism at busy periods. Similarly, just at the moment when traditional markets were being lost to American companies, the union imposed original piece-prices on boots made with cheaper substitute materials. Even where day wages were introduced, their benefits were undermined by widespread restriction of output. The Leicester branch, for example, scientifically managed production by calculating what output should be on the basis of old piece-prices and setting quotas for the men to follow. It was these impediments that led the employers to seek a showdown with the union in 1895. Until this point it was noted how 'supervision was not very rigid, the accounts were loosely kept and most of the data upon which prices were based were mere matters of memory or opinion'. The defeat of the workmen in 1895, however, allowed employers to install 'more exact methods of supervision' as part of a thorough reorganisation of production that stretched into the early twentieth century.[30]

Similar restraints upon productive working existed in virtually all craft trades. Very favourable conditions for the introduction of the Linotype were negotiated by London compositors in the mid-1890s because its full productive capacities were still unknown. But the high wages earned by the machine operators was complemented by a deliberately low output. It was claimed that twice as many ens were set per hour in the United States. Likewise, in engineering the percolation of new methods and machines in the 1890s occasioned a mounting number of shop-floor conflicts as the men successfully defended their craft division of labour. As one observer remarked: 'I have seen factories recently erected . . . with an entirely new equipment in which there are rows of lathes . . . without automatic feed of any description because "we are obliged to have one man to one machine".'[31]

The significance of these impediments to the cheapening of production varied between industry and location. The market structure of printing and the recognition of the key role compositors occupied in the division of labour discouraged employers from mounting the kind of concerted confrontations that were launched in the boot and shoe and engineering industries in 1895 and 1897. In cotton-spinning, the constant work stoppages caused by the increased use of bad cotton were an expense and a trouble for the employers – who were often forced to pay for time lost due to breakages – but the issue did not involve craft autonomy and did not possess the authority content found in other craft trades. The general problem for management in the skilled trades was how to integrate the new structures of production into an ordered system of social relations that would provide ways of reconciling the conflict between new methods and craft restriction. In general, it was quite obvious that traditional paternalism was increasingly obsolete. As we have seen, the viability of such a system rested upon a sphere of independence at the labour process that was at odds with the very purpose of this phase of productive development. The Cadbury's themselves recognised this when, in 1900, they replaced arbitrary methods of industrial discipline with a systematised code of behaviour that was administered according to bureaucratised rules and procedures. This did not, of course, close off the possibility in individual cases of a continued exercise of paternal strategies. In the pottery industry, for example, the celebration of significant events in the owner's family life continued to express the older ties of a reciprocal paternalism. Similarly, shipbuilding employers launched house-building schemes during the war in an attempt to retain their skilled workers and to combat spreading militancy. But the general trend in this period was for traditional paternalism gradually to be transformed into formalised welfare policies that only became common after 1918. Social clubs, canteens, and playing fields were representative examples of these policies, but they did not depend upon the evocation of a paternal atmosphere of good feeling; they were much more a matter of good business calculations.[32]

The most significant response to the conflict between existing work-place relations and new forms of production, however, was more fully to extend systems of collective bargaining. This was most obviously true in those industries where work-place unionism had already established the habits of collective bargaining but where its practice now impeded the development of production. In the craft industries, in particular, the extension and sophistication of collective-bargaining structures provided the principal basis for new means of mediating social relations in industry. These structures tended to supplant the informalities of the mid-Victorian compromise as the main characteristic of production relations. As we shall see, they did not replace the work-place orientation of bargaining, but they did transform its significance. Collective-bargaining systems then, had a dual purpose. On the one hand, they provided a forum to mediate social relations when they broke down and a permanent location for for the bargaining of (often national) conditions. On the other hand, by recognising the legitimacy of union representation in decision-making, they required that the scope and limits of this representation be defined. Thus, it was a general characteristic of these schemes that their procedures not only explained the steps necessary for the resolution of disputes but also explicitly articulated the limits of bargaining by defining the authority of the employer over the organisation and discipline of the work-place.

In cotton-spinning the major issue of the day was the use of inferior cotton which was liable to frequent breakages. A growing series of conflicts fuelled by this issue climaxed in November 1892 when the employers decided on a 5 per cent reduction in wages. A five-month strike followed, ending in the Brooklands Agreement of 1893 which provided a central machinery for negotiations. But Brooklands also addressed the 'bad spinning' issue by prohibiting it as a legitimate cause of strikes. Employers had the right to use whatever cotton they wished and work had to go on while any complaints proceeded through the lengthy procedures. Employer's prerogative was thus explicitly defined and the intensification of labour was implicitly legitimated by the agreement. Intensification was also aided by the stipulation that employers were no longer obliged to pay for time lost due to breakages.[33]

Similar definitions of the rights of employers to initiate change without consultation existed in the procedures of the boot and shoe and engineering industries. In the boot and shoe trade an arbitration system had been established in 1892. The employers' hopes that this would curb militancy proved to be false. The system was locally orientated with boards in each region and the strength of workshop and local organisation and bargaining in the union, therefore, tended to be replicated in the arbitration system. The lock-out of 1895 was launched by the employers precisely to diminish the expanded power of the men and the collective-bargaining system installed after the defeat reflected this objective. The men were denied rights of consultation over changes in the work process before they were initiated; the rights of employers to complete freedom in the methods of work organisation were explicitly affirmed; and bargaining was limited solely to wages and hours.[34]

Similarly, in the engineering industry, the conflict of 1897-8 was the climax to a growing tension over the extent to which employers would be free to reorganise the methods of production. As has been mentioned, local action by craft militants had largely preserved the traditional division of labour on the new machines. Indeed, in 1896 the first ever conference between the ASE and the employers' association occurred on this very issue after strikes in the Northeast had demonstrated the power of the men. The demand for the eight-hour day that emanated from the London shops in 1897 provided the excuse for the employers to confront the union. The real reason was the 'manner of working' and the attempt of the workmen 'to control the business of the employer'. The Terms of Settlement and the Procedure imposed by the employers' victory reflected this authority dimension. Employer authority over work organisation was explicitly recognised, their right to intiate change without consultation was established, and strikes were only legitimate once every level of the Procedure had been passed through. The Procedure was partly an attempt to undercut the local power of shop committees over trade policy and strengthen the position of the central union authority.[35] As we shall see, its consequences were to increase divisions within the union.

Like engineering and shoe-industry employers, the printing industry also faced strongly entrenched structures of local autonomy and bargaining. Leap-frogging wage claims, restrictive limitations on the use of the Linotype machine and on apprenticeship were all common features in the 1890s and early twentieth century. Employers, therefore, worked to secure national negotiating procedures with the Typographical Association (TA) in order better to control these pressures. A national agreement on Linotype wages was negotiated in 1898 amid considerable rank-and-file unrest and in 1910 a joint committee of the Linotype Users Association and the TA established negotiating procedures covering manning and machine issues. Similarly, in 1912, the Scottish employers finally broke the remnants of autonomous regulation in Glasgow printing and established the principle of mutual negotiation over such issues as overtime and apprenticeship ratios.[36]

Such procedures were viable – indeed, natural – where changes in production impacted upon trades that possessed clear traditions of restrictionism and established practices of collective bargaining. Stable social relations could only be re-established by a process of negotiation which enhanced the role and function of trade unionism at the same time as it more clearly demarcated the limits and nature of employer authority over the work process. But the tendency towards intensive labour utilisation was a general theme in this period; alterations in work processes were not confined to the craft industries. In those industries which possessed no prior traditions of craft restriction or organisation and where the habits of collective bargaining were weakly developed, the relationship between the organisation of production and employers' authority assumed somewhat different forms. Changes in the work process and the effort bargain in this sector (and we shall note in particular the gas and railway industries) proceeded generally unhindered throughout the 1880s, secured by the exercise of traditional paternal authority. By the end of the decade, however, these changes had begun to alter the division of labour in such a way as to undermine the viability of traditional authority. The occupational basis for collective organisation was created and the assumptions of paternal social relations were disrupted. It is within this context that the explosion of union organisation amongst the unskilled in the late 1880s must be understood.

The New Unionism and the Labour Process

The first generation of labour historians were quite convinced that the emergence of the new unionism reflected the 'superior attractiveness' of socialist prescriptions for the distress promulgated by the Great Depression. Although this view continues to underlie most accounts, the new unionism has never been seen as purely politically induced.

Attention has been directed to the influence of the trade cycle whose upswing in 1888 allowed the strikes of London match-girls, gas workers and dockers to provide contagious examples of unskilled militancy.[37] And, in addtion, this phase of union organisation is recognised to be closely related to the resegmentation of labour associated with the emergence of the semi-skilled strata out of the old general labourer category. Exactly how these changes altered the nature of social relations and stimulated the initial development of an expanded trade unionism, however, has remained largely unexplored.

It is certainly the case that the Great Depression provided abundant 'flammable material' – as Hobsbawm has put it – amongst the unskilled waiting to be set alight. There were significant technical changes in unskilled work processes in this period, but most often these changes occurred as a gradual accretion of alterations within the context of a managerial policy that took for granted the efficacy of its authority. In the gas works the nature and rhythm of work was gradually modified during the 1880s. It is worth noting that the two major centres of technological innovation in gas working – Manchester and Beckton gas works – were also the original centres of stokers' unionism. George Livesey of the South Metropolitan Gas Company was an avid experimenter. He was one of the first to use new retorts developed in the 1880s that burned with a fiercer heat, demanded more fuel, and increased output by more than 20 per cent. These methods required constant attention and shifted the intensity of stokers' work from an unevenly fluctuating activity, punctuated by long periods of rest, to a continuous confinement in the overheated atmosphere of the retort-house. The number of charges required by retorts increased from two per shift in the 1860s to six in the 1880s and the number of mouthpieces to be tended by each gang doubled from approximately 45 to about 90. Furthermore, the great fuel capacity of the new retorts doubled the amount of coal to be carbonised and increased the size of the scoops and shovels with which it was lifted. In addition, there was the anticipation of imminent mechanisation in the industry. As early as 1883, Livesey had introduced the 'iron man' retort charger at Beckton which improved the ratio of output to labour costs, and by 1888 over 130 of West's retort-charging machines were in operation throughout the country.[38]

The impact of this intensification of work upon the division of labour helped create the conditions for groups like stokers to organise around union collectivities. In the craft industries, the changes in the division of labour associated with new techniques usually involved task simplification and the substitution of unskilled workers to perform the job. In engineering, new lathes allowed handymen to be promoted without the need of craft training. But in trades that were largely unskilled the process tended to work the other way. The effect of changing techniques was to accentuate the pre-existing features of the division of labour and, thus, allow the creation of an occupational distinction. Stoking had always possessed an element of specialisation. Different methods of stoking required particular rhythms of working. Liverpool stokers for example found it difficult to adapt to the demands of London work, in part because the shape and size of the scoops were different. An attempt was made at union formation in 1872 in London and a strike was sparked when a navvy was placed in a stoker's job. But this strike was quickly crushed by the substitution of yardmen and it required the changes of the succeeding 20 years to create a sufficient occupational distinction for a viable union organisation to emerge. We may gain a rough idea of the modification that had occurred by 1889 in this respect by noting that, whereas in 1872 the capital had been plunged into darkness for only two days, it took over a week for blacklegs to restore lighting to Halifax in 1889. Similarly, the former strike had been fairly easily broken. But when Livesey prepared for his confrontation with the union in the autumn of 1889, he erected a dormitory, placed 700 police inside the works and another 3,000 outside to protect the blacklegs.[39]

Changes in the organisation of production during the 1880s worked to strengthen occupational identity in two ways. In the first place, they tended to reduce the number of men in each stoking gang but to provide permanent employment for those that remained. As a consequence, it seems likely that the seasonal nature of stoking work declined during this period. This was not necessarily true for other workers such as yardmen whose numbers were not diminished, for example, by the West machine and may in fact have increased. But, in itself, this must have accentuated occupational distinctiveness and helps explain why it was the stokers who were the centre of new unionism in gas. In the second place, sharpened distinctions within the work-force implied an increased specialisation of work. The tendency of the new methods of retort-firing was to confine stokers to the retort house and to limit their job task entirely to the charging and drawing of retorts. When the Salford gas works was reorganised in 1888 a new division of labour was created which removed the responsibility for wheeling the coal and burnt coke from the stokers and fashioned new job classifications for these tasks. It was calculated that stokers' productivity was increased by 50 per cent by such changes. Thus, by the late 1880s, the simple distinction between yardmen and stokers had shifted into a more complicated division of labour which consisted of stokers, firemen, scurfers, trimmers, coal- and coke-wheelers and yardmen.[40]

The extent to which these changes undermined the traditional basis of employer authority in the industry only became apparent in 1889. The gradual nature of the restructuring of the division of labour, the piecemeal reorganisation of production, and the absence of collective organisation to draw attention to their implications only slowly revealed the contradictions they posed to paternal management. Until the mid-1880s, modest grievances were expressed through the traditional petition, and employers like Livesey were able to exercise an arbitrary paternalism, awarding pensions and other privileges, for example, on a customary and discretionary basis. In 1883 Will Thorne was unable to rouse his Beckton workmates against the iron-man retort charger which reduced gang size and increased work-load. By 1890, however, the Beckton workers struck against a similar machine which it was believed promised to transform them into machine-minders. A gathering restiveness burst forth in a series of strikes in 1886 and 1887 as the prelude to 1889 and prompted the first public reconsideration of managerial methods. Employers had no intention of erecting collective bargaining, however, and their efforts focused around ways to reinforce their traditional authority by such means as reorganising shifts to allow a Sunday holiday.[41] But the explosion in the summer and autumn of 1889 (in the North the strike-wave lasted well into 1890) reflected the collapse of this system of authority. George Livesey complained that 'it was a difficult matter to get the stokers to do the proper amount of work; they would not put the proper quantity of coals into the retorts'. He estimated that 20 per cent less work was done in 1889 than in 1888: 'the allegiance of the workmen . . . was fast passing away'. The demands of the strikes of 1889 were not limited to increased wages and reduced hours. First and foremost, those demands were an effort to impose restraints upon the intensification of work by restricting the managerial organisation of production. The demand for the eight-hour shift was the most obvious example of this. But equally common were attempts to restrict managerial freedom over the deployment of labour. Reductions were sought in the numbers of mouthpieces to be worked by each gang and an upper limit placed on the amount of coal to be carbonised in each shift. In Leeds, Manchester, Birmingham and Beckton efforts were made to secure the closed shop for stokers and yardmen. Stokers also demanded that the new division of labour be formalised by tying job classifications to specific classes of workmen. There were reports that they refused to perform any tasks beyond tending to the retorts and insisted the coal be ready-weighed in preparation for firing.[42]

The extent to which demands could be translated into permanent achievements depended upon the union's success in gaining employer recognition. In the gas industry there was an important distinction between the municipally-owned works of the North of England and the private companies such as Livesey's South Metropolitan. The strikes of 1889 and 1890 had affected virtually every major city in the country. Although the Corporations sometimes offered fierce opposition to unionisation, their monopolistic position made it easier for them to contemplate collective bargaining. Thus, stoker unionism could survive the counterattack of the private companies by retreating into the municipal gas-works of the North where it fused with the growing political presence of labour to secure a grudging acceptance.[43] Within the private sector, however, stoker unionism was severely weakened by the assault spearheaded by George Livesey at his Vauxhall works at the end of 1889. Livesey's strategy was based upon a profit-sharing bonus scheme – an idea that had been touted since the mid-1880s – designed to address the twin problems of productivity and managerial control through a reformulation of paternal social relations.

The men's bonus was linked to the selling price of gas, thus internalising the workers' interest in efficiency. In the event of a strike, the bonus would be forfeited. Long-term labour contracts tied the men to particular gas-works and demanded an explicit obedience to the rights of management to deploy labour as they saw fit. Furthermore, the scheme cleverly played on the divergent interests of the yardmen and stokers. When the scheme was presented in a carefully prepared confrontation in November 1889, the yardmen accepted it immediately. To the unskilled yardmen, the labour-contract clauses offered security of employment and the possibility of occupational mobilty. But to the stokers – who resisted it to a man – the system endowed management with 'the power of making a stoker . . . into a yard labourer'. The stokers' strike was eventually broken and the scheme became a widely copied model elsewhere in the country. By 1914 nearly 250,000 men were covered by descendants of this profit-sharing scheme which survived until the 1920s in the South Metropolitan works as the definition of authority relations.[44]

As a manifestation of the way changes in the labour process were eroding paternal definitions of social relations, the strike wave in the gas-works was typical of the broader themes of the new unionism. After the first flush of organisation in the late 1880s and early 1890s, however, the new unionism sharply contracted to a few isolated centres of organisation until reviving again just before the First World War. One major reason for the partial achievements of this initial phase lay in the strength of the differentiations in the division of labour. Where those distinctions were sufficiently marked they laid the basis for an enduring presence of union organisation which was able to survive trade-cycle recessions and employer counterattacks. But this could only be achieved if the original aims of organisational inclusiveness gave way to a reliance upon stable occupational groups with a recognised place in the division of labour. Thus, stokers soon abandoned the initial effort to organise all gas-workers and were able to sustain a viable – if weakened – unionism throughout the 1890s. This pattern of variable success, which rested upon the extent to which job identification allowed a certain power within the division of labour, would seem to be paralleled in trades of the new unions.

Dock-work, for example, had been greatly altered in the 1870s and 1880s by the demise of sailing ships. Steam-driven ships required larger berths and quicker turn-around time. Expanding forms of subcontracting enhanced intensification and the casuality of labour, but the numbers of permanent men also increased because these changes demanded a continuous core of workers. The expansion of union organisation beyond its traditional centres amongst stevedores seems to have depended upon this group. The union attempted to stabilise labour deployment in London through the union ticket and this was initially accepted by employers. But in London this recognition was withdrawn in 1890 and the well-known free-labour attack in the provinces in 1893-4 (perhaps the most ambitious attempt to reformulate paternal control) caused a rapid crumbling of the union. Unionism could survive only where changes in the division of labour had created semi-skilled occupational groups such as the crane-men who possessed a strategic significance as machine-operators. Even so, the mould of prior social relations had been broken and by 1911-12 sufficient 'flammable material' once again ignited a national strike which helped convince employers of the stabilising advantages of collective bargaining allowed unionism to lay down permanent roots on the waterside.[45]

A further centre of union expansion lay in railway work. Between 1835 and 1875 only ten strikes were found to have occurred on the railways and all were very short-lived affairs. At the end of the

1880s the subservience of railway-workers was broken as 5,000 new members flooded into the Amalgamated Society of Railway Servants in 1889 alone, and by the first decade of the twentieth century the industry had become a centre of industrial militancy.[46] The process by which this occurred was somewhat different from the pattern traced above. But it is worth examining as a particularly clear example of the way the changing relationship between work and authority during this period altered the basis of social relations.

Railway-work rested upon the combination of an iron discipline and paternal welfarism. In return for a military style of obedience, a wide array of occupational benefits and status distinctions were provided. The latter were particularly important. It was revealing, for example, that one of the complaints of the striking Taff Vale railwaymen in 1900 was that the company had failed to deliver new uniforms and the men resented having 'to go around looking more like tramps than anything else'. The acute sensibilities of this status consciousness pointed to one of the curious paradoxes of social relations in railway work. The system allowed and encouraged 'bailiwicks of autonomy' to emerge that stood in apparent contradiction to the tightness of managerial control. Drivers could be punished, for example, for deviations from the timetable; but even directors had to request permission to mount the footplate. Guards, drivers and signalmen in particular possessed strongly developed 'property rights' in their jobs. Engines and vans were 'owned' by certain drivers and guards who would take out only their particular piece of rolling-stock. The same was true of signalmen, alone in their boxes which none could enter without permission. Until the electrical telegraphy brought them out of their isolation, signalmen were solely responsible for the administration of their section of track. Strict job classification encouraged a sense of territorial demarcation which extended even to the unskilled fire droppers:

> They were entirely unsupervised, which in turn was responsible for their strong independent and responsible attitude . . . Foremen rarely interfered with them . . . Rarely did they take an interest in trade unionism . . . Their action was workshop democracy, and the ultimate weapon was 'The Hammer'. When a real grievance could not be solved, they put on the Hammer by going slow. This was only solved by someone at the Superintendent level visiting the lads.

This description perfectly captures the competing tensions and contradictions in railway-work. A highly developed sense of 'independence' combined with a reliance upon paternal bargaining. As Frank McKenna has pointed out, 'within his limited territory . . . a man could often create his own administrative system [and] stamp his own individuality over a certain area or stretch of ground'.[47] These bailwicks (as McKenna calls them) were a result of the needs of production. Drivers had to be entrusted with engines, signalmen with signalboxes, guards with the running of the train. Supervision was impossible beyond the constraints of the timetable and only when things went seriously awry would the worker's responsibility for the details of production be subject to examination. The social inversion of the director asking the driver's permission to come aboard was a ritualistic expression of the safety responsibility of the driver. Quite clearly, the sense of job responsibility encouraged by company hierarchy was perfectly compatible with paternal authority. Indeed, sectionalist grade consciousness was always a conservative force amongst railway-workers. Such systems are delicately balanced, however – as research into the social rituals of early modern France has shown – and always possess a contradictory potential. The dynamic in railway social relations lay in the balance between the sense of job territory and the paternal reciprocities that underlay it. If this balance was violated then the system of authority itself was brought into disrepute. And from the 1880s and 1890s the stability of the system began to be undermined principally by changes in the nature of work, an abrogation of the paternal bargain by changing management styles, and intrusions into the bailiwicks of autonomy.

This process was particularly concentrated in the strategically placed skilled trades of signalmen, guards and drivers. It is convenient to consider signal-work separately because this was the only area of railway labour where technical change seems to have played a significant role in the changing bases of social relations. From the mid-1870s, the skill and responsibilities of signal-work were altered by the adoption of the block and interlocking systems of signalling. The block system of traffic movement worked by keeping trains apart by time rather than distance. A larger portion of responsibility for the safe and smooth operation of the line was thus transferred from drivers to signalmen who supervised movement within their particular block. As a result, the job became sophisticated and skilled. It was said in 1893 that, compared to the 1870s, 'the work of signalling now has become a profession . . . Any man with common sense could act as a signalman before, but now you require a man of some education and good sound judgment . . . a signalman in former times had no responsibilities compared to what he has now, and there is skill as well.' Accompanying the block system was the arrival of electrical telgraphy and the interlocking of points and signals. Points were now controlled by frame levers which were harder to pull then the old 'hung loose' switches. Each section of the line was brought into constant communication with others by means of bell and needle instruments and later by the telephone. Thus, as the work became more responsible so it was becoming more intensified. To permit the passing of one train in some Midland Line boxes involved receiving and sending fifty electrical signals, making twelve entries in the train book, pulling the levers, and visually observing the movement of the train.[48]

If a more integrated system of working intensified the labour, it also broke down the isolation that had traditionally led signalmen to stand apart from union organisation and collective action. By the end of the 1880s this change had become apparent. Union membership amongst signalmen increased decisively during the 1880s and from the 1890s they assumed a leading role in trade movements. There is little doubt that improved communication between the boxes was a major factor in these developments. Raymond Williams, whose father was a signalman, has recounted how they

> talked for hours to each other . . . to boxes as far away as Swindon and Crewe. . . . So they were getting news directly from industrial South Wales, for example. They were in touch with a much wider social network, and were bringing modern politics into the village.

A clear sign that signal work was creating the conditions for modern collective organisation was seen in the leading role signalmen played in the all-grades movement of 1890 on the Midland Railway. Whereas in 1870, for example, efforts to create unity had been weak and fragile, by 1890, it was explained.

> traffic increased, the points and signals were concentrated and interlocked and the block system was introduced, owing to which signalmen found their duties more difficult, responsible, and trying . . . which created discontent with their wages [and conditions] . . . and resulted in meetings of the men being held in the larger centres.[49]

Signalling was unique amongst railway-work in experiencing significant technical change. The most important agency that reshaped social relations on the railways was the transgression upon the 'paternal bargain' that flowed from altered managerial policies. From the late 1880s the changing cost structure of railway business placed a sharp squeeze on profits. Successful labour actions in the late 1880s and early 1890s which reduced hours and increased wages were partially responsible for a rise of 11 per cent in labour costs during the 1890s. These costs were inelastic; but little compensation could be sought in the more elastic cost of materials like coal because these, too, were tending to increase. The expansion of third-class traffic prevented receipts from operations keeping pace with this increase in costs. Nor could these pressures be offset by rate increases because the state, bowing to political pressure from freight customers, refused to allow a commensurate rise in charges. In addition, in response to the growing demands for safety, Parliament was requiring the companies to make heavy capital expenditures. An Act of 1889, for example, required the installation of the interlocking system on lines where it did not already exist. As a result of these combined influences, the rate of return on capital declined from 4.08 per cent in 1886-90 to 3.38 per cent in 1901-5.[50]

The companies' initial response to this situation was to seek greater efficiency and to reduce labour costs by disrupting the structure of grade distinctions, rewards and duties. This was particularly true in freight operations because the limits of passenger traffic efficiency were bounded by the timetable. The surge of militancy in 1888-9 in the Northeast directly followed a reclassification of work which effectively reduced wages and threatened promotion scales. In 1888 the London and North Western Railway adopted the trip method of payment for goods guards, a system of piece-work which tended to reduce wages and encourage the creation of a casualised class of guards who could be called out only when needed. The Midland Railway abolished the guaranteed week in 1886 and imposed a new schedule of harsh fines. In 1893, the Taff Vale Railway began systematically to violate the grade system. Guards and drivers were given extra duties; firemen were substituted for drivers when traffic was heavy; and a new policy reversed traditional promotion from grade by permitting any man to apply for any position whether it was in his grade or not. The search for more efficient working also led to violations of job property rights. In 1900, the North East Railway required guards to take brake vans in the order they came rather than possessing their own: 'it is manifestly expensive, inconvenient, and the cause of much delay in working to have a van stay idle when a man comes off duty instead of running and earning money for the company'.[51]

In addition, the companies used their traditionally unchallenged dominance over labour to secure greater efficiency through tighter discipline. The experience of the Taff Vale Railway provides a particularly appropriate example of this in the light of its later fame. In 1890 a successful strike gained a measure of recognition for collective negotiation and a guaranteed 60-hour week. But in November 1891 Ammon Beasley was appointed manager. Beasley immediately inaugurated a tough, assertive policy towards labour which would eventually turn a financially strapped railway into the most profitable *and* the most densely unionised line in the country. He introduced a policy of instant dismissal with no appeal, refused to recognise the joint committee established in 1890, abandoned the 60-hour working week (that is, the fact that each week's work stands by itself), adopted a more flexible promotion policy and, as we have mentioned, imposed additional duties on guards and drivers. The Taff Vale strike of 1900 was sparked by the explicit abandonment of the 'paternal bargain' on labour deployment when, in violation of traditional practice, a signalman was moved against his wish to a new signal box. But this strike was merely the climax to a decade of eroding respect for the arbitrary discipline of managerial authority.[52]

By 1900, however, the stabilisation of costs began to be sought through better means of traffic management. Much attention was paid to American methods of railway organisation where pooling arrangements, higher train loads and close regulation of traffic flow were identified as the keys to efficiency. Such methods, however, depended upon a constant stream of detailed information which determined the allocation of resources and transmitted decisions through a clearly defined hierarchy of responsibilities. Thus, in the first decade of the twentieth century the methods of railway management began to be revised. Traditionally, freight traffic had been controlled by the 'flow of traffic' principle which rested upon ascertaining the general level of demand in each centre and directing empty waggons towards their location. The disadvantage of this system was its unresponsiveness to sudden changes in demand or in the volume of traffic. Once stock had embarked on its journey, it was difficult to intercept. But neither did this system demand a highly bureaucratised management structure. The new methods of the control system, however, depended upon detailed and accurate information as to the numbers, types, and locations of waggons which was then matched with the needs and resources of all collection points along the line. To operate the control system properly a regular and systematic flow of paper-work on a day-to-day basis was necessary. Just one amongst many channels of information-flow and chains of command ran as follows: station-masters were to send their reports into the depot by 12 noon; the depot was to survey all the station reports for dispatch to the District Superintendent by 2.30 p.m; the latter reported to the General Superintendent by 3.00 p.m. where 'the waggon controller . . . is now in a position to adjust the balance of supply and demand between the several districts'. The system implied a close definition of duties within a hierarchy which could be relied upon to faithfully transmit and execute decisions. At its most sophisticated, the system linked all points in an area by telephone enabling the district controller to issue immediate instructions to particular trains through signalmen. Train controllers had absolute and undivided control over the traffic.[53]

Thus, social relations on the railways were decisively altered. A new level of management control was interposed into the bailiwicks of autonomy by the access of the controller to the signal boxes, drivers' cabs and guards' vans. Customary rights in the instruments of production were also removed; typically, responsibility for loading of goods trains was transferred from the guards to the district controller. In addition, the success of the system rested upon the oral communication of orders 'to ensure the rapid carrying out of plans for moving traffic by giving direct instructions to persons of authority.' Much of the tension caused by the system flowed from the speed ups that resulted.[54] The reliance upon oral communication necessitated frequent contraventions of the printed working rules and brought the system into conflict with the conventions governing social relations on the railways. In 1913 such an issue was the cause of the celebrated strike over Guard Richardson's refusal to attach more vans than the safety regulations permitted. When Richardson appealed this order up the 'paternal' hierarchy to the General Manager, he was told that controllers' orders took precedence.

The problem was not simply that lower-level officials were being given more authority – although that certainly was happening.[55] The real problem lay in the way changing methods of work and styles of management undermined the reciprocities of the paternal bargain. The control system was the climax to a process that had been going on for 20 years. From the 1890s the rules that had previously governed social relations were being changed by policies that contradicted paternal reciprocity. Yet the assumptions of authority had not changed. Thus, at a time when 90 per cent of the Taff Vale men had sent in their notices, Ammon Beasley continued to maintain the fiction that he could not recognise the joint committee because 'it would interfere with the right of every individual member of the staff to appeal to him'. Beasley resisted the negotiating efforts of Richard Bell (General Secretary of the ASRS) because 'I cannot permit the workmen themselves to take the management of the concern out of my hands'. These views were in no way unique. In the late 1890s, Frederic Harrison of the London and North Western dismissed those who refused to promise to remain loyal to the company in the event of a strike, pointing out ' "we claim the right to deal with our servants as we think expedient' ". And Lord Claude Hamilton in 1907 explained the dilemma posed by union recognition to this style of authority:

> How much longer would the men in each department continue to observe the same respect they now have for the head of that department when they know that he would no longer be responsible, except in name, for their pay and control?[56]

The problem, of course, was that this kind of authority could no longer provide a sure basis for mediating or defining social relations. It had begun to break down in the late 1880s when the companies had tried to tie pension rights to work discipline and, instead, had helped to stimulate mass unionism. Similarly, the unremitting use of authority to contravene the bases of social relations on the Taff Vale Railway in the 1890s had undermined the paternal foundations of discipline and stimulated a strong union presence. One kind of collective loyalty had been replaced by another. The climax came in 1900 when signalman Ewington's 'bailiwick' was violated by the order to move to another box. Ewington had strong personal reasons for not wanting to make this move, but he had been a leader in the 1895 strike and the company affirmed their right to insist. In so doing, however, the limits of paternal reciprocity were transgressed, for it was not traditionally done to force such moves against the express wishes of the man. It is, perhaps, significant that this strike was marked by a high level of violence against persons and property, as if to symbolise the full rejection of traditional authority. A similar meaning may be attached to the Driver Knox case in 1912. Knox's dismissal for being reported drunk off duty sparked a general shut-down in the Northeast. The implicit claim of the company to a complete arbitration over life and habits had been accepted in the past because it was part of a total system of social relationships. By 1912 that system had been gutted of any meaningful reciprocity and so the discipline and obedience that went with it also disappeared.[57]

The demise of traditional social relations was matched by the concurrent demise of quiescent, friendly society unionism and the growth in union organisation and militancy. This was a process that occurred largely from 'below'. After the leap in union membership in the late 1880s, a national programme was developed at the 1889 Annual General Meeting of the ASRS and all-grades agitation in the late 1890s forced a more militant spirit upon a cautious leadership. In the 1890s only the North Eastern Railway recognised the formal presence of trade unions, but even there fully-fledged collective bargaining did not exist. Elsewhere, the dilution of disciplinary authority that union recognition implied provided the greatest single obstacle to its achievement. But the threat of a national strike and pressure from the government led a group of 'progressive' railway managers to formulate a conciliation scheme in 1907. The scheme did not bring a new structure of social relations, it represented an attempt to reconstruct a system that would ensure the mediation of social relations without union recognition. Traditional practices were formalised by the scheme. Each case had first to be presented by petition or memorial; representation was organised by grade and limited to men employed by the company; union officials were, thus, excluded, although they could be elected from their grade to their own company board. And, finally, employer authority was explicitly protected and defined: they retained the right to interpret the arbitrators' awards and the discretionary power to exclude disciplinary issues. Amendments made in 1911 were largely minor: union recognition was granted in return for a government agreement which allowed rates to rise in conjunction with labour costs and certain improvements were made in the timely disposal of cases.[58] In spite of these inadequacies, however, the essential breakthrough had been achieved. The companies had been forced to abandon their claims to paternal authority and obliged to turn to collective bargaining and union recognition in order to secure consent and authority at work.

Conclusion

By 1914 the bases upon which labour was represented and organised in society had been decisively changed. The spread of collective organisation signalled not merely the decomposition of the mid-Victorian compromise, but also the main lines upon which social relations were being restructured. For although we have emphasised the elements that disrupted the earlier structures of social relations, the period of the 1880s and 1890s was equally a period when those structures were being rebuilt. This was a process that was wider than production relations; indeed, it was inevitably a political process because it revolved around the question of how labour was to be represented in society. But before we explore that issue, it is necessary to make some fairly general remarks about the way this restructuring worked.

The paradox of the emergence of class as the overriding unit of socio-political organisation and identity during this period was that it occurred within the context of a deeply fractured and segmented working class. We can say relatively little about this here, but it is obvious that the changes in production relations traced above altered the boundaries and relationships between the various sections of the working class. Most importantly, those changes offered different opportunities and threats to different groups. For the semi-skilled or unskilled, the changes seem to have provided not only the need but also the opportunities for collective organisation; for the skilled those changes posed serious threats to the bases of unity. The restructuring of the boundaries and responsibilities of craft skill produced tension not only between craft workers and employers but also within the working class itself. When groups like shipyard-helpers or underhands in the steel industry tried to organise, the hostility of craft workers was a more important impediment than the attitude of employers who, in fact, were often quite indifferent. Craft workers were threatened by the emergence of the semi-skilled and in many unions, such as the ASE, the correct response to this challenge remained unresolved until the early 1920s. Equally, tensions were produced between crafts. Demarcation disputes were endemic and fierce in the 1890s. In the shipyards, for example, boilermakers fought with plumbers and others over the boundaries of job rights. Locally, these segmentations could be of considerable importance, but it cannot be said that they impeded the emergence of a strong working-class presence in society. Indeed the real question is to explain how they could combine with the greater sense of class identity that clearly marked the period. It is quite obvious that the tendency in mid-nineteenth century for such segmentation to override common identity was reversed in the late nineteenth century. There were two broad lines of development that help explain why this occurred.

The first was a pervasive communality of experience. This was a process that extended far beyond the realm of production; it was manifest at virtually every level of experience one cares to imagine. Thus, the demise of local cultural traditions – recounted, for example, in

Flora Thompson's *Lark Rise to Candleford*, or in the mass of folklore gathered at this very moment – and its subordination to national definitions and patterns was surely one powerful and underresearched aspect of this. But within the sphere of production it is broadly true to say that sectional groups confronted similar circumstances. The general experience of intensified work and greater managerial intrusion into the processes of production initiated responses that cut across the boundaries of the particular job. The experience of the Great Depression led printers to abandon their liberal opposition to hours legislation, for example, just as the newly organised were driven to advocate the protection of labour conditions by the state. Engineers and stokers were led to more assertive political and industrial postures both to defend and to gain their different objectives. Both groups, for different reasons and in different ways, were led to the position that social relations no longer could be ordered either on the craft independence of the engineer or the paternal dependence of the stoker.

But the second series of developments was of equal, if not greater, importance. For these tendencies to amount to a changed presence for labour in society, they needed to be articulated and given expression through the organisations and institutions that manifested the immanence of labour. That is, the collective organisations through which labour operated in industry and in politics were not simple reflections of this greater 'class' identity, they were the key agencies in defining the notion of what 'class' meant programmatically and politically. Class as the unit of organisation and loyalty was in part the product of the institutional creations of collective bargaining and the political organisations that represented labour. How large a part is a matter for debate; if it is true that the nature of this organisational presence cannot be read off from 'class' it is equally true that it cannot be understood apart from the socio-economic forces that were creating the imperatives for a rearrangement of social and political relations. It will not do to treat the Labour Party, for example, as purely a creation in the space of politics, if only because 'politics' in the sense of what posture such institutions should assume to represent labour in society was deeply imbricated at all levels of the changes in social relations. It is for this reason, for example, that working-class politicisation during this period was represented as much by such 'cultural' forms as the Women's Co-operative Guild or the Labour churches as it was by the Independent Labour Party. The demise of mid-Victorian social relations forced into the open the question of how the labour estate was to define the roles, responsibilities and programmes that expressed the aspirations of 'class'. Within Labour Party politics and within a wider political context, the implications of these changes in social relations became a central issue of debate. How that question was resolved would be a major determinant in the shaping of labour's modern history.

Notes

1. Avner Offer, *Property and Politics 1870-1914* (Cambridge, 1982), pp. 226-7.

2. On changes in the academic world see T. W. Heyck, *The Transformation of Intellectual Life in Victorian England* (London, 1982); H.A. Clegg, A. Fox and A.F. Thompson, *A History of British Trade Unionism since 1889* (Oxford, 1964), pp. 174-5.

3. Alfred Williams, *Life in a Railway Factory* (London, 1915), pp. 303, 267-73.

4. On these themes in France, Germany and the United States see Michelle Perrot, 'The Three Ages of Industrial Discipline' in John Merriman (ed.), *Consciousness and Class Experience in Nineteenth Century Europe* (New York, 1980); Dieter Groh, 'Intensification of Work and Industrial Conflict in Germany 1896-1914', *Politics and Society*, vol. 8, nos 3-4 (1978); Harry Braverman, *Labor and Monopoly Capital* (New York, 1974); Richard Edwards, *Contested Terrain* (New York, 1979).

5. Groh, 'Intensification of Work'; David Gordon, Richard Edwards and Michael Reich, *Segmented Work, Divided Workers. The Historical Transformation of Labor in the United States* (Cambridge, Mass., 1982), pp. 230-4.

6. On coal see A.J. Taylor, 'Labour Productivity and Technical Innovation in the British Coal Industry', *Ec. Hist. Rev.*, vol. 14 (1961-2); on the railways, see R.J. Irving, 'The Profitability and Performance of British Railways 1870-1914', *Ec. Hist. Rev*. vol. 31 (1978); on gas, see *Journal of Gas Lighting*, 20 June 1892, pp. 1143-8; on pottery, see Richard Whipp, 'Potters, Masters and Unions: Management Strategy and Industrial Relations in the Early Twentieth Century Pottery Industry,' unpublished paper, University of Warwick, May 1982, p. 16.
Labour costs in pottery increased from 33 per cent to 76 per cent of the cost of production between 1890 and 1914.

7. Stephen Meyer, *The Five Dollar Day: Labor Management and Social Control in the Ford Motor Company 1908-21* (Albany, NY, 1981), pp. 162-98. I do not intend to imply that Ford met with unqualified success in this enterprise.

8. Leslie Hannah,'Visible and Invisible Hands in Great Britain' in Alfred Chandler (ed.), *Manageral Hierarchies* (Cambridge, Mass., 1980); Bernard Elbaum and Frank Wilkinson, 'Industrial Relations and Uneven Development: A Comparative Study of the American and British Steel Industries'; *Cambridge Journal of Economics* vol. 3 (1978); S.B. Saul, 'The Market and the Development of the Mechanical Engineering Industries in Britain 1860-1914', *Ec. Hist. Rev.*, vol. 20, no. 1 (1967).

9. Keith Burgess, *The Challenge of Labour* (London, 1980), pp. 77-8.

10. William Lazonick, 'Factor Costs and the Diffusion of Ring Spinning in Britain Prior to World War One,' *Quarterly Journal of Economics*, vol. 96, no. 1 (1981), p. 106; Donald McCloskey, *Enterprise and Trade in Victorian Britain* (London, 1981), Chapters 5 and 6.

11. Bryan Palmer, *A Culture in Conflict. Skilled Workers in Hamilton Ontario,*

1860-1914 (Montreal, 1979), pp. 242-4; David Montgomery, *Workers Control in America* (Cambridge, Mass., 1979); Gordon, Edwards and Reich, *Segmented Work,* pp. 95-7; Dan Clawson, *Bureaucracy and the Labor Process* (New York, 1980).

12. Edward Cadbury, 'Some Principles of Industrial Organization: The Case For and Against Scientific Management', *Sociological Review*, vol. 7, no. 2 (April 1914), pp. 104-6; *The Engineer* 21 March 1902, p. 280, quoting and commenting on a letter from George Barnes on the Gantt system; 14 November 1913, p. 521; *The Engineering Magazine*, (New York), October 1901-March 1902, p. 396; Archibald Kidd, *History of the Tin-Plate Workers and Sheet Metal Workers* (London, 1949), p. 209; ASE, *Monthly Journal*, November 1901; September 1903, p. 98; February 1902, p. 77.

13. W.F. Watson, *The Worker and the Wage Incentive* (London, 1934), pp. 11-12.

14. Keith Burgess, *The Origins of Brltish Industrial Relations* (London, 1975), p. 33; Tom Mann, *Tom Mann's Memoirs* (London, 1923), pp. 34, 36.

15. Lazonick, 'Production Relations, Labor Productivity, and Choice of Technique: British Cotton Spinning', *Journal of Economic History*, vol. 41, no. 3 (1981).

16. Elbaum and Wilkinson, 'Industrial Relations and Uneven Development'.

17. Alan Fox, *The National Union of Boot and Shoe Operatives 1874-1957* (Oxford, 1958), pp. 99-106; R.A. Church,'The Effect of the American Export Invasion on the British Boot and Shoe Industry 1885-1914,' *Journal of Economic History*, vol. 28, no. 2 (1968).

18. Williams, *Life in a Railway Factory*, p. 98; Parliamentary Papers, *Report on 'Gain Sharing' and Certain Other Systems of Bonus on Production,* 1895, Vol. LXXX, (c. 7848), pp. 39, 42-60, 63-106.

19. *Report on 'Gain Sharing'*, p 63; F.A. Halsey, 'The Premium Plan of Paying for Labor', in J.R. Commons (ed.), *Trade Unionism and Labor Problems* (New York, repr. 1967), pp. 278-83.

20. Keith Burgess, 'New Unionism for Old? The Amalgamated Society of Engineers in Britain 1880-1914', unpublished paper, Roehampton Institute of Higher Education, 1981, pp. 2, 8-9; M. Holbrook-Jones, *Supremacy and Subordination of Labour* (London, 1982), pp. 73-74; Richard Whipp, 'Work in the Pottery Industry,' unpublished paper, University of Warwick, 1983, pp. 7-13.

21. *Vigilance Gazette*, November 1888, pp. 12-13 and February 1889, pp. 11-12; Sarah C. Gillespie, *A Hundred Years of Progress* (Glasgow, 1953), pp. 73-5, *The Printing News*, January 1893, p. 11; February 1893, pp. 6-7; July 1893, p. 5; *Scottish Typographical Circular*, December 1897, p. 191; *Typographical Circular*, January 1895, p. 7 and July 1895, pp. 8-9; John Child, *Industrial Relations in the British Printing Industry* (London, 1967), p. 56; Typographical Association, *Extracts from Report of Delegate Meeting*, December 1893, pp. 2, 8-9, 17.

22. Williams, *Life in a Railway Factory*, pp. 183-4; Dempster Smith and Philip Pickworth, *Engineers' Costs and Economical Workshop Production* (Manchester, 1914), p. 85; Arthur Barker, *The Management of Small Engineering Workshops* (Manchester, 1899), pp. 114-31.

23. Charles More, *Skill and the English Working Class 1870-1914* (London, 1980), pp. 187-90; Frank Rose, *The Machine Monster* (Manchester, 1908); *The Engineer*, 31 January 1902, pp. 122-3 and 7 February 1902 pp. 132-42; *The Engineering Magazine*, October 1898-March 1899, p. 704.

24. Holbrook-Jones, *Supremacy*, p. 86; Smith and Pickworth, *Engineers' Costs*, p. 48.

25. William Rowan Thomson, *The Rowan Premium Bonus System of Payment*

by Results, (Glasgow, 1917), pp. 20-25, 35, 54-6; Watson, *The Worker and the Wage Incentive*, pp. 21-2; J. Rowan, 'A Premium System Applied to Engineering Works', Institute of Mechanical Engineers, *Proceedings*, March 1903, p. 209; *Engineering Magazine*, October 1899-March 1900, pp. 204, 449.

26. J.E. Powell, *The Output Problem* (London, 1921), p. 148; Rowan Thomson, *The Rowan System*, pp. 60-61; Rowan, 'A Premium System', pp. 209-17, 227, 238; ASE, *Monthly Journal*, May 1902, p. 85; Smith and Pickworth, *Engineers' Costs*, pp. 52, 154-5; Barker, *Small Engineering Workshops*, p. 16; *The Engineering Magazine*, October 1899-March 1900, p. 63; J. Slater Lewis, *The Commercial Organization of Factories* (London, 1896), pp. xxix, 139; Sinclair and Frank Pearn, *Workshop Costs for Engineers and Manufactures* (Manchester, 1905), pp. 1-2.

27. Williams, *Life in a Railway Factory*, pp. 79-80; Joseph Melling, 'Leading Hands and Industrial Techniques: Workplace Supervision and Management Practice in the British Engineering Trades 1870-1914', unpublished paper, University of Liverpool, p. 32. I am grateful to Dr Melling for sharing the results of his important research with me.

28. Barker, *Small Engineering Workshops*, pp. 103-6, 132; Joseph Melling, '"Non-commissioned Officers": British Engineering Employers and their Supervisory Workers, 1880-1920', *Social History*, vol. 5, no. 2 (1980); Smith and Pickworth, *Engineers' Costs*, pp. 78-9; Craig Littler, *The Development of the Labour Process in Capitalist Societies*, (London, 1982), pp. 53, 87, 92-4.

29. Elizabeth Brunner, 'The Origins of Industrial Peace: The Case of the British Boot and Shoe Industry', *Oxford Economic Papers*, vol. 1 (1949). *Shoe and Leather Record,* 8 January 1892, p. 70, 27 May 1892, p. 1273-4; 6 September 1890, p. 296; 3 July 1891, p. 19; 5 August 1891, p. 1061; National Union of Boot and Shoe Operatives, *Monthly Reports*, May 1889, p. 2; Fox, *NUBSO*, pp. 86-93.

30. Edward Swaysland, *Boot and Shoe Design and Manufacture* (Northampton, 1895), pp. 231-40; Keith Brooker, 'The Northampton Shoemakers' Reaction to Industrialization: Some Thoughts', *Northamptonshire Past and Present* (1980), pp. 151-4; Fox, *NUBSO*, pp. 101-2, 207; *Shoe and Leather Record*, 15 January 1892, p. 122; 29 January 1892, pp. 224; 19 February 1892, p. 441; 11 March 1892, pp. 609-10.

31. *Webb Collection*, B. Vol. LXXIV, f. 33; *Engineering Magazine*, April-September 1899, pp. 384-6; Eric Wigham, *The Power to Manage*, (London, 1973), pp. 30-3; Burgess, *Origins of Industrial Relations*, pp. 60-1.

32. Joseph Melling, 'Employers, Industrial Housing and the Evolution of Company Welfare Policies in Britain's Heavy Industry: West Scotland 1870-1920,' *International Review of Social History*, vol. 26, no. 3 (1981); Richard Whipp, 'Potters, Masters and Unions', pp. 26-34. Edward Cadbury, *Experiments in Industrial Organization* (London, 1912), pp. 69-73.

33. Lazonick, 'Production Relations', pp. 504-5; Clegg, Fox, and Thompson, *British Trade Unionism*, pp. 112-17.

34. Fox, *NUBSO*, pp. 221-3, 231-3; National Union of Boot and Shoe Operatives, *Monthly Reports*, November 1894, p. 2. The 1892 conciliation system in shoe-making was far more favourable to the men; it allowed all issues to be referred to arbitrators where the men were able to argue custom and practice to endorse many restrictions. For a description see Sydney and Beatrice Webb, *Industrial Democracy* (London, 1913), pp. 185-92.

35. *Engineering Magazine*, April-September 1900, pp. 167-8; Burgess, *Origins of Industrial Relations*, pp. 68-9; see ASE, *Monthly Journal*, January 1901, p. 52 and February 1901, p. 59 for examples of the expansion of reorganised production after the 1898 defeat; Wigham, *Power to Manage*, pp. 40, 56.

36. Linotype Users' Association, *Monthly Circular*, June 1899, p. 1; October

1899, p. 1; May 1901, p. 8; *Scottish Typographical Journal*, February and August 1913; A.E. Musson, *The Typographical Association* (Oxford, 1954),pp. 140-43; *Typographical Circular*, January 1899, p. 5; February 1899, pp. 4-5; June 1911, p. 15.

37. S. and B. Webb, *History of Trade Unionism* (London, 1902), pp. 307-3, 385-95; Clegg, Fox and Thompson, *British Trade Unionism*, p. 55; G.D.H. Cole and Raymond Postgate, *The Common People 1746-1946* (London, 1961), pp. 425-6; E.H. Hunt, *British Labour History 1815-1914* (London, 1981), pp. 304-5. The following section largely repeats the arguments presented in R. Price, 'Der *New Unionism* und die Veränderungen des Arbeitprozesses 1880 bis 1920', in Wolfgang Mommsen and Hans Gerhard-Husung, *Auf dem Wege zur Massengewerkschaft* (Stuttgart, 1984). For the best analysis of the economic roots of the new unionism see Eric Hobsbawm, *Labouring Men* (London, 1964), Chapters 9, 10 and 11; James Cronin, *Industrial Conflict in Modern Britain* (London, 1979), pp. 93-6.

38. Frank Popplewell, 'The Gas Industry', in Sydney Webb and Arnold Freeman (eds), *Seasonal Trades* (London, 1912), pp. 175-6; C.E. Brackenbury, *Modern Methods of Saving Labour in Gasworks* (London, 1900), p. 22; Zeriah Colburn, *The Gas-Works of London* (London, 1865), p. 24; Will Thorne, *My Life's Battles* (London, 1925), pp. 64-5; *Journal of Gas Lighting*, 19 October 1880, p. 607; 26 June 1883, p. 1192; 10 November 1885, p. 830; 15 June 1886, p. 1108; 8 May 1888, p. 824; 18 September 1888, p. 517; 2 July 1889, p. 9; 14 May 1889, p. 915, 9 July 1889, p. 65; 26 June, 1883, pp. 1192-4.

39. The importance of relative occupational stability in the formation of the new unions is noted by Hobsbawm, *Labouring Men*, pp. 158-73, 187; *Journal of Gas Lighting*, 17 December 1872, pp. 1033-5 and 7 January 1890, p. 14; *Royal Commission on Labour*, 1893-94, Vol. XXXIV (c. 6894-ix), ques. 26879-885.

40. *Journal of Gas Lighting*, 15 June 1886, p. 1108; 26 June 1883, p. 1193; 18 September 1888, p. 517; Popplewell, 'Gas Industry', pp. 177-78.

41. Thorne, *My Life's Battles; Journal of Gas Lighting*, 20 May 1890, p. 937; on strikes in the 1880s see *Journal of Gas Lighting*, 20 November 1883, p. 887; 6 December 1887, p. 1023; 13 November 1888, p. 854; 18 September 1888, p. 517; 11 December 1888, p. 1038; for discussions on labour management see *Journal of Gas Lighting*, 7, 14 and 21 August 1888.

42. *Royal Commission on Labour*, ques. 26048, 26789-794, 26926-943; *Journal of Gas Lighting*, 14 May 1889, p. 893; 1 October 1889, pp. 633-4; 8 October 1889, pp. 683-711; 15 October 1889, pp. 739, 757; 22 October 1889, pp. 781-2, 793-4; 5 November 1889, p. 882; 1 July 1890, p. 39.

43. For the important Leeds strike see E.P. Thompson, 'Homage to Tom Maguire', in Asa Briggs and John Saville, *Essays in Labour History* (London, 1967); Hobsbawm, *Labouring Men*, p. 169; Clegg, Fox and Thompson, *British Trade Unionism*, pp. 69-70.

44. *Royal Commission on Labour*, ques. 23729-839, 26835-885, 26969, Appendices LI, LII: *Journal of Gas Lighting*, 10 December 1889, p. 1118; 17 December 1889, p. 1145; 12 November 1889, pp. 911, 928; 21 December 1889, p. 1256; 1 July 1890, p. 11; 25 August 1891, p. 311 Smith and Pickworth, *Engineers' Costs*, pp. 65-6; F.G. Burton, *The Commercial Management of Engineering Works* (Manchester, 1899), p. 72; Joseph Melling, 'Industrial Strife and Business Welfare Philosophy: The Case of the South Metropolitan Gas Company from the 1880s to the War', *Business History*, vol. 21, no. 2 (1979).

45. Hobsbawm, *Labouring Men* pp. 222-7; B. Moggeridge, 'Militancy and Inter-Union Rivalry in British Shipping 1911-29', *International Review of Social History*, vol. 6 (1961), pp. 382-3, 409; John Saville, 'Trade Unions and Free Labour: The Background to Taff Vale' in Briggs and Saville, *Essays in Labour History*, pp. 327-9.

46. P.W. Kingsford, 'Labour Relations on the Railways, 1835-1875', *Journal of Transport History*, vol. 1, no. 2 (1953) p. 66; *Railway Review*, 27 December 1889, p. 613.

47. Frank McKenna, 'Victorian Railway Workers', *History Workshop Journal*, vol. 1 (Spring 1976), pp. 58, 66-7; McKenna, *The Railway Workers 1840-1970* (London, 1980), p. 40.

48. Jack Simmons, *The Railway in England and Wales 1830-1914* (Leicester, 1978), pp. 218-22; Society of Telegraph Engineers, *Journal*, vol. 2 (1873), pp. 233-4; *Royal Commission on Labour*, Vol. XXXIII (c. 6894), ques. 26384, 27628, 26517, 26385.

49. See Philip Bagwell, *The Railwaymen* (London, 1963), p210 for an example of signalmen in a leading role in trade movements; Raymond Williams, *Politics and Letters* (London, 1979), p. 24; *Royal Commission on Labour*, ques. 28037.

50. Irving, 'The Profitability and Performance of British Railways'; Geoffrey Alderman, 'The Railway Companies and the Growth of Trade Unionism in the Late Nineteenth and Early Twentieth Centuries', *Historical Journal*, vol. 14, no. 1 (1971), pp. 130, 132-3.

51. *Railway Review*, 22 March 1889, p. 133; 9 September 1889, p. 383; 12 July 1889, p. 325; 8 December 1893, p. 5; 27 October 1893, p. 4. The trip system was later abandoned but reintroduced in 1906 – see McKenna, *The Railway Workers*, pp. 84-5; *Railway News*, 15 Decmeber 1900, pp. 868-9.

52. Bagwell, *Railwaymen*, pp. 137-8, 208, 212; *Railway Review*, 8 December 1893, p. 5; 15 December 1893, p. 4; 29 December,1893, p. 6; 2 February 1894, p. 5; 31 May 1895, p. 1.

53. George Paish, *The British Railway Position* (London, 1902), pp. 14, 31, 100, 239; on the industrial discipline implications of the control system see G.M. M'Donnell, *Railway Management with and without Railway Statistics* (London, n.d.), pp. iv, 8, 13-14, 15, 21-4. On the technical details of the control system see H.M. Hallsworth, *The Elements of Railway Operating* (privately published for the North Eastern Railway, n.d.), pp. 233-42, 337-8.

54. *Railway Review*, 7 March 1913, p. 3; 4 July 1913, p. 5; 14 March 1913, p. 2; 20 June 1913, p. 8.

55. Ibid., 28 February 1913, pp. 1-2 and 7 March 1913, p. 3; Bagwell, *Railwaymen*, p. 339.

56. *Railway Review*, 2 February 1900, p. 10 and 15 December 1893, p. 4: Rowland Kenney, *Men and Rails* (London, 1913), pp. 148-9, 170-71.

57. See *Railway Review*, 15 March 1889, pp. 121-4; 29 March 1889, pp. 150-4; 12 April 1889, p. 169 on the pension funds. It was reported that when the companies abandoned their proposals for company pension funds large numbers of men immediately joined the union. *Railway News*, 25 August 1900, p. 321; McKenna, 'Victorian Railway Workers', pp. 58-60.

58. Bagwell, *Railwaymen*, pp. 129, 138, 203, 268-71; Alderman, 'The Railway Companies', pp. 146-8.

6 CLASS, WORK AND POLITICS 1890-1926

Political Openings

The politics of the age of equipoise began to erode with the Reform Bill of 1867 and, perhaps more importantly, with the Ballot Act of 1871. Men could no longer be marched to the polls by the mining and iron masters of the Northeast and it was surely no coincidence that in the early 1870s collective bargaining was established in those industries. By the early 1900s, employers like Charles Mark Palmer of Jarrow found their political domination under siege by a growing array of Labour candidates. The emergence of an independent labour politics in this period reflected the decomposition of the social relations of the mid-Victorian age. At the local level, the paternal basis of political authority was dissolved as the social relations of production were altered. But this was a lengthy process with considerable regional variation. In some places, the realignment of working-class political loyalties towards the Labour Party was not completed until the mid-1920s.

The realignment of politics, however, was not solely a function of the new presence of Labour as a political estate. Indeed, the emergence of Labour was itself part of wider openings and uncertainties that dominated the total political history of the period. Within the political arena, there was a wide-ranging debate about the nature of the policies and strategies that should form the basis of political alliance and action. The liberal policy consensus that had dominated British politics since the 1830s and 1840s began to be questioned from both left and right. The intellectual revival of socialism and the first stirrings of an anti-free-trade debate in Conservative politics signified the beginnings of the search for new policies to address the external and internal repercussions of the changing world economy and political situation. Classical liberalism as the source of general policy assumptions was progressively abandoned by both political parties. The result was that politics was increasingly riven with uncertainty, upheaval and intensified tension. The 'strange death of Liberal England' theory need not be accepted to see, for example, that after 1906 politics was dominated by seemingly intractable fractures. Debates about the place of women in the body politic, or about the constitutional legitimacy of Conservative intrigues against the Liberal government's Irish policy from 1910, reflected a broader demise of prior political relationships and conventions. Some politicians, most notably Lloyd George, contemplated a way out of the political impasse by breaking the mould of political loyalty entirely. For a short while in 1910 the prospect was mooted of a centre-party coalition drawn from Conservatives and Liberals. But this idea was soon dropped, and Lloyd George opted for a revitalised radicalism that focused on land reform and social welfare.[1] The Conservatives were far more wracked with internal dissension than the Liberals. They, too, were searching for a new programmatic consensus, of which Tariff Reform was the leading contender.

In the event, of course, the war intervened to resolve these uncertainties and alter the political calculus. Liberalism's political and ideological integrity was the major casualty. The Conservatives were the prime beneficiaries as they picked the electoral bones of the stricken Liberal Party. More crucially, however, the war also raised the question of the proper place of Labour within national politics. Before 1918 this had not been a pressing matter. Although the local bases of Lib-Labism were fast eroding prior to 1914, Labour's leaders were more concerned to renegotiate the progressive alliance with Liberalism than they were to replace the Liberal Party in Parliament. But the patched up Lib-Labism that Ramsay MacDonald and Herbert Gladstone had sewn together in their celebrated electoral pact of 1903 was clearly doomed when Arthur Henderson was demeaningly forced to resign from the Cabinet in 1917. The challenge posed by the national organisation of the Labour Party was not merely of electoral dimensions, however. Exactly what Labour's political and programmatic presence signified was unclear and it was this that underlay the political manoeuvrings of the early 1920s. The sensibility to this uncertainty was particularly acute because of the political instabilities that characterised European politics. Domestic militancy fuelled the fear that Britain, too, might be infected with the virus of revolution. Throughout 1920, Kenneth Morgan has written, 'the belief that Labour was the demure front for . . . dangerous assaults on the economic and political structure was Lloyd George's fundamental theme and a major determinant of his strategy'. The same general concern dictated the Conservative Party's attitude to the Coalition.[2] The problem lay in the fact that Labour was not only a political force, it was also an industrial force and these two things were intimately connected. Even if the distinction between 'politics' and 'economics' was formally present at the beginning of Labour's political involvement, that separation could never be absolute.

Labour's political presence could only be mobilised through its industrial structures – as the ILP realised from the start. Real political independence and effective organisation went hand in hand with a trade-union commitment to the Labour Party. Work and politics were inherently intertwined. But if this was so, then the programmatic representation of that connection remained a matter of contention and debate.

The realignment of politics was as much a matter of alternative ideologies and programmes for Labour as it was for the other political parties. Indeed, this matter was more crucial for Labour precisely because the changing relations of production were a prime reason for Labour to claim a political presence. Most modern historiography on the subject of Labour's political emergence mistakenly assumes that the politics and programme of Labourism followed automatically from the trade-union connection. But within both the industrial and political wings of the Labour movement, the programmatic and organisational basis upon which its enhanced presence in society should rest remained indeterminate and very much in dispute. Labour's agenda was not the subject of sophisticated philosophical discourse such as existed within boundaries of Conservatism and Liberalism. The items of this agenda were never reducible to tidy categories because what tended to be at issue was the general stance of Labour towards social and political authority. Nevertheless, it is important to recognise that the context of Labour's history during this period was exactly the possibility of alternative programmes and ideologies. This presumption is as relevant to understanding the disputes within trade unionism over trade policy as it is to understanding the theoretical debates over socialism. The shape of Labour's political agenda was in the process of formation until the early 1920s: it was not explicit with the creation of the Labour Representation Committee in 1900.

The purpose of this chapter is to examine interpretatively the dynamic of this formative stage in Labour's political history. Three interwoven themes will predominate. First, how the issue of what principles should govern the representation of Labour's interest in society was reflected in aspects of the legal limits to collective bargaining. Second, how the question of Labour's political posture within society created tension within the industrial and political sections of the movement. And, third, the process by which these tensions were resolved.

Collective Representation and Responsibility

The growth of collective organisation as the central way the social relations of employers and workmen were mediated raised fundamental questions about the relationship of labour and capital's rights and responsibilities. As we have seen, these matters had always been subject to legal adjudication and in this period there were two separate, but related, issues at stake for the trade unions. The first was the extent to which trade-union purpose was adequately defined by the statutes of the 1870s. The tendency of the law in the 1890s to interpret the statutes as bestowing a corporate status upon the unions was part of a widespread and ongoing concern about the nature and extent of trade-union rights. In 1904, for example, a new Registrar of Friendly Societies tried to tighten the conditions under which union rules could be registered by requiring a more demanding interpretation of the statutes. And the Osborne case of 1909, which enjoined the ASRS from using funds to support parliamentary representation because the statutes had not specified this purpose, was important because it addressed the question of whether trade unions could also have political purposes.

From a rather different angle, there was a growing body of support for the idea that collective agreements be made legally enforceable as a way of ensuring that unions lived up to their agreements. In 1913 the Liberal cabinet was actively considering breaching the voluntarist tradition of the statutes by revising the law to force unions to take more responsibility for the actions of their members. It was at this point that the concern for the legal limits of trade-union responsibility shaded over into the second issue raised by collective mediation of social relations: the question of representative action. If unions did possess a corporate status, they could be expected to exercise an authority over their members. Indeed, aside from the purely legal issue, this matter was implicit in collective-bargaining procedures. Some employer spokesmen, like John Day of the *Shoe and Leather Record*, openly asserted that bargaining rights demanded trade-union responsibility for the actions of their members. Thus, after its defeat in 1895, the National Union of Boot and Shoe Operatives was obliged to provide a monetary guarantee for the fulfilment of agreements. The pattern of industrial-relations law during this period, therefore, was more complicated than a simple reaction to trade-union growth and militancy. Case law addressed the problem of what limits and responsibilities accompanied the new-found rights of trade-union representation in bargaining.[3]

The re-emergence of the crime of conspiracy in the guise of a civil tort, for example, represented an attempt to define the legitimate boundaries of trade-union induced breach of contract. This question was hinted at in the case of *Allen* v *Flood* (1896), one of the few the trade unions won in the 1890s, but it was rejected by the Law Lords who found that the trade-union inspired dismissal of two shipwrights was motivated by a legitimate defence of their own interests. In 1898, however, *Quinn* v *Leathem* directly addressed the issue and found that a union boycott of Leathem and a secondary boycott of one of his customers to induce the dismissal of non-union men were conspiracies to inflict economic damage for purposes that stood outside legitimate trade issues. There were certain parallels between this case and *Trollope* v *London Building Trade Federation* (1895), in which it was found that a union blacklist of employers was an unlawful conspiracy. And both cases stood in sharp contrast to the Mogul case (which had been cited in *Allen* v *Flood*) where a conspiracy of shipowners to expand their business by driving out competitors was held to be lawful. The tendency of these cases to elide a civil wrong into the more serious offence of conspiracy threatened to make unlawful any action which could be construed as interfering with the freedom of the employer to carry on his business in any way he thought fit.[4] The statute of 1825 has explicitly stated the law's purpose to be the protection of employer prerogatives but now the same result was achieved through case-law interpretation of the liberalising statute of 1875.

Precisely the same implications were contained in the efforts more closely to define picketing and intimidation. In *Curran* v *Treleavan* (1891) the recorder's court in Plymouth levied a £120 fine on the local officers of the coal-porters' union for intimidation when they warned Treleaven that continued employment of a non-union gang could lead to a withdrawal of labour. No acts of violence occurred or were threatened, but the Recorder argued that section 7 of the 1875 Act did not limit intimidation only to those acts 'in which a person might be bound over to keep the peace'. Threats directed at preventing a man from doing what he had a legal right to do also could be construed as intimidation if they were an attempt to interfere with the terms of his business. Although this broad interpretation of the intimidation clauses of the 1875 Act was reversed in the Queen's Bench, the same argument was established as good law in the picketing case of *Lyons* v *Wilkins* (1896) and confirmed on appeal in 1899.[5]

In this case, the act of holding out cards urging men not to work was found to be within the statutory definition of watching and besetting because it was aimed at compelling the plaintiffs to change the mode of conducting their business. A secondary picket against one of Lyons suppliers was found to be illegal for the same reason. The definition of legal picketing was thus narrowed to a literal interpretation of the 1875 Act as merely the communication of information. Anything beyond this – including the peaceful effort to persuade, which had been granted in the ignored Act of 1859 – fell within the scope of prohibited watching and besetting. This line of reasoning was followed in subsequent cases until it was contradicted in *Ward, Lock & Co.* v *Operative Printers* (1906) which found that watching and besetting were actionable only if they threatened to give rise to a breach of the peace. And this latter definition was written into the 1906 Trades Dispute Act which expressly allowed peaceful picketing to communicate and persuade.[6]

The most important line of reasoning in the cases of the 1890s, however, was the effort to establish the responsibility of one person for the action of the whole – the principle of representative action. This argument rested upon an explicit interpretation of the trade unions as corporate bodies and it had first appeared in *Temperton* v *Russell* (1893). Joseph Temperton was a builder's merchant in Hull who sued the local building-trades council for losses when he was blacklisted for infringing its rules. Although this action was successful at the local level, the appeals court struck out the representative action part of the judgement while allowing the officers of the council to be sued as individuals.[7] As this was obviously usually a fruitless proceeding against trade-union officials, the precedent was not pursued until the Taff Vale case reopened the issue.

The significance of the Taff Vale case extended beyond the crippling fine of £40,000 that was ultimately imposed upon the ASRS. Perhaps unintentionally,Taff Vale pointedly raised the issue of a union's control over its members. As is well known, the strike against the Taff Vale Railway was launched without the support of the union executive, but Richard Bell, the general secretary, travelled to Taff Vale to mediate in the conflict. Both Bell and J.A. Holmes, the branch secretary, were promptly served with injunctions to cease picketing. But Bell's intervention was rejected by the local strike committee who

> were showing a disposition to treat on their own behalf either with the company direct . . . or through some person of local influence. It was clear that the men could not be controlled by Mr. Bell. . . . The executive committee openly expressed a liking for Sir. W.T.

> Lewis' admirable scheme for a conciliation board [of local men and managers] in preference to a direct representation through their union.[8]

And it was upon this basis that the strike was eventually settled. The judgement against the ASRS by Justice Farwell, however, pointed in quite a different direction. The essence of his finding was that Society was liable for the wrongs of its agents. Two unconnected facts provided the justification for this finding. First, Holmes, quite independently of any 'official' responsibility, had issued a strike circular urging men not to work and, thus, to break their contacts. Second, Bell had put himself, unasked, in charge of the strike. By these actions, it was argued, the Society became liable for Holmes's actions even though he had not acted on Bell's orders.

There was a substantial irony in the Taff Vale case. On the one hand, it emanated from the policies of an anti-union railway manager and the actions of a general secretary whose assumed authority over local affairs was rejected by his constituents. On the other hand, it addressed the question of the responsibilities of trade unions engaged in collective action. In this sense, then, the real importance of the case lay in the way it represented an effort to work out the logic of collective representation for internal trade-union authority. Although it is unlikely that the case decisively affected the nature of industrial conflict, it addressed the growing problem of trade-union control over members that was beginning to pose a serious impediment to the effective operation of collective agreements. The Taff Vale case was obviously bad law unless it was argued that the principle of representative action could be extended to the area of *implied* authority of union agents. And this presented serious problems of legal interpretation because union rules seldom specified the precise limits and boundaries of officials' authority. Thus, in *Denby and Cadeby Main* v *Yorkshire Miners' Association* (1905) the union was found not to be responsible for the actions of members during a strike because the local branch officials had acted contrary to the union rules. Breach of contract by the branch violated the principle of representative action and it could not be regarded, therefore, as acting for the union.[9]

This left the question of representative action untouched and the bias of the statutes of 1906 and 1913 was to evade the issue while restoring freedom of action to the trade unions. It is, however, important to realise that a fairly general consensus in the trade-union and political worlds accepted the logic of Farwell's finding. Union leaderships welcomed the decision as the opportunity to rein in their more militant members and initially were unwilling to press for its reversal. Their ultimate change of heart reflected the scale of the award (not announced until 1904), the intensity of rank-and-file protest and the refusal of the Conservative government to negotiate a bargain. Outside the Labour movement, the consensus was even stronger. The Royal Commission on Trades Disputes (1903) had recommended some union liability for damages, the Liberal government's law officers took the same view, and a majority of the Liberal Cabinet was against a total reversion of this position. The Trades Disputes Act of 1906 which exempted the unions from liability, therefore, flew in the face of most informed opinion. It did so partly because many Liberal MPs had been elected on the promise to reverse Taff Vale and, perhaps most importantly, because of a unilateral concession by the Prime Minister himself who, in reply to a question in the House, committed the government to statutory repeal.[10]

The question of union responsibilities, however, was equally pertinent in the collective-agreement systems that expanded from the 1890s. These systems were among the most signal emblems of the Labour movement's new presence in society and they may properly be regarded as epitomising the new configuration of social relations between employers and workmen. But their ability to maintain industrial peace was continually tested, and with it the credibility of the trade-union commitment. A common characteristic of the labour unrest was the paralysis of union discipline and in many industries by 1914 serious doubts surrounded the continued existence of the systems of mediation. This was not simply a matter of collective bargaining failing to deliver adequate economic rewards. It was probably true that the collective-bargaining procedures held wage increases to a lower level than was potentially attainable given the relatively tight labour market from 1909. But industrial militancy was more profound than merely an economic matter, as the government's chief mediator, George Askwith, continually noted. The essential stimulus to the labour unrest came from the operation of agreements which tended to expose for debate fundamental questions of organisation, strategy and politics. These systems were one of the sources of the wider politicisation of labour during these years, and it is as important to see them in this light as it is to see them as the arena for economic bargaining.

The problem lay in the way the procedures of collective agreements tended to exclude and restrict certain issues from bargaining, delay the resolution of grievances, and prohibit strike action. Union representation was discouraged by the railway conciliation scheme of 1907 and, in railways, the boot and shoe industry and engineering, the employers retained considerable discretion over what issue was a legitimate cause for collective negotiation. The systems thus provided plenty of fuel for industrial militancy; but their central purpose was to provide channels of mediation for the resolution of disputes, not to address the substantive issues themselves. Thus,the necessity for local-level organisation was inherent in national collective agreements and was accentuated by the extensive changes that were occurring in the conditions of production. Indeed, modern workshop organisation in Britain may be dated from this point. However, the priorities of these local centres could not always be meshed with the national function of the trade union as an institution of mediation. Thus tensions were created in trade unionism that went to the heart of the policies and strategies they followed in order to fulfil their function of worker representation in industry. We may best see how this developed by looking at some representative examples.

The conciliation structures on the railways underscored industrial tensions because they seemed further to undermine traditional social relations without providing a fully equitable replacement. The personal petition continued to be the first step for the resolution of grievances, yet there was a consistent pattern of employers' refusing to deal seriously at this level because of the presence of higher levels of appeal. In addition, until 1911, the system worked with extreme deliberation and grievances which remained unresolved for months on end were then settled by awards which were binding for four to six years. This might not have mattered had the period been one of unambiguous gains in the standard of living and stable social relations, but neither of these conditions obtained. A rising cost of living combined (after 1909) with falling unemployment to afford the opportunities for militancy. The disciplinary hierarchy was in the process of being reorganised and tightened. And, with the renewed pressure on company profits after 1907, there were increased efforts to devise more efficient ways of working. The result was that the conciliation system came to be seen as merely another strategy by which the railway companies expanded their control over work-processes and evaded effective bargaining or regulation of working conditions. Speed-ups, greater intensity of working, employers' reclassification of grades to avoid awards, reductions in pay and allowances endorsed by arbitrators, were all identified with the very system that from an institutional union perspective represented a partial retreat by the companies from their traditional anti-unionism. Thus, outside of union officials, it was hard to find any positive enthusiasm for the system. Apathy and low voter turnout characterised board elections. In May 1911, for example, the highest number of votes cast anywhere was in the East Central district of the Midland region where one man secured 1,500 votes.[11]

It is hard to judge how divorced the union was from all this, but the surprise that greeted the 1911 strike suggests a complacency that was blind to reality. One week before the spontaneous strike explosion of July 1911, an editorial in the *Railway Review* remarked on the need to amend the system because of its delays but conceded that this would have to wait until the agreement expired in 1913. Yet warning signals were clearly posted. A strike of Hull porters in February 1911 epitomised the frustrations with the system. They had been demanding a wage parity with the record keepers for five years on the grounds that they were frequently called upon to do checkers' work. When the company responded by dismissing the strikers, other departments came out in support. A return to work was secured only by the promise that the case would be taken up at the next meeting of the local board.

This did not imply that militant sentiment aimed at making the conciliation boards work better or faster: that was the priority of institutional unionism. Although militancy had no focus of expression, nor a specific programmatic presence within union structures, there was little doubt that the main focus of anger was the system of collective agreement. In that sense the authority of the mediators of social relations was being challenged. As the *Railway Review* remarked, 'the most remarkable feature of the situation is the dissatisfaction of the men with the present system of Conciliation Boards and especially with the spirit in which they have been worked'. Indeed, the original locus of the strike of 1911 lay amongst Liverpool goods workers who took wildcat action for an increase of wages and the settlement of grievances that had not been resolved through the conciliation structures. Stoppages then spread spontaneously to Manchester, Bristol, London and elsewhere. Like many strikes of the period, this was very much a rank-and-file affair, overriding the sectionalism that plagued the railway workforce. The unions responded creatively. By 15 August they had called for a national stoppage to begin two days later. Overcoming their traditional divisions, the unions secured modifications in the Conciliation Boards to establish the principle of full recognition and were finally prodded into serious action on grade unity, which culminated in the formation of the National Union of Railwaymen in January 1912. The Boards were not abolished, however, and this ensured continued dissension within the union. Protest meetings were held against the acceptance of the Report of the Royal Commission appointed to examine the system. At Swansea, J.H. Thomas faced a rowdy meeting which condemned the way the union had accepted the Report without testing membership opinion; other meetings condemned the way the settlement reinforced sectionalist representation on the boards.[12]

In cotton-spinning, the Brooklands agreement of 1893 created a formal procedure for the resolution of disputes, established long-term wage settlements and limited yearly fluctuations to 5 per cent either way. As we have seen, this routinisation of social conflict came just at the moment when employers were shifting to lower-quality cotton to maintain their competitive position. Thus, breakages and stoppages were more likely at the very instant when continuous, uninterrupted working was essential to maintaining real earnings. The result was an effective speed-up. By 1910, this problem was also affecting weavers and the industry was beginning to be infected with the labour unrest. Spinners had been locked out in 1908 and a wage-cut imposed. Secret negotiations in July 1910 resulted in a five-year freeze on wages which accentuated the bad spinning problem and resulted in a growing number of small-scale stoppages and militant dissatisfaction with the meagre results of collective bargaining under Brooklands. A weavers' strike in 1911 over the attempt to expand the closed shop ended amidst recrimination about the conduct of negotiations. In 1913 the spinners went on strike and temporarily withdrew from Brooklands to secure a modification of the delays involved in grievance resolution. This failed to resolve the problem and led to increasing tension within the spinners' amalgamation over the commitment to the Procedure. Open revolt broke out in the spring of 1914 in Middleton and Oldham, two of the largest districts, after the union agreed with employers to extend the temporary agreement reached in October 1913. Like similar revolts on the railways, in building and engineering, this one threatened a crisis of authority in the union. Special meetings to agitate the bad spinning question were called by district committees at which demands were heard for a direct action policy of 'no agreements, satisfactory spinning, or we close your mills'. The union officials reacted strongly; the meetings were condemned as unconstitutional, leading members of the district committees were forced to resign and prohibited from holding office again. Like most other revolts this one did not force a change of policy. Its importance lay in the way it demonstrated the common problem of an increasing dissension within labour that followed from policies and strategies that were implicit in the structures of collective agreements.[13]

In the engineering industry, the situation was somewhat more complicated. Technical changes tended to reinforce the traditions of localist organisation. The premium bonus system, for example, could only be monitored by plant bargaining through workshop committees. Thus, from the 1890s there was a growth in 'unofficial' organisation and an increase in the role of shop stewards who were recognised for the first time in the union rules of 1896. This thickening of local autonomy, however, tended to contradict the implications of the Procedure of 1898 whose purpose was to enhance central authority in the union. Thus, after 1898 divisions within the union became much sharper. One faction led by George Barnes accepted the defeat of 1898 and was prepared to abandon craft opposition to rationalisation in return for certain concessions on overtime and the mutuality of piece-rates. Premium bonus was recognised in the Carlisle agreement of 1902, and in 1907 an agreement was reached which strengthened the trade-union position on overtime, apprenticeship ratios and piece-rates in return for a more precise definition of employer rights over machine-manning. This policy came into increasing conflict with the craft militants organised in the workshop committees. In 1903 the union executive supported an employer wage-cut on the Clyde, and forced an end to a strike by suspending the men's benefits. A revolt in the Northeast against the agreement of 1907 forced Barnes's resignation, and the initiative passed to the localities where a revival of craft militancy succeeded in restoring control over machine-manning and in resisting efforts to expand premium bonus and the division of labour. By 1911 and 1912 the workshop committees had established a virtual alternative structure of union authority displacing even the sympathetic district committees. In Manchester, for example, shop committees took over the bargaining functions of the district committee on issues such as piece-work. And on the Clyde, as the war began, a district-wide stewards' committee was preparing to take action against non-union labour in defiance of the 1907 agreement and Executive Committee instructions. By contrast, the official union structures were profoundly split. In 1912 two rival executives physically contested possession of headquarters and a ballot on the Terms of Settlement and Carlisle agreement resulted in a majority for their abolition. The 'old' executive which had won the struggle at headquarters, refused to accept this and in 1914 negotiated a temporary procedure with the employers (the York Memorandum) which remained in effect until 1922. In the meantime, as war clouds loomed, the employers were once again contemplating the need for a national confrontation to restore the viability of the collective-agreement system.[14]

These intra-union tensions require some explanation and conceptualisation. In the first place, they revealed the divergent priorities that changes in the work-process and the operation of collective agreements stimulated in various sections of labour. This was frequently no simple matter. In engineering, for example, Barnes's general policy of expanding the boundaries of union membership seems to have been favoured by those skilled setters-up who had been created by the new division of labour. These people were likely also to hold radical political opinions which reinforced their acceptance of a dilution of the craft character of the ASE. But the old craft centres remained powerful enough effectively to impede this and other 'modern' policies. Indeed, as the war years were to show, the strength of workshop bargaining ultimately lay with those who were intensely suspicious of the encroachment of the semi-skilled. However much the advanced shop stewards on the Clyde may have recognised the virtues of abandoning craft mentality, for example, they were as restrained by its presence as officials like George Barnes who wished to accept the new relations of production as the basis for a new *modus vivendi* with employers.

In the second place, whatever the precise configuration of these tensions, it is inadequate to regard them simply as forces which fragmented labour. They were a product of the changing basis of social relations and, as such, they reflected the problems of power and authority that flowed from those changes. This was the reason why these tensions were so likely to assume the character of 'revolt' and why they were so politically charged. Implicitly or explicitly, they posed a challenge to the bases of authority upon which the new structures mediating social relations between capital and labour rested. As such, they often threatened to disrupt the internal cohesion and authority within union structures themselves.

And this leads to a third consideration. The tensions within unions were ultimately power struggles between divergent strategies and policies. As such, any analysis must address the question of how power was organised and distributed within the unions.[15] The failure of most of the oppositional currents was due not so much to the weakness of their support, nor even to the deficiencies of their arguments, but more to the difficulties of translating collective opinions into policy. It was revealing, for example, that the question of how to translate the grievances of the workshop into the sphere of collective agreements was not systematically addressed within institutional unionism during these years. Although the extent to which pressure from below could modify or alter union policy varied from case to case, there was general resistance from the leadership to the search for alternative systems of internal organisation that would mitigate or resolve the tensions that came from divergent priorities. For very good reasons, union leaderships remained tied to the structures of collective agreements that large sections of their memberships found objectionable. The attitude of union leaders to these questions is hard to judge. They generally resorted to various devices that aimed to defuse or deflect substantive discussions. The Welsh miner's leader, Mabon, for example, was known to break into 'Land of My Fathers' when faced with dissatisfied constituents. Jimmy Thomas's attitude to dissent was more cynical – but he is, perhaps, an extreme case – 'if the buggers are giving you trouble – give them a mass meeting. That shuts them up.' Others within his union had a different conception of the mass meeting as the source of negotiating sovereignty, however, and much of the unrest in the NUR in 1912 was based upon the inadequacy of consultation with the membership.[16]

These tensions, then, were more than just factional struggles within unions. They were the product of a process that derived from the changing basis of social relations and the new responsibilities of unionism as one mediator of those relations. As such, they raised questions about the nature of power and authority that conjoined with a wider debate on those issues in Edwardian England. It was inevitable, therefore that union militancy should possess a political dimension because in its inchoate and unsystematic way it addressed the question that was central to the changing place of labour in society: upon which programmatic, ideological and organisational basis should labour participate in the politics of the nation? It was for this reason that the tensions over union policies were frequently part of a wider politicisation. Those who wished to pursue a more aggressive industrial policy were forced into a consideration of the nature of union government and the institutional linkages of politics. Thus, in the Durham Miners' Association there was a close association between groups opposed to executive policy and ILP branches. In South Wales a more radical association occurred. And in Lancashire spinning, the demise of union authority opened the way to a more splintered political attachment which included growing support for the Labour Party.[17]

The Openness of Labour Politics

The process of the politicisation of labour was far more than a matter of the issues and tensions that were stimulated by the law or the workings of collective agreements and it is now necessary to backtrack for a moment to complete the picture. Both political and economic bases of social relations were being undermined by a complex series of factors which often contained a high degree of local variation.[18] These changes were located on a wide front, but they obliged a reorientation of values and perceptions which permitted alternative conceptions of political and social relations to attain a relevance they had not previously possessed. The presence of a concurrent intellectual debate about socialism was both a reflection of this reorientation and the main source of ideas that could fill the openings it created.

The growth of local government, for example, diminished the need for patrician involvement in the institutions of urban life. By the early twentieth century, the aristocratic urban presence had been relegated largely to ceremonial functions and positions. Similarly, large urban employers began to withdraw from their presiding social presence. In Crewe, for example, recreational institutions were traditionally sponsored by the railway company, but by the 1880s these services had fallen into the domain of the municipality. The company's gift of £10,000 for the construction of Queen's Park in 1887 was the last major act of social paternalism. When the town council requested assistance in enlarging the town baths – which the company had built in 1866 – they were informed that this was now the municipality's responsibility. Undoubtedly, the single most common factor in the abandonment of paternal social relations was the new economic pressures on employers. In the Deerness area of Durham, for example, the changing economic structure of the coal industry from the 1880s led to hardened attitudes towards labour demands. This then assumed its own dynamic which fractured the labour community between those who advocated militant industrial and political postures and those who remained committed to the tightly integrated religio-political structures of Methodism and Liberalism.[19]

One particularly noteworthy example of this process was sparked by the Manningham Mills strike of 1891, long known as the moment of the creation of the Bradford Labour Union, one of the precursors of the ILP. The firm of S.C. Lister & Co. was an archetypal practitioner of paternal social relations. As late as 1889, two of its directors lived in the immediate vicinity of the factory. The work-force enjoyed what they believed to be a close relationship with the firm and remained unorganised and strike-free. This relationship was rudely disrupted when the company responded to the McKinley Tariff by cutting the wages of skilled silk- and plush-weavers by between 15 and 33 per cent. The resulting strike and the naked use of authority – including troops – to disperse meetings solidified the community support enjoyed by the strike and stripped away the mask of paternal reciprocity. Although the strikers were eventually starved back to work, these circumstances allowed the message of independent political action preached by socialists like Fred Jowett to gain a relevance it had hardly possessed before. Within a year, Ben Tillett had mounted a serious parliamentary challenge to the Liberals in West Bradford, the Labour Union had secured control of the Trades Council, and a network of Labour Clubs had been created. Lib-Labism remained a force to be reckoned with in Bradford, but henceforth the solidity of its representation of working-class politics was shaken.[20]

And this seems to have been typical. The shift from Lib-Labism to independent working-class politics was a gradual movement. Different tendencies co-existed within the same organisation, reflecting the political flux of the period. It is well known, for example, that Keir Hardie's break with Liberalism was reluctant and initially quite tentative. And Hardie's experience was typical of miners in general who abandoned Lib-Labism only after the reluctance of Liberals to open up their political machinery had demonstrated its irrelevance. In the boot and shoe trade, opposition to the cautious policies of Thomas Inskip (general secretary of NUBSO until 1894) did not necessarily translate into a support for socialism, although the most militant branches were those where the ILP was strongest. But the changing relations of production forced even those who were not socialists to alter their political perspectives. Thus, in the debate over labour representation in 1894, Charles Freak, who supported the notion without committing himself to socialism, illustrated the way this worked:

> If a man introduced a machine which made things much quicker than before and cheaper, the patent should not be bought up by capitalists who could rig the market and make a big profit for themselves. Such patents ought to be bought by the government, and worked for the good of the people.[21]

These kinds of connections were made elsewhere. In printing, the search for new strategies to meet the changing conditions of the trade was a constant preoccupation in the 1890s. A prime focus was the necessity for political action to control the uses of machinery – a theme that represented a decisive shift from the non-political attitudes to these questions in the mid-Victorian period and was more reminiscent of early nineteenth-century efforts to connect economics and politics. Similarly, amongst engineers, there was a growing belief that political action was necessitated by the failure of the 1898 conflict and the consequent shift in the balance of power in social relations. Thanks to machinery, it was argued,

> the employing class receive a larger proportion of the nation's wealth . . . The struggle for existence is fiercer today than it was fifty years ago, unemployment more frequent . . . Fifty years ago the workmen received a subsistence wage; the workmen of today receive no more.[22]

If the social and political experience of increasing numbers of workers was opening the way to alternative bases of political action, the question of what kind of programme of action and organisation remained a matter of considerable debate and uncertainty. The eclectic intellectual roots of mainstream British socialism are clear enough. It drew upon a disparate body of dissenting religious thought, mainstream social criticism of the Ruskinite tradition, and liberal indivvidualism.[23] This produced a strong tendency to regard with suspicion the theoretical programmes and analyses of what Ben Tillett called the 'chattering, continental magpies'. Labourism's appeal – perfectly expressed by Robert Blatchford's *Merrie England* – was informed by the moral image of an organic, harmonious national policy. Until 1918 it failed to provide any clear programmatic expression of socialism apart from the immensely detailed, technocratic analyses of the Webbs. In all probability this proved to be a strength rather than a weakness and, certainly, it may be argued that such eclecticism was consistent with the history and traditions of working-class culture in Britain. But it is also important to realise that this collection of values did not proceed unchallenged; it faced a continual and growing competition from alternative tendencies of thought and action. Although these alternatives remained largely trends rather than fully developed theories of organisation and programme, they are worthy of note because their presence ensured that this period was one in which the possibilities of Labour politics remained undecided and open. By the early 1920s those uncertainties had been resolved, but the process of resolution was less one of intellectual debate and more one of economic and political struggle, victory and defeat.

This challenge was present at the very beginning of organised socialism in Britain, before it began to take organisational shape in the legislative orientation and limited aims of the LRC. As Stephen Yeo has demonstrated, there was a period when socialism attempted to mobilise around the task of 'making socialists' in a visionary effort to create the culture of a 'new life'. The emblematic symbol of this creative and dynamic phase was, of course, the *Clarion* newspaper with its network of clubs and societies. This effort was essentially flawed because it failed to address the politics of 'what is to be done?'. As Blatchford himself confessed, 'I approach this question with great reluctance. The establishment and organisation of a Socialistic state are the two branches of work to which I have given least attention.' This void meant that the exigencies of how to fuse fellowship, unity and primitive democracy within a strategy for advancing political power were never seriously examined. Into the void left by Blatchford and others like him moved, quite naturally, the analysis of the Webbs whose answer to 'what is to be done?' contained no place for notions of democratic organisation other than those of bureaucratic structures of representation. The separation of the various spheres of the movement was inaugurated in the mid-1890s when the Clarion movement devolved into a purely recreational body and the labour churches disintegrated into historical curiosities.[24]

Nevertheless, as it became increasingly apparent that Labourism had no conception of programmatic action other than piece-by-piece legislation, so criticism mounted. Indeed, the ideological vacuum seemed to be celebrated by the Webbs and Ramsay MacDonald who pointed out that socialist legislation did not have to be implemented by socialists. By 1907 the essential irrelevance of the Labour Party in Parliament fuelled a growing dissatisfaction with the whole basis of Labour's political organisation. Thus, the flawed and mercurial Victor Grayson who carried the Colne Valley constituency in 1907 against the cautious wishes of the leadership became a focus for the yearning for something more positive and mobilising than a politics that consigned Labour to a mere appendage of Liberalism. The sharp criticism of the vacuous tactics pursued by the leadership of the ILP in 1908 and 1909 was the political equivalent of the 'rank-and-file' revolt within trade unionism a few years later. Both drew inspiration from the same well-springs of a desire to discuss the possibility of new directions of action and organisation. The ILP leadership declined to enter into an introspective debate and re-evaluation and restored 'discipline' by threatening to resign on an essentially minor vote of censure. By 1911 the marginalisation of the rebels was complete and they broke away to form the British Socialist Party.[25]

The most serious challenges to Labourism, however, were provided by those tendencies and groups that grew directly out of the conflicts in industry and gathered under the aegis of syndicalism and guild socialism. Neither was purely marginal to Labour politics during these years and both reflected the centrality of issues of power and authority in labour's internal discourse. Syndicalism made deep inroads into virtually every major union by 1914, its entrance assisted by the way systems of collective agreement exposed to view issues of accountability and power. It also provided a meeting ground for those dissatisfied with the limitations of parliamentary politics and the restraints imposed upon trade-union policies by the operation of the collective-agreement systems. Although syndicalism's organisational presence was more problematic than its description (by Cole) of the 'temper' of industrial militancy before the First World War, it was by no means negligible. The Amalgamation Movement, for example, was particularly strong in building and engineering, and elsewhere unofficial reform or vigilance committees represented syndicalist centres of opposition. But the main significance of syndicalism lay in the way it contributed to the widening agenda of policies and strategies. Under syndicalist influence, the notion of workers' control attained a widespread currency in the period 1912-22 and, indeed, came to pose a serious alternative to nationalisation as the main conception of socialisation.[26]

This demand reached the agenda of the railway workers' union in 1912, 1914 and 1917 and in the Miners' Federation of Great Britain (MFGB) it displaced the official policy of nationalisation in 1918. Indeed, a detailed presentation before the Sankey Commission of 1919 for a scheme of control similar to that outlined in *The Miners' Next Step* actually found its way into the Labour Party programme in the 1922 election. In engineering, the demand for workers' control had by this time become a virtual orthodoxy. The old syndicalist Tom Mann was for a while general secretary of the ASE. The demand for joint committees to run industry began to be heard from 1915, and the notion of 'encroaching control' towards a complete worker domination of industry found a ready audience amongst engineers accustomed to the practice of work-place autonomy. Even in the aftermath of the 1922 defeat, it was argued that only on the basis of strong workshop organisation could trade unions gain the knowledge necessary for them to 'fulfil the wider economic task for which they ultimately seem destined, viz. the control of industry . . . it is around this issue of workshop control that the decisive battle between capital and labour will be fought'.[27]

Guild socialism was potentially even more significant than syndicalism. Not only did it have a more impressive body of 'theory', but, for a while, it seemed likely to secure a significant presence within the institutions of labour. A product of the growing dissatisfaction with Labour's policies in the early 1900s, guild socialism quickly shed the medieval patina of its original founder, J.A. Penty, and between 1912 and 1922 its adherents were to be found occupying positions of some influence. Until 1915, for example, guild socialists controlled the Fabian Research Committee and were a noisy, challenging presence at Fabian summer schools. Similarly, from 1918 to 1922 they controlled the Labour Research Department, one of the few centres within the organisational structure of the party which could serve as a conduit to the stewards' and workers' control movements. During the war guild socialism's pre-eminent exponent, G.D.H. Cole, was attached to the ASE, established close contact with the shop stewards' movement and was a key influence in propagating the ideas of the collective contract and encroaching control. It was a testimony to the influence of these currents that by the end of the war the Webbs were forced to pay less attention to efficiency as the essence of socialism and give more emphasis to the rearrangement of power and authority through participatory democracy.[28]

The challenge posed by these tendencies, however, was less organisational and more of one of ideology and ideas. At the heart of these alternative approaches to the place of labour in politics was the effort to formulate strategies and programmes that would reconstitute economic and political democracy in ways that were absent from the analysis of the Webbs and others. Syndicalism was identified by one observer as lying at the heart of the labour unrest of 1910-14 because it raised the question of 'the struggle for complete democracy . . . the futility of political democracy by itself'. Syndicalism stood in opposition to the state collectivism and social welfarism that dominated progressive thought before 1914; it saw both as agents of a state bureaucratisation that threatened a domination ' "even more rigid than it is today" '. Suspicion of the growing reach of the state placed syndicalism in association with a much wider body of thought in Edwardian England. Not all of it was 'progressive' and within the working class the residues of liberal individualism continued to fuel an opposition (of sentiment, at least) to the welfare reforms. Indeed, there was something to be said for the logic of these various arguments. The motivation of welfare measures lay more in the desire to remove inefficiencies in the labour market than it did to enlarge freedom. The virtue of syndicalism was that it tried to address the changing relationship between freedom and authority, but it never managed to provide an adequate linkage between its programmatic analysis and the inherent working-class suspicion of the state expansion of the period.[29]

Syndicalists were concerned to search for a structuring of authority relations that would ensure accountability and subject each institution to democratic control. Thus, opposition to nationalisation as the definition of socialisation lay in the fact that it would not change the essence of social relations which would still be determined by the need 'to extract as much profit as possible'. The democratic intention applied as much to union organisation as it did to the state. Indeed, syndicalists saw the two as integrally related. Trade unions could only play their proper role within an industrial democracy if they were themselves fully accountable to their members. *The Miners' Next Step*, for example, envisaged a

> Central Production Board who, with a statistical department to ascertain the needs of the people, will issue its demands on the different departments of industry, leaving to the men themselves to determine under what conditions and how the work should be done. This would mean real democracy in real life. . . . Any other form of democracy is a delusion and a snare.[30]

Oddly enough, the questions syndicalism raised about how power and authority should be arranged found no resonances in mainstream Labourist thought. This was illustrated by the anodyne response to the labour unrest by Ramsay MacDonald in his book *Socialism and Society* which argued with a crass biological determinism that socialism was an inevitable organic stage of economic growth. The absence of any consideration of power and authority relations reflected the conventional belief in Labour circles that the organisation of power was purely a matter of controlling the machinery of state through Parliament. This absence was typical, too, of Labour's major intellectual theorists, the Webbs. In a sense, it was to Fabianism that currents like syndicalism and guild socialism posed the greatest challenge. In contrast to the Fabian emphasis upon bureaucratic collectivism as the means of resolving the problem of economic distribution, these tendencies recognised the integral relationship between this question and power and authority throughout production and the state. The Webbs recoiled with horror from any suggestion that there were alternative ways of addressing economic organisation to the growth of 'expert' administration. G.D.H. Cole was quite right when he remarked that the Webbs approach conceived

> the mass of man as persons who ought to be decently treated, not as persons who ought to freely organize their own conditions of life; in short [their] conception of the new social order is still that of an order that is ordained from without, and not realized from within.[31]

It was, of course, the guild socialists and particularly Cole who replaced the 'temper' of syndicalism with a more thorough consideration of how socialism meant reordered power relationships throughout society. The key to this effort was the recognition that Labourism had so far failed to address the question of power at any level beyond the parliamentary. For Cole the question was: how could socialism expand the areas of freedom in society? Thus, 'power relationships in economic and social systems [were] . . . the central issue for social analysis and social action'. The 'hard centre' of guild socialism rested upon a 'conception of an active, self-governing community' which achieved the amelioration of conditions through the distribution of power in society. The actual structure of this community would be achieved by expanding the definition of democracy beyond the political act of voting to mean a participatory control over every aspect of life in which man had a functional interest: for Cole, 'genuine democracy would only be realized in a system of coordinated functional representation'. Under this system the state would actively reflect collective will and sovereignty rather than simply embodying sovereignty, as the Fabians assumed. In this way, Cole argued, the syndicalist fear of an intrinsically repressive state would be removed. Correctly structured, the state would serve as the expression of community and fellowship.[32]

The emphasis upon participation and decentralisation in guild socialism allowed it to speak directly to the experience of workshop militancy and bargaining. The work-place was seen as the key area for the expansion of freedom and control in society. There were three reasons for this. First, production was the location where those issues were acutely meaningful to working-class life. Second, work was a laboratory where the 'habit of control' could be learnt in preparation for its expansion to the rest of society. And third, capitalism was most vulnerable at the work-place where the strategy of 'encroaching control' could actively undermine established power and authority relations. The relationship between guild socialism and the shop stewards' movement was thus very close, and between 1916 and 1919 encroaching control was at the centre of both guild-socialist and shop-steward strategies. The workers' committees patterned after the Clyde Workers' Committee were constructed upon participatory principles. Stewards were elected on an all-grades basis, each shop elected delegates to local workers' committees, no committee was to possess executive power, and all questions were to be referred back to the rank and file.[33]

Neither syndicalism nor guild socialism should be regarded merely as the intellectual flotsam pried loose by the fractures of the period. Both movements signified the surfacing of certain continuous themes in the tradition of working-class organisation and represented the most ambitious effort to date to legitimate and theorise on those themes. Workshop organisation in British labour had always focused around questions of power and authority over the work-process; it had always possessed a localist focus; and it had always structured action around forms of primitive, participatory democracy. These themes were conspicuously absent from mainstream Labourist thought, but they were integral to syndicalism and guild socialism and the centrality of work-place authority in social relations during this period anchored their meaning and relevance within organised labour. The challenge they posed was to reconsider how power and democracy were to be organised in the face of changing conditions of production. In that respect, they flew in the face of traditional conceptions that were culturally and historically deeply entrenched at all levels of society, including the Labour movement. Under those circumstances, the failure of these alternatives to progress beyond often vague dissent cannot be attributed solely to their gaps and inconsistencies. Naturally, they contained internal tensions. Guild socialism and the shop stewards' movement were by no means fully integrated, for example. The latter possessed its own intellectuals like John Maclean and J.T. Murphy. Furthermore, by 1919 the Russian Revolution and Bolshevism provided an alternative body of analysis and strategy which undermined the assumptions of guild socialism, splintered the movement, and eventually displaced it as the programme of the shop stewards' movement.[34]

More important to understanding the limitations of these alternatives, however, were the political and economic circumstances under which they developed. The survival of both guild socialism and the shop stewards' movement depended upon a quiescent reaction to their growth from employers, the state and the mainstream labour institutions. Survival also depended upon the continued existence of an industrial militancy and tension that was not necessarily coincident with these alternative strategies and organisations but which clearly provided them with a potentially growing base of support and made their prescriptions relevant. The presence of this militancy was also important in keeping the political situation fluid and providing the opportunity for alternative ideas and policies to obtain a hearing. By the early 1920s these conditions no longer obtained. The multi-layered challenge to political and industrial stability was defused. The workshop movement was decisively defeated; encroaching control halted and reversed; and the debate between alternative strategies and policies closed. The key elements in this process were the contradictory and ambiguous tensions between the state, the unions and the workshop movement; the marginalisation of alternative strategies and the triumph of Labourism particularly within the Labour Party; and, finally, the erosion of the economic conditions for work-place action by the depression of the early 1920s.

The Hegemony of Labourism

The necessities of the war dictated that the distance traditionally maintained between the state and industrial relations be finally and explicitly abandoned. As in the other areas where the boundaries of the state expanded, the effects of war were to accentuate and generalise trends already in progress. Since 1905, active use of the 1896 Conciliation Act by socially progressive bureaucrats in the Board of Trade had developed the precedents for state intervention in production relations. The creation of a separate Labour Department in the Board of Trade in 1911 headed by the ubiquitous George Askwith signalled the professionalisation of state conciliation in industrial relations. A prior reliance upon the occasional charismatic intervention in disputes by a Rosebery or a Lloyd George was replaced by a more bureaucratic process of continuous monitoring and strengthening of the machinery of collective bargaining.[35]

But the war forced a much deeper involvement by the state. Employers like William Weir, who was appointed Director of Munitions for Scotland, clearly saw the war as the opportunity to enlist state support in his long-term effort to displace the impediments of craft restriction to labour-process reorganisation. Dilution, in particular, could not be achieved simply by devolving responsibility onto the unions, although this was probably what most would have preferred. The problem was the ASE, whose refusal to sign the Treasury Agreement in March 1915 signified its deep reluctance to enter into any formal relationship. Considerable concessions, such as the promise of a post-war restoration of trade practices, were necessary to overcome this reluctance. Although the union was willing to join in supervising the development of dilution procedures and policies, it was well aware that their implementation would depend upon the reaction of craft militants. Thus, the executive was far less willing to play an active role in the execution of dilution.

By the end of 1915, however, it was clear that an essentially voluntarist policy of labour mobilisation would not work. State and employers' labour policies were extremely vulnerable to labour's growing awareness of its new shop-floor power. The South Wales miners' strike in July 1915 forced the government to take the mines under control and grant generous wage increases. On the Clyde there was militant talk about using the opportunity to secure high wages and bring masters and government to their knees. The employers were reluctant to confront craft militancy alone. A strike at Langs on the Clyde in August 1915 forced the Ministry of Munitions to allow the ASE virtually to dictate the terms of settlement. Various investigations of industrial unrest begun in 1915 defined the central domestic political and social issue of the war. Beneath the wage demands, concluded the British Association, lay 'the desire of workpeople to control their own lives and have a determining voice as to the conditions under which they shall work'.[36]

Events on the strategically crucial Clydeside were the main determinants of government policy towards labour militancy; it was there that workshop organisation was most effectively carried out, in the Clyde Workers' Committee. State policy developed in a gradual, tentative way and until the end of 1915, the government was restrained by the absence of any suitable legal instruments to use against the leadership of the Clyde Workers' Committee. At Christmas 1915, Lloyd George made a personal visit to the Clyde factories in an attempt to remove the opposition to dilution. The turbulent and insulting reception he received probably tipped the balance towards the tougher measures long advocated by Weir, and by the beginning of 1916 elements of such measures were in place. The Munitions of War Amendment Act and an expanded Defence of the Realm Act provided the legal basis for the arrest and deportation of militant strikers in March 1916 when a strike over dilution crippled the Clyde. The government moved to force the pace on dilution. Commissioners were appointed in each region, and provision was made for trade-union representation. Dilution was negotiated on a plant-by-plant basis which had the fortunate by-product of straining the united front the CWC was trying to maintain on the issue. When David Kirkwood, the Parkhead steward, negotiated a separate agreement with the Commissioners, the possibility of a common policy collapsed. This set the pattern for the rest of the war and it ensured an important separation between the revolutionary militants of the CWC and the more conservative craftsmen on the shop-floor.[37]

But the policy of the government also served to legitimate and strengthen shop-floor organisation. Kirkwood had insisted upon a workshop committee to monitor the dilution agreement and this became a general feature. In any case, negotiations on a plant basis could only be conducted with the stewards. On the other hand, the limits of this co-operation were also clearly drawn to keep it firmly within the bounds of collective bargaining. Consultation, not control, was the only legitimate right of these committees, and this forced the militants of the CWC to scale down their original demand for an equal say in control to a share in control. In addition, there was to be no recognition of the unofficial workers' committees. The government determined on this from the beginning when Lloyd George refused to negotiate with the unofficial CWC during his visit in December 1915. Both the government and some employers favoured the integration of shop committees into the industrial-relations system, but only if they were responsible to the official union structures.[38]

An important stage in this policy was marked by the shop stewards' agreements of 1917 and 1919, which granted stewards official bargaining recognition. However, this merely registered what had already been achieved in engineering by informal means and, indeed, the stewards' influence may have contracted under these agreements. Allan Smith, secretary to the employers' association, later claimed that in accepting these agreements, the employers had helped defeat the challenge to union authority from the shop stewards' movement. Thus, the stewards were presented with a serious dilemma. The theory and practice of the stewards' strategy rested upon a theory of 'encroaching control' in the workshop. Little attention was paid to the question of how to consolidate power within the trade-union structures. In part, this was due to the suspicion of the function of leadership and, in part, to the belief that as presently constituted the trade-union structures were themselves a major part of the problem. Thus, the reaction to the agreement of 1919 in particular was divided. On the one hand, like the Whitley councils the government was also propagating, it was argued that 'to become embodied in the constitution of the trade union would be little short of death'. On the other hand, not to try and capture official posts threatened to surrender to the officials the stewards' influence over the mass membership. Thus, *Solidarity*, the paper of the stewards' movement, reluctantly recommended a vote in favour of the 1919 agreement but urged a complementary strengthening and expansion of the workers' committees. By 1921 the dilemma of what attitude to take towards participation in official structures was resolved, but in the meantime, the stewards had been progressively marginalised by government policy and driven into an increased dependence upon official trade unionism.[39]

The major preoccupation of government policy until about 1922 was to stabilise a delicate and unstable industrial and political situation, and the tactical wizardry of Lloyd George was stretched to the full as he sought to defuse the labour crisis by isolating 'extremism'. The government's task was assisted by the ambiguous relationship between what Cronin has called the 'movement of insurgency' and the trade-union leadership. In some cases, workshop committees were destroyed after the war with the acquiescence of union officials. Even those leaders like Robert Smellie who adopted the vocabulary of 'direct action' had no clear idea of how, or to what ends, it should be used; others, like Jimmy Thomas, unalterably opposed the notion. Government policy played on these divisions to strengthen the moderate leaders against what Tom Jones (the Cabinet Secretary) termed the 'mutiny of the rank and file'. A crucial stage in this process was the 40-hour strike on the Clyde in 1919. The ASE was badly divided on the issue. Some militants were demanding a 37-hour week, but the union had just settled nationally for 47 hours and was in no position to endorse the steward-led demand for 40 hours. The government moved decisively to exploit this division. Tanks were sent to Glasgow, gunboats moved up the Clyde, and Willie Gallacher and other activists were arrested. A sharp lesson was delivered to direct action and the legitimacy of official agreements was reinforced. To allow the strike to succeed would have been to allow established political and industrial order to be discredited. The defeat of the strike delivered a 'fatal blow to the unofficial movement' and marked the beginning of the marginalisation of militant industrial action. But a discriminating diplomacy greeted the concurrent demands of railwaymen and miners. In

September 1918 and August 1919, the railway workers threatened strike action to secure shorter hours and higher wages. A national rail strike was too serious to contemplate. So was a national coal strike, and the miners' demand for nationalisation in 1919 was successfully stalled with the promise of a Royal Commission. The moment for the miners to achieve control of the mines thus passed. On another level, the redeeming of the promise to restore trade practices in engineering strengthened the credibility of official trade unionism as it used the opportunity to take 'up many claims originally formulated by the shop stewards' and workers' control movement'.[40]

At the same time, the structures that sustained militant policies were undermined by their own internal failures. The doomed experiment of the building guilds by the iconoclastic Malcolm Sparkes discredited the practicality of guild socialism. The evident failure of the shop stewards' movement to alter trade-union policy or structure eroded belief in encroaching control and drove home the logic of Lenin's strictures against 'workerism'. Thus, from 1919 the politics of the shop stewards' movement drifted away from guild socialism towards Communism and the political wilderness.[41] Meanwhile mainstream Labourism was asserting its predominance. Official trade unionism was remobilised, direct action and unofficial organisation were discredited, and Labour politics were revitalised under the firm control of Arthur Henderson, Ramsay MacDonald and Sydney Webb.

The formation of the national Labour Party in 1918 injected a disruptive and uncertain influence into electoral politics. Until the Conservatives quite deliberately decided to risk (under the most favourable political circumstances) the experiment of a Labour government in 1924, it was not exactly clear what this implied for the conduct of politics. In retrospect, however, a major paradox lay at the centre of the emergence of the Labour Party. The stimulus for the party's formation came from the wave of radicalism that characterised the pre- and post-war years. The formalisation of the party's loose local structures into a national organisation in 1918 was not so much a logical culmination to the organisational efforts of the past two decades as a response, in Arthur Henderson's words, to the 'militant democratic consciousness' of the masses. The formation of the Labour Party was not a reflex to a resurgent, oppressive capitalism but, rather, to the model of Bolshevism which – as the Leeds Convention of 1917 showed – threatened to fuse with the indigenous militancy and radicalism. But if the

Labour Party's creation was unthinkable without this context, then the end result was that socialism became weaker within the party than it had been before 1918.[42]

This was especially apparent at the organisational level where the initiatives of Henderson and Webb effectively squeezed the socialists out of the ILP. Similarly, the insertion of clause 4 into the party's constitution promising common ownership of the means of production was not intended by Webb to be an expression of working-class politics, but more to appeal to middle-class professionals believed to be committed to the 'efficiency' of state socialism. In addition, a central control descended upon rival power centres and ideological tendencies that challenged Labourist orthodoxies. The demands of the regions for local autonomy were swept aside; executive hostility to co-operation with the Communist Party existed before that organisation had exposed its own peculiarities. Most important, those centres where alternative strategies to Labourism remained unbowed – the Labour Research Department, the advisory committees, and the *Daily Herald* – were either disbanded or bought firmly to heel. The result was that by 1923 the debate over alternative policies and strategies was effectively closed off. A parallel clarification of Labour's policy effectively narrowed the range of aspirations: the levy on capital and workers' control were dropped from the programme in 1923. Indeed, all serious thinking on policy-planning came to a virtual halt and was not to be revived until after 1931. The ILP remained the only source of innovative thinking, but it was increasingly inconsequential in policy circles and its proposals were generally ignored. By 1923 the hegemony of political labourism in the party had effectively marginalised those elements which represented a broader political line than that countenanced by the political and trade-union leadership.[43]

But it is impossible to divorce these political developments from the parallel isolation of the shop stewards' movement and the discrediting of the strategies associated with industrial militancy. From 1919 the political credibility of Labourism was increasingly enhanced as the plausibility of alternative tendencies like direct action declined. The experience of the Clyde illustrated one variant of this process. The defeat of the 40-hour strike was balanced by the construction of a successful local political machine – albeit one that stood to the left of the national party. Similarly, the failure to achieve nationalisation of the railways or mines, the disastrous episode of Black Friday, and the subsequent defeats of the miners strike in 1921 and of the engineers in 1922, were matched by the growing success of the Labour Party in national politics.[44] Thus, the ultimate triumph of political Labourism depended as much upon the economic defeat of Labour as it did upon the internal manoeuvrings of the political leaderships.

The absence of an unchallenged consensus in Labour politics was mirrored at the level of national policy-making. Significant sections of employers and government were in favour of developing a progressive response to industrial and political instability that would continue the wartime co-operation between unions, employers and the state. Some employers, like Charles Renold, a leading exponent of scientific management were concerned to erect 'a new constitution for industry' which would extend 'the right of labour to concern itself with the general conduct, aims, methods and results of . . . industry'. The machinery of management would be rearranged to enable 'responsibility and power to be shared with the workers' through the inclusion of workshop committees in collective bargaining. As long as militancy remained a serious threat, these options remained open. Although this conciliatory tendency was never more than a minority sentiment amongst employers and by 1921 was of little importance, within government it retained a stronger presence. Lloyd George's commitment to a socially progressive policy of reconstruction was probably genuine. Its viability was always fragile, however, because of opposition from those who wanted a return to 'normalcy' whereby social and economic policy would be guided by orthodox monetary considerations. Throughout 1919 and 1920, the necessity to appease labour forced the subordination of monetary issues to the priority of domestic peace and the hope of reconstruction continued to flicker. Britain left the gold standard in March 1919 and did not fully return until 1925. But the policy struggle was decided by early 1921 when the onset of the slump and the labour movement's refusal to back the miners with a general strike seemed to presage the taming of labour. At that moment the calls for 'economy' in social expenditure reached irresistible proportions.[45]

The social implications of orthodoxy were quite clear. Improvements in working-class conditions would depend upon the vagaries of international trade and the ability of the pound to remain artificially strong. The exposure of British industry to world competition was most problematic in the old export industries but it was precisely there that the obstacles to the smooth operation of this policy were the greatest. This was especially the case in engineering and mining where the structures of militancy were deeply entrenched. And it was in those industries that the central social battles were to be fought for the triumph of the political economy of normalcy. In engineering, the continued survival of workshop organisation impeded the necessity to reduce costs by efficient methods; in mining, the obstinate resistance to lowered standards of wages and work stood in the way of generalised reductions.

As early as 1918, it was recognised that the competitive success of the engineering industry depended upon the adoption of more efficient managerial organisation. Once the fragile possibility of securing this by co-partnership was removed, the central strategy became the diminution of worker restrictions at the production process. And the nexus of conflict came to centre on the question of the regulation of overtime. Within the union, it was claimed that, during the war, workshop bargaining had secured the right to shop-steward consultation on overtime. Whether this was true or not, a general effort was certainly made through 1920 to restrict and gain control over the working of overtime, particularly in Lancashire.[46] This led to an agreement in September 1920 which limited overtime to 30 hours a week in any given month but was ambiguous on the rights of consultation. And in December 1920 the union circularised its district committees claiming the rights of mutual consultation on the basis of the prior consent clause in the Procedure of 1914. This transformed the issue for the employers into a crucial question of authority. The consent clause was intended only to apply to general conditions of work, not to specific managerial instructions. If the right of prior consent were admitted on overtime there was nothing to stop it being extended to all other issues that had to do with the execution of work. Indeed, this was already a problem. The immediate post-war years saw an expansion of shop-committees and bargaining and a greater influence for militant policies within the union itself. The initiatives for organisation and action increasingly shifted from the district committees to the shop-floor committees. There were constant struggles (which the men frequently won) on prior consultation over machine-manning, apprentices, and the operation of premium systems. Conferences were held in the spring of 1921 to try and resolve these contentions but they met with no success. For the worker, the appearance of growing unemployment gave the issue a crucial economic dimension because restrictions on overtime and other working practices would maximise available work. But such restrictions posed a basic challenge to the employers' strategy for coping with the depression. Economics and power were inextricably bound together.[47]

By the summer of 1921 the union was beleaguered. In June it accepted a wage reduction which sparked off a further series of conflicts in those areas like Sheffield where workshop bargaining had secured piece-rates 50 per cent above the national average. In November, the employers demanded a further reduction and moved to reassert their control over the workshops. A memo was presented to the AEU insisting that the decision to work overtime rested solely with the employer and restating the clause of 1898 that gave employers the right to initiate any changes in the workshop before the exhaustion of discussions through the Procedure:

> The employers contend that if British industry is to maintain its appropriate place in . . . the world there must be freedom to the management to introduce such changes in the works as may be necessary for the proper development of the industry.[48]

Under the threat of a lock-out, the executive accepted this ultimatum and recommended union approval, but a ballot registered a 15,000 majority against this interpretation of the overtime agreement and workshop efforts to enforce prior consultation continued. The employers now proceeded to broaden their attack and in March 1922 demanded that all 50 unions engaged in engineering-related work accept the memo – which suggests that restrictions were also common in areas like shipbuilding and foundry work. When this was rejected, a lock-out was inaugurated. The government established a court of inquiry whose report was sympathetic to the employers and by the middle of June union resistance had been broken. The AEU voted by a large majority to accept the integration of the memo into the Procedure.[49]

The 1922 agreement, which nominally remained in force until 1975, signified the completion of the process begun in 1898. Collective bargaining was combined with a precise definition of how authority relations in the industry were to be ordered and a clear delineation of the spheres of responsibility between unions and employers. At the workshop level, of course, the situation was more ambiguous, but there is little doubt that employers immediately took the opportunity to erode the gains achieved by the men over the previous decade. The resistance of the National Union of Foundry Workers to payment by results was finally overcome. Violations of piece-work agreements were widespread. Employer control over the division of labour was enhanced by the removal of restraints on machine-manning, the freedom to introduce new systems of production, and the spread of the open-shop principle. The already weakened shop stewards' organisation crumbled. At the Clyde centres of Beardmores, Fairchilds, John Brown and North British Diesel, for example, victimisation effectively discouraged workshop organisation and by December 1923, it was reported that 'those shops, once solidly organized, are now about the worst in the district as far as membership is concerned . . . we cannot get members with sufficient guts to function as shop stewards'.[50] Although there were to be significant exceptions to this trend both within engineering and elsewhere, the 1922 conflict ensured an employer-dominated balance of power in production for most of the inter-war years.

The general strike of 1926 marked the final stage in the marginalisation of industrial and political militancy. The defeat of the miners' strike of 1921 destroyed their hopes of a national wages system and the issue since then had been whether they would have to face another reduction in wages and conditions. But the miners also represented the last important stronghold of the militant radicalism of the war and post-war years. Once they were defeated, that spirit was driven back into purely local 'little Moscows' of the Northeast and South Wales and its few remaining representatives within the labour movement, like A.J. Cook, were thoroughly discredited.[51] In the second place, and more significantly, the defeat of the miners was important for a complete return to the political economy of normalcy. A temporary revival in prosperity in 1924 led to slightly better wage conditions but these were almost immediately abrogated by the downturn in early 1925. The unexpected unity of Red Friday forced the government to reintroduce a wages subsidy just at the moment it returned to the gold standard. The careful preparations that were made to confront and defeat the expected strike in 1926 reflected the importance of the issue: if the miners won, the economic strategy of the 1920s would suffer a serious political defeat and the basic direction of industrial and social policy would be thrown into doubt. The government was right to argue that the strike raised constitutional issues: the credibility of its national economic policy was at stake.

For labour politics, however, the defeat of the strike consolidated labourist policies and established the unassailable position of the moderate faction of the labour leadership for the rest of the period. From this position of confidence, alternative organisational strategies and policies were regarded with intense disdain and hostility. This was, perhaps, understandable in the case of the Communist-led Minority

Movement which was contained by a concerted offensive long before the gyrations of Comintern policy destroyed the movement in the early 1930s. Less defensible was the suspicion directed at the National Unemployed Workers' Movement which was unfairly branded as a Communist front and effectively isolated by the studied neglect of the TUC – whose own efforts on behalf of the unemployed were notably unenergetic.[52]

Equally revealing was the fate of an attempt to revive the debate between workers' control and nationalisation as the best means of socialising industry. In the aftermath of the débâcle of 1931, when a serious re-examination of Labour's policy positions could no longer be avoided, a contest emerged between those who wanted direct worker representation on the boards of nationalised industry and those who wanted 'public' representatives chosen on the basis of expertise. At the TUC in 1931 and the Labour Party conference in 1933, resolutions were passed in favour of the former. But the proposals ultimately formulated by the TUC General Council and the policy committee of the Labour Party's National Executive ignored these resolutions and representation by ability alone (which did not, of course, preclude worker appointees) was maintained against constant references back. Statutory representation of workers on governing boards was a far cry from syndicalist notions of workers' control, but the intensity with which this debate was conducted throughout the mid-1930s suggests the issue was not merely semantic:

> The outcome would determine the final distribution of power within the enterprise, which in turn raised fundamental questions about the role of public ownership in capitalist society. A major element of worker representation would redistribute power . . . whereas Morrison sought to leave the basic power structures unchanged.[53]

The theory of workers' control had been essentially truncated after Cole's retreat into quietism from 1923. But the victory of the Morrisonian definition of nationalisation in the shape of the public corporation was less a function of superior intellectual argument and more of its reasonableness as 'practical politics'. The success of Herbert Morrison's flagship public-service body, the London Passenger Transport Board, provided a shining contrast to the political problems believed to be associated with a syndicalist-sounding alternative. The dogged evasion of conference resolutions on worker representation

To

LAMBETH

Memorandum

reflected the essential determination of Labourism to avoid transgressing the boundary between political power and authority relationships in the economic realm.

Conclusion

In a curious way, the failures of Labour in the 1930s have come to be blamed upon those elements and factions that were pressing alternatives to labourist strategies. According to one authoritative account the pressure of the 'left' inhibited 'the Party leadership [and restricted] its room for manoeuvre'. Yet the real question about Labour politics is why left-wing tendencies aroused an immediate reflex of fierce opposition? The evidence of the 1920s – when the 'centre' operated in a total ideological vacuum and the 'left' was the only source of policy proposals – hardly suggests that if the left had produced different kinds of proposals it could have captured the party. It was power both in a political and philosophical sense that was at issue.[54]

The determined hostility demonstrated to alternative policies reflected the logic of Labourism far more than the fear of subversion. The failures of 1918-26 were the failures of those strategies, organisations and personalities who were identified with the search to fuse industrial militancy with political action. By 1926, the use of industrial power to influence national policy and the discussion of ways fundamentally to reorder social and political authority were excluded from the agenda of Labour politics. The partnership between Fabian political reformism and trade-union economism was established as the means by which the amelioration of working-class conditions was to be sought. Within Labour's political discourse, then, the nature of production relations and action at the industrial level could only comprehended as purely economic and as not relevant to issues of power and authority. The result was that the relationship between work and politics that had lain at the heart of Labour's political debates was now broken. The Labour Party became the party of the working class just at the moment when it embraced this strategy. In the 1920s and 1930s this separation was reinforced by the one act of political revenge to follow the general strike. The Trades Disputes Act of 1927 prohibited political strikes and imposed financial restraints upon trade-union support for the Labour Party. This attempt to cripple the party's finances was rather easily evaded; the importance of the Act was to enshrine in law the distinction between the separate spheres of industrial and political action.[55]

It must be stressed that the Labourist formulation of the relationship between labour and society was not a predetermined product of working-class history. On the contrary, it emerged as the decomposition of older structures of social and political relations opened a process of debate and struggle within the Labour movement, the working class and between labour, state and employers. This complex (more complex than we have managed to portray here) dynamic interacted upon the mosaic of complementary and contradictory attitudes, tendencies, and values that composed the cultural, political and industrial experiences in the history of labour. Labourism was one particular composite of these elements, but it was neither more nor less indigenous than guild socialism, syndicalism, or, for that matter, working-class Toryism. It is true that the weight of tradition and culture both within the working class and within society at large tolled heavily against the putative alternatives to Labourism. The Webbs were more compatible to the British tradition of reform than the young G.D.H. Cole; Ramsay MacDonald was a more appropriate political leader than Jimmy Maxton; J.H. Thomas was more of a consensus figure than John Maclean. But, in the final analysis, the triumph of one set of ideological assumptions over another, or the dominance of group personalities over others, did not merely reflect their more accurate representation of British working-class consciousness or history. They reflected the process of history as it was played out at the time, in which there were winners and losers and in which some alternatives were eliminated while others remained viable.

Notes

1. Robert Scally, *The Origins of the Lloyd George Coalition* (Princeton, 1974); Avner Offer, *Property and Politics 1870-1914* (Cambridge, 1982), pp. 364-81.

2. Maurice Cowling, *The Impact of Labour 1918-1924* (Cambridge, 1971), pp. 30-44; Kenneth Morgan, *Consensus and Disunity* (Oxford, 1979), p. 214; James Cronin, *Labour and British Society* 1918-1979 (London, 1984), Chapter 2.

3. Daily Mail, *What the Worker Wants* (London, 1912), pp. 129-31; H.A. Clegg, A. Fox and A.F. Thompson, *A History of British Trade Unionism since 1889* (Oxford, 1964), p. 318; H.V. Emy, *Liberals, Radicals and Social Politics 1892-1914* (Cambridge, 1973), pp. 268-74. K.D. Ewing, *Trade Unions, the Labour Party and the Law* (Edinburgh, 1982), pp. 17-18.

4. Cyril Grunfeld, *Modern Trade Union Law* (London, 1966), pp. 420-4; K.W. Wedderburn, *The Worker and the Law*, 2nd edn (Harmondsworth, 1971), p. 346.

5. *Western Morning News*, 8 and 9 January 1891 and 10 September 1891.

The case was considered of sufficient significance to warrant a notice by *The Times*, 10 January 1891, p. 7 and 12 January 1891, p. 9; *Curran* v *Treleavan*, (1891) 2QB, p. 562.

6. Grunfeld, *Trade Union Law*, p. 442; *Lyons* v *Wilkins* (1896) 1 Chancery Division, 825-34, (1899) 1 Chancery Division, 269-70; G.R. Rubin, 'The Strengths and Weaknesses of the Picketing Law', *Industrial Relations Journal*, vol. 4, no. 2 (1974), p. 58. The Barnsley weavers were fined £11,000 in a similar case in 1901 – see, David Howell, *British Workers and the Independent Labour Party 1886-1906* (Manchester, 1983), p. 66.

7. R. Brown, 'The Temperton v. Russell Case (1893); The Beginning of the Legal Offensive Against the Unions', *Bulletin of Economic Research*, vol. 23 (May 1973).

8. *Railway News*, 8 September 1900, pp. 407-8.

9. Clegg, Fox and Thompson, *British Trade Unionism*, pp. 326-9; Arthur Shadwell, *Industrial Efficiency* (London, 1909), p. 567; Bob Hepple, 'Union Responsibility for Shop Stewards', *Industrial Law Journal*, vol. 1, no. 4 (1972), pp. 202-5.

10. Clegg, Fox and Thompson, *British Trade Unionism*, pp. 317-25, 393-5; K.D. Ewing, *Trade Unions, the Labour Party and the Law*, pp. 22-5; John Wilson, *C-B. A Life of Sir Henry Campbell-Bannerman* (London, 1973), p. 505.

11. *Royal Commission on the Working of the Railway Conciliation and Arbitration Scheme of 1907*, 1912-13, Vol. XLV (Cd. 6014), ques. 5680, 5695, 5803, 6309-402, 7453; Philip Bagwell, *The Railwaymen* (London, 1963) pp. 278, 280-81; Charles Watkins in *The Industrial Syndicalist*, May 1911; *Railway Review*, 19 May 1911, p. 3.

12. *Railway Review*, 16 June 1911, p. 1; 10 February 1911, p. 9; 11 August 1911, p. 8; 18 August 1911, p. 1; 5 January 1912, p. 8; Bagwell, *Railwaymen* pp. 290-9, 309.

13. Lazonick, 'Production Relations, Labour Productivity and Choice of Technique in British and U.S. Cotton Spinning; *Journal of Economic History*, vol. 41, no. 3 (1981), pp. 504-5; Joseph White, *The Limits of Trade Union Militancy. The Lancashire Textile Workers 1910-1914* (Westport, Conn., 1978), pp. 75-9, 85-7, 104-7, 173-8; *Cotton Factory Times*, 6 March 1914 p. 5; 3 April 1914, pp. 1, 5; 13 March 1914, p. 5; 17 April 1914, p. 4; 24 April 1914, p. 4.

14. James B. Jeffreys, *The Story of the Engineers 1800-1945* (London, 1945), pp. 165-7; Jonathan Zeitlin, 'The Labour Strategies of British Engineering Employers 1880-1914', unpublished paper, 1981, pp. 33-36; Keith Burgess, 'New Unionism for Old? The Amalgamated Society of Engineers in Britain 1880-1914', unpublished paper, 1981, pp. 16-20, 31; *The Socialist* (Edinburgh), July 1914, p. 84.

15. Charles Sabel, 'The Internal Politics of Trade Unions' in Suzanne Berger, *Organizing Interests in Western Europe* (Cambridge, Mass., 1980); J. Zeitlin, 'Trade Unions and Job Control: A Critique of Rank and Filism', unpublished paper 1982.

16. Howell, *British Workers*, p. 27; James Hinton, *Labour and Socialism* (London, 1983), p. 113; *Railway Review*, 2 February 1912, p. 1.

17. Howell, *British Workers*, p. 45; White, *Limits of Militancy*, p. 173.

18. For this see Howell, *British Workers*, where one of the major themes is the slowness with which the spaces opened in both the trade union and political spheres for the socialistic ILP to enter.

19. David Cannadine, *Lords and Landlords. The Aristocracy and the Towns 1774-1967* (Leicester, 1980); Allan Redfern,'Crewe: Leisure in a Railway Town' in John K. Walton and James Walvin (eds), *Leisure in Britain 1780-1939*, pp. 117-36; Robert Moore, *Pit-Men, Politics and Preachers. The Effects of*

Methodism in a Durham Mining Community (Cambridge, 1974), pp. 89-92, 188.

20. J. Reynold and K. Leybourn, 'The Emergence of the Independent Labour Party in Bradford,' *International Review of Social History*, vol. 20, no. 3 (1975); Joyce, *Work, Society and Politics: The Culture of the Factory in Later Victorian England* (Brighton, 1980), p. 26; Jonathan Schneer, *Ben Tillett* (London, 1982), pp. 68-76.

21. Fred Reid, *Keir Hardie. The Making of a Socialist* (London, 1978); Roy Gregory, *The Miners and British Politics 1906-1914* (Oxford, 1968), pp. 61-4, 131-2; Howell, *British Workers*, p. 106; Fox, *The National Union of Boot and Shoe Operatives 1874-1957* (Oxford, 1958), pp. 190-6. Inskip was forced to resign in 1894 as a result of his opposition to independent labour representation.

22. For examples of this in printing see *Typographical Circular*, January 1895, p. 7; July 1895, pp. 8-9; September 1894, p. 7; September 1895, p. 7; December 1898, p. 1; Robert Gray, *The Labour Aristocracy in Victorian Edinburgh* (Oxford, 1976), pp. 170-6; ASE, *Monthly Journal* February 1898, pp. 9-10.

23. Stanley Pierson, *Marxism and the Origins of British Socialism* (Ithaca, NY, 1974); Robert Currie, *Industrial Politics* (Oxford, 1979).

24. Stephen Yeo, 'A New Life: The Religion of Socialism in Britain 1883-1896,' *History Workshop Journal*, no. 4 (1977).

25. Stanley Pierson, *British Socialism: The Journey from Fantasy to Politics* (Cambridge, Mass., 1979), pp. 158-68.

26. Bob Holton, *British Syndicalism 1900-1914* (London, 1976); Branko Pribicevic, *The Shop Stewards' Movement and Workers' Control 1910-1922* (Oxford, 1959), pp. 65-74. On the direct relationship between the structure of industrial relations and syndicalism see R. Price, *Masters, Unions and Men: Work Control in Building and the Rise of Labour 1830-1914* (Cambridge, 1980), pp. 246-58.

27. Pribicevic, *Shop Stewards' Movement*, pp. 5, 46-7; Bagwell, *Railwaymen*, pp. 370-2; G.D.H. Cole, *Self-Government in Industry* (London, 1917), pp. 223-4; Cole, *Trade Unionism in Mining* (Oxford, 1923), p. 70; Andrew Taylor, 'The Miners and Nationalization 1931-36', *International Review of Social History*, vol. 28, no. 2 (1983), p. 177; AEU, *Monthly Journal* August 1922, p. 52.

28. Margaret Cole, 'Guild Socialism and the Labour Research Department' in Asa Briggs and John Saville, *Essays in Labour History 1886-1923* (London, 1971); A.W. Wright, *G.D.H. Cole and Socialist Democracy* (Oxford, 1979), pp. 63-5.

29. Henry Pelling, *Popular Politics and Society in Late Victorian Society* (London, 1968), Chapter 1; Fred Henderson, *The Labour Unrest* (London, 1912), p. 135; Roy Hay, 'Employers and Social Policy in Britain: The Evolution of Welfare Legislation 1905-1914,' *Social History*, vol. 4 (1977). Resistance to statism remained focused on its disruption of social and family life: see M.J. Daunton, 'Down the Pit: Work in the Great Northern and South Wales Coalfield 1870-1914', *Ec. Hist. Rev*. vol. 34, no. 4 (1981), p. 592; Dave Douglass, 'The Durham Pitman' in Raphael Samuel (ed.), *Miners, Quarrymen and Saltworkers* (London, 1977), pp. 266-70.

30. R.J. Holton, 'Syndicalist Theories of the State', *Sociological Review*, vol. 28 (1980), p. 14; South Wales Unofficial Reform Committee, *The Miners' Next Step* (London, repr. 1973), pp. 32, 34.

31. J. Ramsay MacDonald, *Socialism and Society* (New York, repr., 1970); Wright, *Cole and Democracy*, pp. 55-8, 71.

32. Wright, *Cole and Democracy*, pp. 22, 34-6, 50-1, 75, 100-1.

33. Ibid., pp. 28, 60. 90-1; Pribicevic, *Shop Stewards' Movement*, pp. 95-8, 126.

34. James Hinton, *The First Shop Stewards' Movement* (London, 1973),

Chapter 12; Margaret Cole, 'Guild Socialism' p. 280; Wright, *Cole and Democracy*, pp. 99-100.

35. Roger Davidson, 'Social Change and Social Administration: The Conciliation Act in British Industrial Relations' in T.C. Smout (ed.), *The Search for Wealth and Stability* (London, 1979). On the development of state policy generally see the interesting essays in Kathleen Burk (ed.), *War and the State* (London, 1982).

36. Iain McLean, *The Legend of Red Clydeside* (Edinburgh, 1983), pp. 30-1, 33-4, 39-40, 43-4; Hinton, *The First Shop Stewards' Movement*, pp. 31-2, 128, 142, 144; A.W. Kirkaldy (ed.), *British Labour: Replacement and Conciliation 1914-21* (London, 1921), pp. 165-8.

37. McLean, *Red Clydeside*, pp. 40, 52-61, 63-7; William Gallagher, *Revolt on the Clyde* (London, repr. 1980), Chapter 6.

38. G.D.H. Cole, *Workshop Organization* (Oxford, 1923), pp. 67-70; Cole, *Trade Unionism and Munitions* (Oxford, 1923), p. 109; McLean, *Red Clydeside,* p. 85; Pribicivec, *Shop Stewards' Movement*, pp. 114-20; Wayne Lewchuk, 'The Role of the British Government in the Spread of Scientific Management and Fordism in the Inter-War years'; *Journal of Economic History*, vol. 44, no. 2 (June 1984), pp. 355-61.

39. Keith Middlemas, *Politics in Industrial Society* (London, 1979), pp. 128-9; Wigham, *The Power to Manage* (London, 1973), p. 103; Pribicivec, *Shop Stewards' Movement*, pp. 90-1; *Solidarity*, March 1914, p. 7; June 1918, p. 2; July 1918, p. 6; September 1919, p. 1; August 1919, p. 2.

40. For attacks on workshop organisation and the failure of unions to protect them see Pribicivec, *Shop Stewards' Movement*, p. 103, n. 1; *Solidarity*, 18 February 1921, p. 8; Tom Walsh, *The New Triple Alliance* (London, 1921), pp. 1-7; Cronin, *Labour and British Society*, Chapter 2; Hinton, *Labour and Socialism*, pp. 109-12, 115-16; Middlemas, *Politics in Industrial Society*, pp. 143-4, McLean, *Red Clydeside*, p. 131.

41. Frank Matthews, 'The Building Guilds' in Briggs and Saville, *Essays in Labour History*. The formation of the AEU reflected the failure of the shop stewards' movement decisively to influence ideas on trade-union structure. The Union was essentially created by a fusion of existing stuctures and there was no attempt to restructure it along the lines of greater participatory democracy: see *Solidarity*, August 1919, p. 1. See Gallagher, pp. 251-3, for his conversion from workerism by no less an authority than Lenin himself. See also, Pribicivec, *Shop Stewards' Movement*, p. 104.

42. Ross McKibbin, *The Evolution of the Labour Party 1910-1924* (Oxford, 1974), pp. 92-3, 105; J.M. Winter, 'Arthur Henderson and the Russian Revolution,' *Historical Journal*, vol. 15, no. 4 (1972), pp. 770-3.

43. McKibbin, *Evolution of the Labour Party*, Chapter 9, esp. p. 245; Morgan, *Consensus and Disunity*, pp. 226-32.

44. McLean, *Red Clydeside*, Chapters 13 and 14.

45. Charles Renold, *Workshop Committees* (London, 1921, revised edn); Morgan, *Consensus and Disunity*, pp. 23, 25, 58, Chapter 3. The one attempt to explore the political economy of these years as it impacted upon labour is the stimulating essay by John Foster, 'British Imperialism and the Labour Aristocracy' in Jeffrey Skelley (ed.), *The General Strike 1926* (London, 1976).

46. *Report of the Departmental Committee Appointed by the Board of Trade to Consider the Position of the Engineering Trades after the War*, 1918, Vol. XIII (Cd. 9073); J.E. Powell, *The Output Problem* (London, 1921); AEU, *Monthly Journal*, May 1920, pp. 68-70; June 1920, p. 32; January 1921, pp. 28-30, 48; February 1921, pp. 30-3, 49, 50; October 1920, pp. 37, 43; January 1922, pp. 60-1.

47. *Report of a Court of Inquiry Concerning the Engineering Trades Dispute*

of 1922, 1922, Vol. VIII (Cmd. 1653), pp. 6-9; Arthur Shadwell; *The Engineering Industry and the Crisis of 1922* (London, 1922), pp. 47-51; AEU, *Monthly Journal*, April 1921, pp. 10-11 and May 1921, pp. 12-15. The war years also saw the extension of workshop bargaining to industries beyond engineering – this subject has yet to be researched. For the docks and other examples see *Solidarity*, 25 February 1921, pp. 3, 8; 4 March 1921, p. 8; 8 April 1921, p. 8; 24 April 1921, p. 8; R. Bean, 'Custom, Job Regulation and Dock Labour in Liverpool 1911-39,' *International Review of Social History*, vol. 28, no. 3 (1982).

48. AEU *Monthly Journal*, June 1921, pp. 14-19; September 1921, p. 25; October 1921, p. 10; *Report of a Court of Inquiry Concerning the Engineering Trades Dispute* p. 20.

49. AEU, *Monthly Journal*, February 1922, p. 12; Wigham *Power to Manage*, pp. 118-23.

50. Wigham, *Power to Manage*, pp. 124, 127; AEU, *Monthly Journal*, September 1922, p. 19; November 1922, p. 51; December 1922, pp. 52-4; February 1923, p. 25; December 1923, pp. 24-5; September 1923, p. 20; June 1923, p. 23; August 1925, p. 24. Shop stewards' organisation had been eliminated from Coventry by 1921: see Richard Whiting, *The View from Coventry* (Oxford, 1982), pp. 48-9.

51. G.A. Phillips, *The General Strike* (London, 1976), pp. 31, 43-6; Stewart MacIntyre, *Little Moscows* (London, 1980).

52. Howell, *British Workers*, p. 108; Roderick Martin, *Communism and the British Trade Unions 1924-1933* (Oxford, 1969), pp. 57, 93-9, 102, 135-6, 151; Ralph Haybourn, 'The National Unemployed Workers' Movement 1921-36', *International Review of Social History*, vol. 28, no. 3 (1983).

53. Taylor, 'The Miners and Nationalization', p. 182; Trades Union Congress, 64th, 65th, 66th, 67th *Annual Reports*; Jim Tomlinson, *The Unequal Struggle? British Socialism and Capitalist Enterprise*. (London, 1982), pp. 71-9.

54. Ben Pimlott, *Labour and the Left* (Cambridge, 1977), pp. 194, 198-200.

55. Ewing, *Trade Unions, the Labour Party and the Law*, pp. 62-3.

7 PRODUCTION AND PREROGATIVE 1926-1947

Introduction

The unity to the period between 1926 and 1947 may not be readily apparent. From the débâcle of the general strike until the outbreak of the Second World War, Labour's history was marked by a series of reversals. The ambiguous effects of the depression – long-term unemployment and the growth of new industries – in no way mitigated the basic vulnerability of Labour's position in society. The disaster of the Labour government of 1929-31 merely compounded that weakness and ushered in a more complete Conservative political hegemony than before. Labour's position was then suddenly reversed by the emergency of 1940 when a full political partnership was the necessary condition of national survival, and by 1945 the rehabilitation of Labour was completed with the moment of sweetest electoral triumph. In 1947 the most accomplished Labour government of the century stood at the pinnacle of its success. The Welfare State was in the process of construction, the political attachment of the working class to the Labour Party was never firmer, and the socialisation of industry was in its first bloom. These signposts are well known and need no repetition. We are concerned with a slightly different rhythm within labour's history, one which underlay these grand developments.

The consequences of labour's defeats in the early 1920s was to allow employer prerogative a more total freedom than it had ever known before. This was the crucial context within which the various economic responses to the depression were played out because it permitted both the worsening of working conditions and the reorganisation of production to be untroubled by social constraints. It is hardly surprising, therefore, that the 1920s and 1930s were marked by high growth rates and extensive rationalisation. Then, from the late 1930s, as rearmament became a priority, the limits to managerial freedom began to be more tightly drawn. And by the time the Coalition government was formed in 1940, the sharing of national power was mirrored at the work-place. The price for output was a reversal of the production-prerogative equation of the 1920s and 1930s. This reality was legitimised and reinforced by state policy which, out of sheer necessity, endorsed the joint regulation of production. Unlike after 1918, however, the inheritance of wartime was not totally lost. Workshop bargaining and organisation were established as central features of industrial relations in post-war Britain. Given the political context, it was unthinkable that there would be a repeat of the post-1918 assault on labour. On the other hand, by 1947 the possibility of building upon the balance of power in work-place relations to create new structures of social relations was decisively rejected and industrial relations were effectively divorced from national politics where they lay virtually ignored for about twenty years.

The Depression in the Workshops

The inter-war depression marked a fundamental shift in the basis of the British economy. The primacy of the traditional, Victorian industries of growth was displaced by a more diversified structure signified by the rapid expansion of the 'new industries'. The two social faces of the depression – deprivation and unemployment contrasting with growth and relative prosperity – were to some extent interdependent. An expanding car industry was surely assisted by the collapse of the labour market in South Wales which freed up certain categories of mainly young workers to move to new locations. Thus, worsened conditions combined with rates of growth that were unmatched since mid-Victorian times. The stagnation of the pre-1914 period was replaced from the early 1920s with 'rapid technical progress and structural change' in which 'the pace of productivity growth accelerated enormously'. During the 1920s and 1930s industrial output increased by 60 per cent; even in the years of deepest depression, it grew by 17 per cent. In mining, lengthened working days and reduced wages were married with real improvements in productivity – reversing the general trend since the 1880s. And in textiles between 1929 and 1932 traditional techniques of intensification – such as increasing the number of weaving looms per worker – resulted in a 40 per cent increase in productivity.[1] The depression provided a more crucial stimulus to the reorganisation of production than at any time since the industrial revolution and two broad aspects of this development require notice: first, the spread of rationalised production techniques; and, second, the related, but not coterminous, extension of the Bedaux system of scientific management.

Rationalisation was not only a function of improved techniques. The 1920s, in particular, were marked by an intensive phase of merger and consolidation in industry not seen again until the 1960s. A deepened concern with professionalised, scientific management was the natural counterpart to this development. It was during the depression that the managerial function came to be clearly identified with a technical, scientific expertise. The war had shown the possibilities of rationalised production. Flow-line principles were first introduced for the manufacture of army trucks, and in some critical industries, such as machine tools, the pressures of war had directly stimulated state-directed reorganisation. In 1915 the Department of Scientific and Industrial Research had been established to lend government support to the fusion of science and industry. It was widely recognised that economic success in the post-war years was contingent upon the rationalisation of production, the economic use of resources, better layout and improved managerial techniques.[2] The extent to which this actually occurred should not be overestimated: rationalisation in the true sense of the term was most visible in new industries, like Imperial Chemical Industries (ICI), whose capital requirements and technical base allowed an easy integration of mass-production methods. These developments were probably much weaker in other industries, but few sectors remained totally untouched. Coal-mining, for example, saw longwall methods more widely introduced, replacing the small work-groups with large teams under closer supervision. Mechanisation increased quite dramatically. Between 1921 and 1930, the number of coal-face conveyors jumped from 800 to 2100 and by 1930 about 30 per cent of coal was cut mechanically, as opposed to 8 per cent in 1913; in Scotland the percentage was even higher. There were consequent changes in the division of labour. Hewers were less likely to be responsible for setting props or drilling holes and this contraction in job responsibility was paralleled by a similar diminution of discretion as the work processes became more integrated and supervised.[3]

The new motor-car industry first introduced the continuous flow principle of factory organisation in the early 1920s. Two years after Morris took over the Hotchkiss engine works he increased production from 300 to 1500 engines per week. Similarly, the number of employees per car at Austin fell from 55 in 1922 to 10 in 1927, the increased labour intensity being secured by a variety of means including mechanisation, the abolition of overtime and a premium bonus system. Control of the work-force was ensured by a strict bureaucracy which administered the testing and grading of workers who were monitored by a dense hierarchy of supervisors, foremen and charge hands. The big Morris works at Cowley did not see the automatic assembly line until 1934; until then chassis were pushed around from one work-group to the next and the work sharply subdivided into single-purpose operations. Even this marked an enormous improvement over the pre-war system of stationary chassis construction, however, and by 1926 as many cars were being produced in a week as had previously been produced in a year. The mechanical assembly line doubled this rate of production with the same size of labour force.[4]

As always, it is difficult to make firm generalisations about engineering. Certain processes remained hard to rationalise: aircraft engines were not mass-produced, for example, until the second half of the war. And old-fashioned plant continued to cause many bottlenecks during the war years. After 1930, Bedaux methods spread but the major gains in output were probably achieved by rate-cutting and changes in the division of labour. Thus, in July 1931 overtime and shift payments were cut and piece-rates reduced from 33⅓ per cent to 25 per cent above time-rates. The 1920s and 1930s illustrate how deskilling is more often a function of depression than technical changes because skill privileges are difficult to maintain in a collapsed labour market. Thus, by 1935, 57 per cent of engineering workers were classified as semi-skilled compared to around 44 per cent in 1916. It was reported from Bolton that two-thirds of the turners' traditional roller-turning work was now performed by youths.[5] Although dilution had been proceeding in an *ad hoc* manner since 1922, the greatest single impetus to rationalisation was provided by rearmament. In particular, rearmament required the concentration of the highly skilled in the tool-room and the substitution of the semi-skilled on the high speed, mass-production machines that performed routine jobs. By 1938 a widespread dilution had been carried out which reorganised skill distribution between the highly-skilled tool-room workers whose position rested upon their craft skill and the semi-skilled whose position rested upon their integrated role in the mass-production system.

Integral to these developments was the changing emphasis in managerial theory. Until the mid-1920s management thought remained dominated by the industrial psychology approach epitomised by the Quaker industrialists. Although they were by no means opposed to reorganising production, this tended to be placed in the context of trying to stimulate a corresponding partnership with labour through consultation and persuasion. As late as 1923, for example, Taylorist assumptions were criticised in the new *Journal of the National Institute of Industrial Psychologists* in favour of achieving increased output through collaboration and partnership. But by then managerial theory was already shifting towards the technicist search for greater efficiency on the basis of managerial expertise which displaced the trade unions from the central focus they had occupied in the minds of the Quaker group. In Urwick's standard work, *The Management of Tomorrow*, published in 1933, there was only one reference to the unions. Although some remnants of partnership remained, such as the works councils, they were no longer regarded as the beginning of a new structure of industrial relations but, as at Mond's ICI, as purely consultative contributions to rationally organised production. Such schemes were especially likely where the commitment to scientific management was strong. But organised labour regarded them with a considerable, and justified, suspicion. As Mond himself pointed out, the purpose of the works councils was '"to bind them [the men] more closely to the Company's interest than to the interest of the working classes"'.[6]

The new commitment to a strategy of scientifically organised production was illustrated most clearly by the popularity of the Bedaux system. Appropriately enough, the Bedaux organisation first opened an office in Britain in 1926 and from the late 1920s its methods spread rapidly. By 1929 about 250 firms had adopted Bedaux and possibly as many again had been touched in some way by its techniques. As Craig Littler has pointed out, 'the history of scientific management in Britain in the inter-war period is largely the history of Bedaux'. The system promised productivity increases of 50 per cent by time-and-motion study which purported to guage the exact degree of effort and rest necessary for a particular job. As with the other offshoots of Taylorism, Bedaux supposedly assessed the amount of required energy without leading to sweated overwork. The attractions of Bedaux may have been increased by its similarity to the premium bonus system – which G.D.H. Cole claimed it had replaced by the end of the 1930s. Like premium bonus, it established a sharply regressive relationship between increased output and pay and depended upon extensive record-keeping and bureaucratisation which mystified the relationship between work and wages. The advantage of Bedaux over premium bonus, however, lay in its provision of a method for measuring and dividing the work (into the famous 'B' units) instead of leaving it to the trial and error of management. A further advantage was its adaptability. Although the system was particularly suited for continuous-process industries where routinisation was the key requirement, the measurement of time and motion could be used on virtually any job. Thus, a study of blend-pulling in a tea factory resulted in an increased productivity of 70 per cent. And there were Bedaux schemes in textiles and extensive efforts to install it in engineering – although since its main aim was to increase output its deskilling function was secondary. Craft workers opposed it as much for its speed-up implications as anything else. Indeed, the most disruptive effect of Bedaux was on lower-level supervisors who formed the main centre of opposition to the system.[7]

Thus, the system met with mixed success. There were prolonged struggles at Wolsey hosiery where the introduction of a Bedaux plan occasioned the first strike in the company's history and destroyed the old paternal pattern of social relations. Similarly, the system met with resistance at Richard Johnson's wire factory where it coincided with the final destruction of the craft methods of wire-drawing. In engineering, where it was an alternative to straight reduction of piece-rates, there were strikes at Boulton and Paul, Luvax, Henry Hope and Venestas, some of which secured modifications in the system. Even in textiles, there were reports that opposition had softened its provisions.[8]

But the emergence of scientific management in Britain contained some revealing contrasts with its original introduction in the United States at the end of the nineteenth century. Two features, in particular, were generally absent in Britain. The first was the way Taylorism in the United States was part of a structural shift in class relations which occasioned a real crisis and a clear defeat for the claims of craft autonomy. The second was that Taylorism served as an ideological expression of the emergent claims to status and position in society of expert engineers and managers. In Britain, on the other hand, scientific management was introduced subsequent to the defeat of craft militancy and organisation and in the context of a depression which further weakened the labour movement. More a manifestation of pre-existing managerial prerogatives than part of an offensive to secure them, scientific management was not associated with a managerial crusade to restructure economic and social relations. In Britain the key break in class relations had occurred with the rupturing of the mid-Victorian compromise in the late nineteenth century which had been largely accomplished without the necessity for a distinctively 'managerial' ideology. The impact of scientific management did not establish a self-confident and distinctive managerial identity. Even innovative companies like ICI were remarkable for the 'gentlemanly' tone that pervaded their managerial and technical strata. This lack of associational or ideological identity was illustrated by the weakness of the various societies that catered for managers. As late as 1939 the Works Managers' Association had recruited a bare 900 members from a pool of 25,000. At another level, it was represented by the satirisation of management experts as the ridiculous figures of fun caricatured in the 1950s film *I'm Alright Jack*. Thus, managerial identity remained weakly developed and its ideological ethos remained defensively encased in a culture whose values were mainly derived from an anti-industry, aristocratic patrimony.[9]

At bottom, scientific management tended to degenerate into merely another technique to expand output on the cheap. Beneath the pseudo-scientific mumbo-jumbo, the main burden of Bedaux was the simple speed-up. Craig Littler's case studies confirm what was pointed out at the TUC in 1932, that 'there is no attempt to increase productivity by labour-saving devices'. Indeed, the original schemes bore some resemblance to the 'gain-sharing' experiments noted in the 1880s. Foremen and overseers were paid a premium for driving the worker to surpass the 'normal' pace of 60 B-units of work per hour. Any rationalisation that did occur could also occur without the Bedaux system itself.[10]

Scientific management thus entered decisively into British industry possessing neither a developed ideological presence, nor an integral relationship to restructured class and authority relations. The ironic consequence was that the traditional structures of social relations in production were left undisturbed. Craft and workshop militancy and organisation, for example, may have been at low ebb in the 1920s and 1930s but they remained structurally unchallenged as continuous features of social relations in production. Indeed, sporadic manifestations of these themes occasionally erupted in the period.

In those parts of shipbuilding that were not closed down, for example, boilermakers proved able to protect their craft division of labour from rationalisation. In the early 1930s, the Shipbuilding Employers' Federation tried to lessen their reliance upon skilled platers by reclassifying the welding of plates to the ship frame as semi-skilled work. The failure of national negotiations in 1933 shifted the initiative to the plant level where local militancy and the platers' control of pre-existing welding work on the bulkhead allowed them to establish their claims to all welding. This particular case may have been somewhat unusual in the success it attained, but restrictive custom and practice continued to impede changes in working conditions in the docks in the early 1920s and workshop organisation may be seen in operation in railways, engineering and the new car industry.[11]

On the railways, for example, the mid-1920s saw a revival of the vigilance committees that had first appeared in the 1890s. The origins of these committees lay amongst the London engine-cleaners, a group of unskilled workers sharply affected by redundancies and transfers following the amalgamation of the companies in 1923. Since engine cleaners had no secure representation within the trade-union hierarchy, the vigilance committees' function was to monitor trade-union responses to various efforts by the companies to erode the 1919 Condition of Service agreement. A further phase of rationalisation in the 1930s, accompanied by grade reclassification, redundancies and wage cuts, stimulated the expansion of these committees to cities in the North, the publication of a newspaper, annual conferences, and the infiltration of trade-union organisation. Like workshop organisation in engineering, vigilance committees acted to resist the local-level manifestations of pooling arrangements and other consequences of rationalisation. The work-to-rule was their most important tactical weapon but it would also seem that they were sometimes able to negotiate local depot agreements. Just how successful these efforts were is difficult to know; Frank McKenna claimed that 'many a man's livelihood was saved by vigilant local departmental representatives refusing to agree to staff reductions often against trade union advice'.

There was an ambiguous relationship between Vigilance Committees and trade-union officialdom. The NUR instructed branches to refuse to acknowledge or read material from Vigilance Committees and there were claims that officials often refused to support their workshop actions. As a pressure group, however, they may have forced a greater accountability from trade unions. McKenna implies that mass agitation and frequent works-to-rule in 1935 and 1936 ended the practice of 'local staff representatives [agreeing] something with management and then [telling] the men afterward', and that 'this . . . workshop floor leadership [emerged] not as an alternative to the official leadership of the time but as a supplementary group of knowledgeable local representatives. Around these local committees revolved most of the active members of the trade union branches.' Like so much else in the history of workplace industrial relations, however, any accurate assessment of their effects and influence will have to await more detailed local research.[12]

In engineering a fleeting revival of workshop organisation and action occurred in 1925 and 1926 following the breakdown of national wage negotiations. In London, Manchester, Sheffield and Nottingham the number of stewards increased and shop committees organised meetings to agitate for wage demands and against overtime and speed-ups. An interesting strike at Hoe's Engineering in London was, perhaps, symptomatic of this movement. Negotiations on the wage demand were conducted by shop stewards, their failure was followed by a go-slow, the introduction of non-union men and a stay-in strike. A general stoppage began on 12 January 1926 when the day shift 'rushed the foreman [who had informed them they could not clock on unless they promised to work] and forcibly entered the factory'. After several days, the Engineering Employers' Federation entered the dispute, threatening the union with a national lock-out unless it ordered the men to return to work and adhere to the Procedure. Two aggregate meetings were held at which unsuccessful efforts were made to get the men back to work and after the second the Executives involved issued a statement instructing a return to work. Eventually, it would seem the men agreed to place the dispute in the proper hands of the district committee. For the union officials this was the essential victory. Since 1922, they had understandably insisted upon a more centralised control of industrial relations to avoid provoking another lock-out. A rules revision following the 1922 débâcle had reduced the autonomy of workshop bargaining, requiring that 'workshop conditions [were] to be controlled by the District Committees subject in all cases to the approval of the . . . Executive Council'. In May the district committee secured the dismissal of the non-union men and work was resumed. By September a premium bonus system had been introduced without consultation and the shop stewards dismissed.[13]

Finally, it is important to note that the origins of workshop organisation in the motor-car industry date from this period. A stay-in strike by non-unionists at Austin's Birmingham factory in May 1929 against the new grading system that accompanied the introduction of flow-line production resulted in the mutual negotiation of rate-fixing and the appointment and recognition of shop stewards. By August, it would appear that these gains had been lost, although similar strikes were reported in 1936 and 1938. The most significant of the workshop actions, however, was the Pressed Steel strike at Cowley in 1934 which began in the semi-skilled press-shop and was led by immigrants from South Wales who had brought their traditions of organisation with them. The AEU was weakly represented in the factory and it joined the strike only towards its end. As Richard Whiting has demonstrated, however, the repercussions of this strike were felt throughout the local political structures: 'The growth of the Labour Party in the south-east of Oxford, the formation of local housing associations to combat high rents, the unusually active Communist Party, are all difficult to explain except in terms of that strike.' At the work-place this initiative resulted in union recognition, the spread of union organisation throughout the factory, and the establishment of a stewards' organisation which by 1936 had expanded its activity beyond the boundaries of the formal disputes procedure. In 1937, for example, stewards secured direct negotiating access to higher management. But a series of unofficial strikes over piece-rates in 1936 irritated the union officials who complained that ignoring the constitutional machinery hampered '"any efforts which the union could make on their behalf"'. And by 1938 the company also came to see the justice of this complaint as it was provoked by 13 strikes in almost as many weeks over piece-rates and boy labour. Thus, in 1938, negotiating rights beyond their own department were withdrawn, one of the leading stewards who refused to accept this was fired, and others were denied re-employment. The union made few efforts on their behalf and strikes for their reinstatement were unsuccessful. A roll-back of gains followed this defeat, piece-prices were reduced and workshop organisation neutralised. In spite of these limitations, however, the achievements of this spate of activity were impressive in an industry whose seasonal market fluctuations engendered employment insecurity. About half the work-force was permanently unionised; the habits of sectionalism had been breached; and precedents established – if only temporarily gained – for the mutual negotiation of manning-levels and piece-rates.[14]

But, as Whiting makes clear, this was a unique case in the motor-car industry. More common was the situation at the main Morris plant where union recruitment efforts in the 1930s yielded unimpressive results. As one car worker recounted, in the radiator shop 'the first man to put his name down as a shop steward got the sack on the spot', and the atmosphere of fear ensured that union membership remained weak and liable to fluctuation. The solid core of unionists was composed of a group of left-wing activists who, until 1938, remained largely isolated. Sectionalism was rife, not only between the skilled and semi-skilled, but also between the various work-groups: 'in the canteen each section tended to sit with themselves . . . And most shops kept themselves apart.' Managerial policy was based not only on fear and divisions, however. In the 1920s, Nuffield's paternal welfare policies and force of personality had combined with a deliberate policy of high wages. By the 1930s, a more sophisticated, bureaucratised welfarism had been developed which included sick-clubs, profit-sharing, holidays with pay (long before the Act of 1938 stimulated their spread), and a pension scheme. These relatively advantageous conditions – which were better than trade-union standards – were the carrot to the stick of seasonality and unemployment. They had not been achieved by trade-union action and were likely to be jeopardised by it. Thus, trade unionism in this instance was an essential irrelevancy.[15]

It would be too much to claim that this reflected the general significance of institutional unionism for national politics; but it would not be an overly exaggerated claim. The defeat of the general strike may have strengthened the position of the moderate leadership, but it also diminished their political importance in the councils of state. This was more than just a reflection of the declining affiliations to the TUC between the mid-1920s and the late 1930s. It reflected the shifting political balance both within government and in national politics. Before the general strike, Baldwin's Minister of Labour, Arthur Steel Maitland, had wished to foster friendly relations with the trade unions but the Trades Disputes Act – passed over his objections – put an end to that policy. Similarly, although some employers favoured capitalising upon the strength of the moderates in the labour movement after the general strike to fashion a national policy of co-operation, they did not represent a consensus view. Most employers saw no reason to endow a weakened labour movement with a share in economic policy-making. If there was to be co-operation, they wanted it on an industry and plant level where the power equation was relatively straightforward. It was this and the onslaught of the deepest phase of the depression in 1929 that made the Mond-Turner talks on union–industry co-operation an ultimate non-starter.[16]

Similarly, none of the governments in the 1930s were interested in according a consultative role to the trade unions. MacDonald kept the unions at arms length in his concern to demonstrate that Labour could govern in the 'national' interest; Baldwin temperamentally preferred to do nothing; and Chamberlain was wary of the concessions that would be necessary in return for Labour's co-operation over rearmament. Thus, even during the rearmament period, the trade-union presence at Whitehall was shadowy. There was no consultation over conscription, for example, and Chamberlain was unwilling to win Labour support by repealing the Trades Disputes Act. Labour's revenge came a few months later when their refusal to co-operate politically with Chamberlain in a national government catapulted him out of power. By May 1940, of course, only a full partnership with Labour would suffice to meet the national emergency. And by that time, too, the balance of power at the work-place had been transformed and the basis laid for the considerable gains that were to be made during the war. The foundation for this revival rested upon the opportunities created by rearmament and, specifically, upon the absence of planning or co-operation with Labour at the national level.[17]

Rearmament and Revival

The Chamberlain government was determined to pursue rearmament by indicative planning rather than by the direct compulsion of industry and labour. The fear of doing otherwise was dictated by the desire to avoid the problems of the First World War when the national mobilisation of labour had created enormous difficulties. Chamberlain's memories of this may have been particularly acute because he had been a notable failure as Director of National Service. Thus,

> the Cabinet dared not upset industrial harmony by opening negotiations over dilution, new training schemes, or transfer of labour, which could be achieved only by lengthy negotiations and which, if successful, might have led to social and economic disruption similar to that of 1915-16.

Those ministers who did press for the compulsory direction of resources were dismissed in 1938. Even contacts with industry were kept to a minimum, with the exception of the aircraft companies who treated the state as if it were their personal treasury.[18] The paradox of this policy, however, was that although it kept the labour question out of national politics, it enhanced the local power of labour in those areas where bottlenecks and shortages occurred. This was particularly true, of course, in the core armaments industries and especially in the aircraft industry which, from the beginning, received priority in the drive to rearm. The revival of workshop organisation began in that industry in the mid-1930s and, by the end of the decade, as war production expanded, it had spread throughout the engineering sector.

Labour shortages plagued rearmament from the start. It could hardly be otherwise. If compulsion and direction were ruled out, how could skilled men be persuaded to move to where the jobs were? Acute shortages occurred in the building industry, whose role in the construction of air bases and shadow factories made it second in importance only to engineering. By 1937, the remaining unemployed in building and engineering were elderly craftsmen whose long-term absence from the work bench made them ill-suited to the type of work now available. In May of that year it was estimated that only 50 per cent of unemployed engineers were suitable for immediate employment. This problem was enhanced by the shortage of apprentices. Since the early 1920s, the importance of apprenticeship as a route into skilled engineering had declined as part of the general shake-out of craft labour. The number of apprentices had fallen from 78,161 in 1929 to 52,741 in 1933 and their wages gap with the skilled increased; but the demand for skill increased with rearmament and apprentices were at a premium. A rash of wage strikes by apprentices in 1937 signified their new importance.

Since national agreements on dilution and reorganised production were not addressed by government policy, these questions had to be handled at the local level. There was something to be said for this focus because even if national agreements had been reached the problem of their enforcement would have still remained. Negotiating with district union officials on workshop questions was recognised to be more appropriate than dealing with national officers, but agreements with '"work people themselves are likely to be even more effective"'. The importance of workshop bargaining was thus implicitly recognised by employers who wanted to avoid negotiating a national policy for dilution because of the restriction it could impose upon their freedom to redesign production and deploy labour efficiently. Those needs varied from industry to industry and plant to plant and could be best handled by *ad hoc* lower-level negotiations. Thus, not until the very eve of war, when acute labour shortages demanded wholesale dilution, were negotiations conducted on general principles to guide the reorganisation of production.[19]

From 1935, then, workshop organisation and bargaining were stimulated by the reliance upon plant-level agreements to secure war production. At Armstrong Whitworth, for example, in 1936, the uncertainties over how to organise the construction of all-metal aircraft led to the gang system of work organisation. This system virtually handed over to the gang responsibility for organising the execution of work. Gang leaders were elected who kept track of the work and money and who could be removed only with the gang's agreement. Foremen were transformed into a service resource dealing with such issues as supply hold-ups.[20]

The most immediate catalyst which revived workshop organisation was dilution. A strike at Hawker's Brockworth factory in March 1935 over dilution and premium bonus marked the beginning of the movement. The *New Propellor*, perhaps the most impressive rank-and-file publication ever issued, came out of this strike, as did a national meeting of aircraft shop stewards which called for the absorption of all skilled men prior to dilution. This was not achieved, but a fairly wide degree of local mutuality was secured. Thus a strike at Parnell's in July 1936 ended the employers' attempt at unilateral dilution and secured prior notice and consultation on the substitution of semi-skilled men. Similarly, at the Harland Woolf and Hawker factories shop committees gained control over the supply of labour for vacancies and the closed shop. At Fairey Aviation, in April and May 1938, workshop action successfully prevented the expansion of boy labour on rib-work. In the newly established shadow factories workshop organisation was slower to start, but by 1938, for example, the Rover shadow factory was sufficiently well organised to secure mutuality over time-and-motion studies. An attempt to downgrade skills in the milling shop at Rolls Royce where trade-union organisation was weak led to a mass meeting and withdrawal of the system. Strikes over the use of semi-skilled men on skilled jobs were very common by the late 1930s.[21]

In its many guises, dilution was a major stimulant to revived workshop organisation but it was by no means the only issue or feature of the movement. As early as 1936 the agenda of the shop stewards in the aircraft industry had lengthened to include a reversal of the 1931 agreement, control over apprenticeship, a close working relationship between the union and stewards, and removal of the employers' right to initiate changes in the work process before the completion of the appeal procedure. These demands did not represent a programme that could be systematically pursued: workshop bargaining does not form a 'movement' in that sense of the term. They were important, however, because they reflected the new assertiveness of labour and the historical continuities that existed in work-place bargaining. The actual themes that run through the workshop bargaining of the late 1930s illustrate these points – in many instances they contained echoes of past achievements and prefigured the direction of the post-1945 period. The origins of the 'informal' system of industrial relations of the 1950s and 1960s lie in the immediate pre-war years.[22]

First, there was the vast expansion of shop stewards' organisation. In Coventry alone the numbers of stewards increased by 260 between 1935 and 1937. Following the Brockworth strike, the formation of the National Council of Aircraft Industry Shop Stewards, and the publication of *New Propellor*, which provided a focus for local organisation, stewards' committees were established at such major factories as De Havilland and Fairey Aviation. Extensive links began to be established between the various plant organisations, often through the common ground of Communist Party membership. It had been such contact that allowed the Brockworth strike to be successful. And here lay the origins of the combine committees of the late 1950s and 1960s. By August 1937 the National Council was represented at 49 factories, and, by April 1940, when the movement merged to become the Engineering and Allied Trades Shop Stewards' Council, this number had grown to 109.[23]

A second theme of this thickened workshop organisation was one that was to lie at the heart of the shop stewards' movement after 1945:

the demand for mutuality over various conditions of work. Pricing committees in the skilled tool and sheet-metal shops were often the initial signs of a revived workshop organisation. This reflected, of course, the widespread pressure on piece-rates that had dominated the previous decade and a half and the popularity of Bedaux time-and-motion schemes. Mutuality over piece-rates was one of the first things *New Propellor* propagated, arguing that shop committees should share responsibility with the rate-fixer and in the event of disagreement a shop meeting should have the final decision. It is unlikely that the sovereignty of the shop meeting became custom and practice, but there is no doubt that considerable, if varying, degrees of mutuality were achieved. By early 1936 the shop committees had achieved mutual control over rate-fixing at Faireys and A.V. Roe and in 1938 strikes secured the same rights elsewhere. Conferences between shop stewards and management on these issues also increased to become a frequent feature of shop-floor industrial relations. At Fairey's Stockport factory access to time-records was gained in late 1936. By 1938 custom and practice had established new rights to be defended.[24]

A third manifestation of the growing power of workshop organisation was the gradual improvement in working conditions. From Arthur Exell's account of Morris Motors in the 1930s, it is clear that war brought an increased sense of freedom from the oppressive discipline of the inter-war years. But in the aircraft factories the foundations for this were laid earlier. Smoking rules were relaxed, as were those that governed visits to the lavatory. The renewed confidence of the shop-floor workers was revealed by the reappearance of strikes against obnoxious men and 'bullying' supervisors. An embargo on overtime at Hawkers secured improvements in ventilation and concessions in such areas as the availability of refreshments. Informal action by London ship-repairers secured a wage increase against the wishes of the AEU, and at Armstrong-Whitworth's Baginton factory a strike against non-union labour in the erecting shop enforced the closed shop throughout the factory. As war approached and the pace of production increased, canteens became a favourite object of action. Fairey Aviation's canteen at its Stockport factory was boycotted until the standard of food was improved.[25]

The final set of issues that provided the focus of an expanded workshop organisation and bargaining revolved around the preparations for meeting the anticipated hazard of mass bombing. A high degree of co-operation was required to organise against air raids and this became a key means of mobilising and extending the demand for joint regulation.

Unilateral management control over air-raid precautions was challenged by stewards' committees from the summer of 1939. At Hoover, for example, meetings were held to force negotiation on the distribution and allocation of fire-watching and at Vickers the right to inspect ARP arrangements was secured by the stewards' committee. A significant boost to stewards' organisation was provided by this issue – in some places union organisation spread on the basis of the need to organise the factory against the expected air raids. In other places, stewards' committees readily transformed themselves into ARP committees; elsewhere, the issue stimulated an encroaching regulation of other, related, questions. At Napier, for example, stewards helped to organise the black-out and then went on to demand payment during air raids and better transportation facilities.[26]

By the outbreak of war, then, the groundwork had been laid for the transformation of industrial relations. Work-place organisation had re-established itself, had begun to encroach upon managerial prerogatives, and had secured considerable gains in the core war industries. It is important to emphasise that this had been achieved within the context of the voluntarist organisation of war production. In contrast to the First World War, the partnership of joint regulation at the work-place *preceded* the establishment of co-operation at the national level. With the end of the phoney war and the full political and economic mobilisation of 1940, however, voluntarism was replaced by state regulation.

Production, Prerogative and War

By the summer of 1940, survival, let alone successful prosecution of the war, demanded full economic, social and political mobilisation of the nation. Churchill understood this, noting that in this war the front line ran as much through the factories as through the battlefields. The central reality of the war was the 'strategic fact that labour rather than machinery or capital had become the scarcest and most prized industrial commodity'. It was this recognition that underlay the broad policy approaches of the war. In addition, the near loss of the war in 1940 threatened to shake the nation's faith in the reliability of governance by the traditional élite. As Orwell remarked in 1941, although England resembled a 'family' it was a family with the wrong members in charge. Cynicism and scepticism were, perhaps, the dominant mood of the early years of the war and government was acutely sensitive to this fact. Thus, mobilisation was not only more urgently required than had been the case in 1914–18 (when it was not fully attained until 1917), but it could not be achieved by a simple appeal to patriotism.

The declaration of war aims in 1940, the promise of an expanded democracy, the beginning of planning for the post-war era at the very nadir of military fortunes, all reflected the necessity to mobilise around the theme of a 'people's war'. The *democratic* tone that underlies much of the war – from Monty's studied informality, to the self-governing communities in the underground railway ('tube') shelters – represented the very real shift in the political balance that mobilisation caused. Ernest Bevin's accession to the Ministry of Labour with a power second only to that of Churchill conveniently epitomises this shift. Within three days of taking office, Bevin had drawn up a plan for the full mobilisation of labour and began the promulgation of the vast expansion of state regulation and control it required.[27]

Perhaps one of the most revealing paradoxes of the war from May 1940 was the enormous sense of liberating freedom that accompanied this dictatorial mobilisation. Beyond the 'psychological' reason that this marked the end of the drifting policies of phoney war, lay a more important fact which factory worker Arthur Exell identified when he recalled:

> Everyone felt confident then; Essential Works Order had come in, and we could feel our feet a bit. And the bosses didn't dare do anything, they just had to produce the stuff, and the men could enjoy themselves a lot more. We had a lot of sing songs, . . . In Cases the men used the hammer a lot; and the jerry cans had to be tapped, all the way round the top and the bottom, and this tapping was the beat of the music and they were singing to it.

The main effect of the draconian state regulation of the labour contract was to diminish enormously the prerogatives and powers of the employers. It was true, of course, that the regulations also covered strikes and industrial action, but the law had to be used sparingly as the futile attempt to prosecute strikers at Betteshanger colliery in 1942 demonstrated. The relative labour peace of the war cannot be explained by the efficacy of the law and there was a great reluctance to invoke the full power of the state against labour. Thus, efforts to rationalise shipyard work practices were blocked by the obstinate conservatism of the craftsmen. Only 3 per cent of shipbuilding labour were dilutees, compared to 30 per cent in engineering.[28]

The Essential Works Order was the keystone to state regulation of labour relations and gave Bevin virtually unlimited power to direct and control production. As part of this, EWO specified minimum working conditions and guaranteed wages; it also established a strict disciplinary regimen under the control of National Service Officers. Given the critical role of manpower in production, however, the net result was not to reinforce employer discipline – as had been the ultimate effect of legislation in 1916–18 – but rather to redefine discipline as being outside the sphere of employer prerogative. Under EWO, employers lost the right arbitrarily to dismiss men and even relatively minor offences were subject to arbitration. In practice this meant that disciplinary issues tended to become subject to joint regulation as a way of avoiding National Service Order intervention. Thus, work committees were frequently granted the right to handle a variety of disciplinary matters such as absenteeism. When Mass Observation investigated workshop relations in 1942 it found that EWO had made a real difference:

> Many managements . . . speak nostalgically . . . of those days when 'there was discipline in industry'. Most workpeople believe that management are longing for those days to return and that ahead of them lies a return to the quick sack and the unexplained instability. . . . [But] for the time being the boot is on the other leg; it is the skilled worker who can worry and upset the boss.[29]

The effect of mobilisation on social relations, then, was not so much to increase state power as to force a vast expansion of shop-floor organisation and joint regulation. The complexities of the National Arbitration Award of 1942 in the engineering industry, for example, stimulated workshop bargaining because its interpretation could only depend upon the particular circumstances in particular factories. The increase in shop-floor negotiation reinforced the spread and sophistication of stewards' organisation and responsibility. Indeed, the war marks the real entrenchment of shop stewards as a distinctive feature of British industrial relations.

By 1943, the stewards' movement was demanding that joint regulation be enshrined in a law that would endow them with a legal status and define the obligations of management to negotiate. A survey of over 140 enterprises during the same year listed the areas subject to joint regulation: in 120 cases, health, canteens, and welfare were within its purview; in 82, redundancy and transfers; in 106, transport; in 97, absenteeism; and, in 110, stewards had the effective right to hold meetings on the premises. Specific examples of joint regulation are plentiful.

By national agreement with the government, stewards and the AEU exercised a power of veto over dilution. At Sterling Engineering, the shop stewards ran the welfare organisation and canteen; at the De Havilland factory in May 1943 they demanded control of the canteen and when this was granted claimed productivity increases of 25-61 per cent. In a Scottish aircraft works a productivity increase was achieved in return for the right to elect charge-hands. At Fairey Aviation, rate-fixers were allowed to discuss time and prices only with the elected pricing steward who 'is at liberty to examine the planning and layout of any job. If he is not satisfied with this, or with the method of production, he can suggest an alteration or have the matter gone into through the JPC.' At Vickers no premium prices could be altered without the consent of the stewards.[30]

Joint worker-employer regulation of canteens was a favourite target for workshop organisation, and the reasons for this deserve some consideration. This was an issue that had figured quite prominently in the pre-war activities of the stewards and was typically one of the first issues an organised stewards' committee raised for discussion with management. During the war, it bore directly upon productivity because the better the conditions of work, the better 'the good-will and time keeping of its workers'. An AEU enquiry into production committees in 1942 found that the good faith of a management was commonly judged by the state of its lavatories and canteens. The radio show 'Workers' Playtime' was the insufferably condescending response of the BBC to this relationship between canteens and output. The state encouraged these initiatives. Bevin secured authority empowering him to order the establishment of canteens and by 1944 over 5,000 had been established under this sanction and a further 6,800 by company initiative. But this was not purely a matter of production norms; it also related to factory social relations. The canteen was an important focal point of the factory; 'it is a place in the factory which is *common* to all workers. Just as the symbol of the factory to management is the office, the canteen serves that purpose for workers who have no such symbol at their point of work.' The canteen was the location that best expressed the worker community of the factory, the place where meetings of the whole factory were held – though they frequently had to be fought for – and in that sense it was an expression of worker power and solidarity. Thus, securing control or influence over the running of the canteen was not a trivial or diversionary matter; it linked directly into the enhanced status and power of the shop-floor worker. That it also satisfied the desire of the Communist Party and the National Government for productivity does nothing to detract from that fact.[31]

Joint regulation, however, was not so much an expression of wartime unity and co-operation as their condition; it was a fact of factory life without which war production could not have been fulfilled. Neither state nor union policy created this aspect of the wartime social consensus, but rather built upon an impetus that already existed. Indeed, both management and unions looked with some suspicion upon workshop and steward organisation. There was widespread fear in management 'about getting out of this position [of government control and joint regulation] after the war'. And trade-union officials were found by Mass Observation to

> desire more say in the affairs of the land but seldom any strong wish for anything like joint management or more actual control in industry. The higher trade unionists are intimately wedded to the present system of boss and worker, and some of them feel that the end of this system might mean the end of them.

Indeed, Mass Observation concluded:

> We find industry, in all the leadership sections on both sides, thinking predominantly in terms of the return to something like the pre-war structures, whereas the rank and file (and most other sections of the community) are tending more and more to think in other terms.

Thus, when the early joint production committees began to surface in 1941, the Executive Council of the AEU 'condemned the so-called unofficial shop stewards' committees and instructed its members to have nothing to do with them'. Naturally fear of Communist influence had much to do with this, although Bevin's suggestion for precisely the same committees also received a cool reception from the AEU.[32]

Joint production committees composed of worker and employer representatives were one of the most significant developments of the war in the workshops. Intended to devise improvements in productivity, they evolved out of the existing reality of workshop organisation and growing joint regulation. In many cases, they were the result of stewards' agitation and sometimes were merely transformed stewards' committees. About one-fifth of JPCs were established before they received official sanction in March 1942 and 60 per cent of those had been formed on worker initiative. Thus, in Jack Murphy's factory, the stewards' committee sent a letter to the manager proposing a joint effort to increase production and out of the meeting came a workers' production committee which led to an overarching JPC to serve as a forum for discussion on the organisation of the factory. Furthermore, the invasion of Russia in June 1941 allowed the Communist activists in the stewards' movement to shed their inhibition about all-out co-operation in the war effort and actively press the formation of joint production committees.[33]

Until that point, *New Propellor* (which was dominated by Communist Party members) had emphasised the necessity of joint regulation as a defence against an expansion of managerial prerogative in the cause of production. It had played down the official party line that the war was a conflict between two imperialisms. Indeed, it is important to appreciate that the Communist Party was far more a creature of the historical traditions of social relations in industry than their Svengali. As Hinton has remarked in his study of Coventry factory politics, 'Communist militants found themselves up against rank and file resistance to the abandonment of established work practices in the interests of war production'. At Barrow, in 1943, for example, the opposition of both AEU officials and Communist stewards to an unofficial strike against the national arbitration award failed to prevent a renegotiation of the basic rate or an abolition of the premium bonus system introduced in 1902. Similarly, at Dalmuir Royal Ordnance Factory, the enthusiasm of Communist support for the removal of craft standards resulted in a loss of influence to smaller, more radical political groups. Nevertheless, the situation was transformed in June 1941. Stakhanovite virtues were extolled, absenteeism condemned, doubts about co-operation with management were stilled. At either period, the effects were the same: to bargain production for prerogative, expand the area of joint regulation and, to that extent, alter the balance of power in production relations. Thus, in October 1941, and with a clear political conscience, a national conference of stewards could call for 'workers . . . to use their organizational strength to wipe out the inefficiences, the redundancies, the horrible bloomers and blunders of capitalism'.[34]

Within the AEU pressure began to mount for the creation of production committees and in January 1942 the Ministry of Supply stepped in and invited the AEU to discuss their establishment in the ordnance factories. An agreement between the AEU and Engineering Employers' Federation to establish committees in factories of more than 150 employees followed in March. Shop-steward initiative remained important, however, because there was no obligation on management to agree to the formation of production committees, but that pressure already existed and they spread rapidly throughout 1942. By June 1944 about 4,500 were in existence.[35]

JPCs were not universally effective. Some were perpetually moribund and in other places they were regarded with contempt by the workers who elected the least-highly regarded men or, in one case, boys, to membership. The core of worker resistance to the committees lay in certain parts of the north where an old craft mentality fed suspicion of anything that smacked of co-operation with management. On the Clyde, for example, the Glasgow District Committee of the AEU was split on the issue of JPCs. A considerable number 'were opposed . . . because they believed they would enable the employers to intensify exploitation when peace returned'. Some Royal Ordnance Factories refused to set them up for similar reasons. Even amongst Communist stewards opposition was not unknown.

The JPCs were not confined to engineering, although they were probably most extensive in that industry. There were yard committees in shipbuilding, pit committees in coal-mining, site committees in building, and depot committees on the railways. They further stimulated and reinforced factory organisation and inter-factory links. JPCs' most visible impact on factory conditions, however, was in the sphere of welfare, where they presided over improvements in canteen facilities, sanitation, tea-breaks, and time allowances for smoking. The mandate to discuss and recommend ways to maximise the utilisation of machinery, however, allowed them to extend their purview beyond welfare issues. How far they intruded into other areas is unclear. In theory, JPCs were advisory and consultative and were excluded from discussing wage and piece-price questions; in fact, it was impossible to maintain these demarcations. At least 20 per cent of the committees regularly discussed issues like piece-rates and bonuses and some were even reported to be involved in discussion of company finances. Management was continually fearful that they would go too far '"and begin to ask about profits. That'll be the end for me. I shall have to let the whole show slide if they insist.'"[36]

The most common topic for discussion, however, was discipline. Indeed, in the shipyards the joint committees had grown out of yard committees originally established to deal with the problems of absenteeism. The admission that discipline was a legitimate area of joint regulation represents one example of the trade-off between production and prerogatives that formed the basic experience of shop-floor social relations during the war. The committees were not merely collaborating with managerial discipline, they were redefining its very nature. A pertinent example of this is provided by Arthur Exell. The arrival of women into the radiator plant and the intricacies of the jobs they were assigned, led to a high degree of frustration and absenteeism. Exell was approached by the works manager to help resolve the problem, a JPC was set up and a bargain struck: 'One of the things we promised was that we could see to it that people came to work, providing they were in the union, if they weren't in the union then we had no control over them.' And management which had previously resisted unionisation was obliged to accept the closed shop.

Another story Exell recounted, however, gets to the heart of what the JPCs signified for production relations. Some difficulty was encountered in achieving the required output on an important job. The JPC were called in to discuss the matter, which resulted in the adoption of their suggested change in the organisation of the work. As Jack Murphy pointed out in a similar connection, the very fact of JPCs openly discussing the organisation of production was an enormous change over previous experience. Decision-making at the point of production was no longer simply a preserve of management; enhanced workshop organisation and the JPC had injected a new democratic openness into the organisation of work and legitimated the rights of joint regulation.[37]

From 1944 the shop stewards were increasingly preoccupied with the peacetime future of joint regulation. The movement called for a controlled return to peacetime production and legislation permanently to establish wartime co-operation at the work-place in order to meet the productivity challenges of the post-war world:

> If goods and services are to be produced as efficiently for the requirements of peace as they have been for war, then government control of production and prices, priorities and allocation of material must be continued . . . workers in the JPCs and shop steward committees have . . . played their part in influencing and controlling programmes, contacts and movements of materials. This will be just as necessary in the post-war period.

It was urged that JPCs be continued, that their consultative rights be extended to cover expected redundancies and dislocations in the return to peacetime conditions, and that legal recognition be granted to workshop organisation. These demands were reflected to some extent in the interim report of the TUC Reconstruction Conference in 1944 which envisaged a series of works councils and consultative machinery in public industries and the expanded function of JPCs in private industry.[38]

Similarly, the response of the shop stewards to the economic crisis of 1947 was to argue the necessity of expanding joint regulation as a means of mobilising the same initiative and energy that workers had displayed during the war. They urged that JPCs be made mandatory, with wide powers – extending even to company finances – and that consultation by management should be compulsory:

> Workers must play a greater part in the management of their factories. . . . Workers must have the right to know about the firm's future policy, and about the work ahead . . . how the profits are distributed; and they have a right to be consulted on matters concerning their working conditions.

Exactly the same sentiments were expressed in the motor-car industry – which had been quickly identified by stewards as badly in need of modernisation: 'Increased production here means giving the workers a real voice in production through JPCs with wide powers in the factories and consultative machinery at every level.' And on the railways there was a flurry of discussion in 1946 about the inadequacies of the government's nationalisation schemes, workers' control and the need to strengthen and extend JPCs and shop stewards' organisation.[39]

The argument that workshop bargaining should be fully and legally integrated into the industrial relations system was an interesting anticipation of similar proposals that were to emerge from the concern over industrial relations in the late 1960s. After the war, however, these notions possessed fairly serious political implications. On the one hand, they were based upon experiences that had been legitimated by the state and, more generally, by the leftward shift in values and assumptions that accompanied the war. On the other hand, therefore, they did not aim solely at rectifying dysfunctions in the aid of efficiency (which was the case in the late 1960s) but pointed toward the perpetuation of a reordered hierarchy of social relations in industry. But the viability of these arguments clearly depended most centrally upon the attitudes and policies of the state which was unwilling to endorse the implications of this policy. Indeed, it is extremely improbable that these proposals attained a presence within the policy-making processes of the state. Thus, they remained confined to the marginal sphere of rank-and-file organisation with an occasional appearance at centre-stage events such as union conferences. Equally, it is important to remember that there was some degree of indeterminacy to the whole drift of Labour government policy after the war. The dominant mood of the first two years of the government was that certain options remained open in both domestic and foreign policy. Until the turning point of the summer of 1947, it was, therefore, possible to visualise a policy that permitted the expansion of joint regulation.

The determining factor for domestic policy was the kind of economic policy that would be pursued which, in its turn, was increasingly bound up with the wider international political economy. There were two broad economic policy alternatives facing Labour in 1945: a bilateral negotiation of agreements on a country-to-country basis which would be compatible with a continuation of planning and controls; or, an 'Atlanticist' policy of dependence upon American loans in return for a liberalisation of the British economy and the opening of the Empire to American capital. It is clear that this choice was not evenly balanced. In the context of the post-war international chaos, the immediate emergence of great-power tensions, the necessity to maintain great-power status, to say nothing of the evident unwillingness of the Americans to subsidise socialism by free loans or a continuation of lease-lend, the weight of the advantage clearly lay with the Atlanticist option. The first American loan of October 1945 had been made conditional upon the liberalisation of trade, the end of imperial preferences and the convertibility of sterling from 1947. Nevertheless, the bilateral alternative continued to be discussed until 1947, in part because the exact posture and role that the United States would assume in international affairs remained somewhat unclear. Hugh Dalton, for example, continually toyed with the option of a wholesale reduction of Britain's overseas commitments and the adoption of a bilateralist policy. The choice was not finally forced until the *annus horrendus* of 1947 exposed the full extent of Britain's economic and, therefore, international weakness. The decision to remove British forces from Greece and Palestine revealed the necessity for the United States to assume the role of world policeman and coincided with the success of Bevin's policy of pulling America into a commitment to the reconstruction and defence of Europe. Economic bankruptcy was only staved off by the American loan and Marshall Aid, both of which obliged the government to reduce economic intervention and remove controls.[40]

Dalton's cheap money, expansionist policies were replaced by the grim, puritan austerity of Stafford Cripps. Harold Wilson's bonfire of controls in 1948 signified the virtual end of wartime planning and the substitution of fiscal planning through the budgetry process. Naturally, this ended any hopes – however slender they may have been – that joint regulation of production would continue. As early as 1946, Cripps, who was the commanding figure in economic policy after 1947, poured scorn on the idea that workers were capable of any role in managing industry. The nationalised industries had no place for worker representation. Thus, although some JPCs survived into the post-war era, most rapidly disappeared after 1947.[41]

Indeed, since 1944 the structures of wartime workshop bargaining and organisation had been under increasing pressure from employers. The unease management felt about the implications of joint regulation has already been noted, and after the invasion of Normandy a harder posture was evident in industrial relations. A minor strike-wave in early 1944 was met by regulation IAA which imposed strong penalties on industrial disruption and was used against the protests over redundancies that were appearing as preparations were made to return to peacetime production. A strike at Humber's Coventry works in January 1945 over the efforts of the works manager to tighten discipline exemplified the growing tensions. The complaints against the manager ranged from his abolition of the custom of allowing older men to leave work early to a refusal to continue the practice of weekly meetings with the stewards. Jack Jones described the manager as '"harsh, rigid and unbending"' and another steward explained that

> It is the general impression in the works that we gathered from the meetings we attended, that it is part of an attempt to prepare for post-war conditions, and that cooperation in the industry for the successful prosecution of the war, which has been so distinct a feature of wartime relations, has now to give way to a changed atmosphere of pressure from above.[42]

There was a growing hostility to negotiating with stewards and JPCs. At Armstrong-Whitworth in April 1945, the directors responded to efforts to raise the question of peacetime production by claiming that 'they only had the right to know the plans of the company'. Strikes against the victimisation of stewards began to be reported in the *Metal Worker* (as *New Propellor* became after April 1946) during 1946. And by 1948 there was widespread tension over attempted rate-reductions, redundancies, time and motion and refusal to negotiate with stewards. The quickened pace of the offensive in 1948 was coincident with the change in government economic policy and the implementation of Marshall Aid which sent Anglo-American productivity councils into the factories to investigate restrictive practices and conduct Bedaux-type studies. Surely by no coincidence, a widespread condemnation of restrictive practices was mounted which reflected the work-place implications of an Atlanticist economic policy. Productivity was now defined as a matter of free market stimulation rather than as integral to planned production. Trade-union leaders added their voices to the campaign. A special conference of trade-union executives placed the burden of peacetime productivity solely upon the removal of restrictive practices and failed to address, for example, the question of the re-equipment of industry. Even Jack Tanner, the old syndicalist and Minority Movement supporter, but now president of the AEU, was reported to endorse this line.[43]

The purpose of the employers' offensive was to undermine mutuality. At the Humber factory in Coventry, in 1946, an important attempt was made to destroy the tool-room agreement that had kept local piece-prices high during the war. Although this failed, similar attacks had to be faced elsewhere in 1948 and 1949. At Austin and De Havilland (where Reg Birch was a strike leader), efforts were made by management to assert a unilateral control over rates. The introduction of time-and-motion men 'sitting behind the man on the machine for days and weeks without placing a time or price on the job' was seen as an attempt to 'get back to a system of observing and spying, like the inhuman Bedaux system'. This strike was successful in maintaining the stewards' role in the negotiating process, but the issue was not resolved until a sit-in strike in April 1950 resulted in an agreement that ensured some mutuality over time-studies and rate-fixing.[44]

As this would suggest, the success of the employers' counter-offensive of the late 1940s was only partial. On the one hand, there is no doubt that workshop organisation and bargaining were in an essentially defensive posture until the mid- to late 1950s and it seems likely that stewards' organisations declined after the war. The success of the Labour government's policies and the widespread support they received from the working class kept industrial conflict at a low level until 1953. On the other hand, the counter-attack was not pressed. The key feature of the immediate post-war period was the crumbling of the possibility of building upon wartime social relations of production, but it was a gentle erosion compared to the situation after the First World War. The recognition of joint regulation as the central feature of work-place social relations was withdrawn. With the decision of the government to abandon an economic strategy of domestic planning, there was no place for workshop organisation or shop stewards in the formal structure of industrial relations. The result was that workshop bargaining and organisation was driven back to its localist roots and could survive only where its strength and particular circumstances permitted – which actually turned out to be quite extensive. Thus, at De Havilland, for example, workshop organisation was too deeply entrenched to be rooted out, but it had to fight to maintain the prerogatives secured since 1935. By contrast, Standard Motors decided to pursue a policy of collaborative industrial relations on the basis of the wartime experience. Agreements in 1947 and 1949 formalised the customs and practices established over the previous decade.[45] But this case was quite unique and was so out of tune with the rest of the industry that the company was forced to sever its connection with the Engineering Employers' Federation. However, it stands as a reminder of the direction industrial relations could have taken after the war had the experience of the past ten years been built upon rather than rejected.

Conclusion

The marginalisation of the workshop movement of the Second World War was not accompanied by any crisis in social and political relations. Unlike the First World War, or in Japan after the second, the greatly strengthened organisational presence of labour at the work-place was not linked in to struggles over national politics or policies. Although at the local level there were resonances of alternative policies and ideas – especially on the question of worker representation on the boards of nationalised industry – they possessed no real political significance. The failure to build post-war industrial relations around wartime joint regulation meant that workshop organisation continued to exist as a purely economic, local phenomenon which practiced 'encroaching control' over managerial prerogatives, but did so apart from the wider world of Labour politics. As such, it reflected the successful decoupling of politics from the economic and social structures through which Labour's support was mobilised. James Cronin has pointed out how the 'enduring weakness of British social democracy' has lain in the 'growing lack of correspondence between social structure and political allegiance or, more precisely, between the possibilities inherent in the shifting social structures and their actual crystallisation or mobilisation in politics'.[46] Between 1945 and 1951, of course, this discordance was largely inconspicuous, but what needs to be stressed is that the containment of workshop organisation as a purely economic phenomenon has provided one of the major characteristics of Labour's organisational and ideological stance since 1918. The consequence was that Labourism's void at the work-place was filled by the Communist Party. This presence within the wartime stewards' organisation did not reflect the manipulation of King Street, but rather the ability of individual militants to represent the main tradition of workshop bargaining and militancy. Furthermore, the Communist Party had no thoughts of trying to generate any wider political challenge on the basis of the achievements of wartime organisation. Soon after the war the Party dissolved its work-place branches and continued to call for a national government long after others on the left abandoned the idea. Thus, in this respect, too, the separation between politics and economics was accentuated.

Indeed, the general paradox of the wartime transformation of production relations and the shift in political attitudes was that they reinforced that separation. The need to mobilise labour by accepting an industrial and political partnership dictated the development of a wartime 'consensus' on economic and social policy. At one level, this was reflected in the wider acceptance of broadly socialist notions of what constituted a just and fair society. Even *The Times* endorsed an extension of social welfare and, for a while, the active search for egalitarianism became a consensus value; the domestic policies of wartime resulted in a real diminution of the extremes of wealth. Furthermore, those who composed the 'middle opinion' of the inter-war years were able to secure a major role for their policies of technocratic reform. Reconstruction was a far more serious matter than it had been in 1914-18 and received a broad support within both political parties as leading representatives of middle opinion like Macmillan came to play a dominant role in the Conservative Party. Although there were divergences of opinion as to the exact shape of the economic and social policies that should be pursued after the war, there was a basic consensus around the priorities of full employment and social reform. The Labour Party was clearly most qualified to carry out such policies and, in retrospect, there should have been no surprise over the results of the 1945 election.

Confounding widespread expectations within the working class, the return to peacetime economy was not accompanied by a reversion to large-scale redundancies and deprivation. To the contrary, the energetic implementation of the Welfare State effected a genuine improvement in the conditions of working-class life. The reforms of the Labour government of 1945-51 marked the finest achievement of the policies of Fabian statism and they seemed fully to justify the Labourist formulation of the 'British road to socialism'. Thus, unlike the First World War, Labour's success in carrying out the policies of the wartime consensus allowed the separation between politics and economics to be seemingly resolved. With full employment and the Welfare State, the question of production relations no longer seemed relevant to the political economy of Britain. The total absence of such questions – and many others – from Anthony Crosland's monumental paean to Fabianism, *The Future of Socialism*, published in 1954, reflected the extent to which these matters played no part in the agenda of Labour's socialism. The irony was, however, that the very success of these policies of full employment and the Welfare State established the labour-market conditions for workshop militancy, bargaining and organisation to thrive within the purely industrial sphere of post-war society. During the next 20 years, this presence eventually was to ensure that production relations would, once again, become a problem for national politics.

Notes

1. Derek Aldcroft and Harry Richardson, *The British Economy 1870-1939* (New York, 1970), pp. 220, 225ff; Sean Glynn and John Oxborrow, *Interwar Britain: A Social and Economic History* (London, 1976), pp. 94-5; Noreen Branson and Margot Heineman, *Britain in the Nineteen Thirties* (London, 1971), pp. 143-4; J. Stevenson and Chris Cook, *The Slump* (London, 1976), pp. 8-9.

2. Aldcroft and Richardson, *The British Economy*, pp. 230-3; D.H. Aldcroft, 'The Performance of the British Machine Tool Industry in the Inter-War Years', *Business History Review*, vol. 40 (1966).

3. Stuart MacIntyre, *Little Moscows* (London, 1980), pp. 114; Aldcroft and Richardson, *The British Economy*, p. 229; J.H. Mitchell, 'The Mechanization of the Miner', *The Human Factor*, vol. 8, no. 4 (April, 1933).

4. Frank Woolard, 'Some Notes on British Methods of Continuous Production', *Proceedings of the Institution of Automotive Engineers*, vol. 19 (1924-5); Patrick Fridenson, 'The Coming of the Assembly Line to Europe' in Wolfgang Kohn, Edwin T. Layton and Peter Weingart (eds.), *The Dynamics of Science and Technology* (Dordrecht, Holland, 1978), p. 163; Roy Church, *Herbert Austin* (London, 1979), p. 100; R.C. Whiting, *The View from Cowley* (Oxford, 1983), pp. 30-1.

5. David Lee, 'Beyond Deskilling: Skill, Craft and Class' in S. Wood (ed.), *The Degradation of Work* (London, 1981); Richard Croucher, *Engineers at War 1939-1945* (London, 1982), p. 9; James Hinton, *The First Shop Stewards Movement* (London, 1973), p. 63; AEU, *Monthly Report*, August 1925, p. 4; January 1931, p. 16; May 1931, p. 19; July 1931, p. 11; February 1931, pp. 14, 21; August 1931, pp. 25-33; March, 1933, p. 14; April 1933, p. 17; September 1933, p. 22; Wigham, *The Power to Manage* (London, 1973), p. 134.

6. John Child, *British Management Thought* (London, 1969), pp. 55-63, 70, 75, 87, 103; C.S. Myers, 'The Efficiency Engineer and the Industrial Psychologist', *Journal of the National Institute of Industrial Psychology*, vol. 1 (January 1923); Helen Jones, 'Employer Welfare Schemes and Industrial Relations in Inter-War Britain', *Business History*, vol. 25, no. 1 (March 1983), p. 64ff.

7. Craig Littler, *The Development of the Labour Process in Capitalist Societies* (London, 1982), pp. 108, 111-14, 127, 141-3; G.D.H. Cole, *British Trade Unionism Today* (London, 1939), p. 94; Trades Union Congress, 64th

Annual Report, 1932, p. 422; H.M. Vernon, 'Effect of a Bonus on the Output of Men Engaged in Heavy Work', *Journal of the National Institute of Industrial Psychology*, vol. 4 (July 1929).

8. Littler, *Development of the Labour Process*, pp. 118-27, 128-40; Mick Jenkins, 'Time and Motion Strike', *Our History*, no. 60 (Autumn 1974). The deskilling at Johnson's had first been attempted in 1898: see ASE, *Monthly Report*, September 1898, p. 6 and October 1898, p. 70; AEU, *Monthly Report*, May 1930, p. 30; August 1930, p. 26; May 1931, p. 26; August 1931, p. 36; October 1931, p. 29; December 1933, p. 8; May 1934, p. 24; TUC, *Bedaux System of Payment on Results*, 1933, p. 8.

9. David Gordon, Richard Edwards and Michael Reich, *Segmented Work, Divided Workers. The Historical Transformation of Labor in the United States* (Cambridge, Mass., 1982), Chapters 3 and 4; David Noble, *America by Design* (New York, 1974); Susan Merkle, *Management and Ideology* (Berkeley, 1980); Littler, *Development of the Labour Process*, pp. 194-5; Martin Weiner, *English Culture and the Decline of the Industrial Spirit 1850-1980* (Cambridge, 1980), pp. 148-50, 151-4; Child, *British Management Thought*, p. 111.

10. TUC, 64th *Annual Report*, Littler, *Development of the Labour Process*; W.F. Watson, *Bedaux and Other Bonus Systems Explained* (London, 1932), p. 30.

11. Jim McGoldrick, 'Crisis and the Division of Labour: Clydeside Shipbuilding in the Inter-War Period' in Tony Dickson (ed.), *Capital and Class in Scotland* (Edinburgh, 1982), pp. 158-79; see R. Bean, 'Custom, Job Regulation and Dock Labour in Liverpool, 1911-39', *International Review of Social History*, vol. 27, no. 3 (1982) for the way custom and practice were carried over to the formalised system of industrial relations in 1911 and impeded modernisation in the early 1920s.

12. Frank McKenna, *The Railway Workers 1840-1970* (London, 1980), pp. 129-34; *Railway Vigilant*, February 1933, pp. 3-10; March 1933, pp. 6-11; April 1933, p. 4; October 1934, pp. 4-6.

13. AEU, *Monthly Report*, March 1926, pp. 9-17; April 1926, pp. 10-12, 25-31, 45-9; May 1926, pp. 13, 45; September 1926, p. 35.

14. Church, *Herbert Austin*, pp. 150-51; AEU, *Monthly Report*, May 1929, p. 27; Arthur Exell, 'Morris Motors in the 1930s Part II', *History Workshop Journal*, no. 7 (Spring 1979), pp. 58-60; Whiting, *Cowley*, pp. 63, 75-81.

15. Exell, 'Morris Motors, Part II', pp. 33, 61-65; Whiting, *Cowley*, pp. 85-7.

16. Keith Middlemas, *Politics in Industrial Society* (London, 1979), pp. 194-7; G.W. McDonald and Howard F. Gospel, 'The Mond-Turner Talks 1927-1933: A Study in Industrial Cooperation', *Historical Journal*, vol. 16, no. 4 (1973); Wigham, *Power to Manage*, pp. 128-32.

17. Middlemas, *Politics in Industrial Society*, pp. 255-61, 263-5.

18. A.J.P. Taylor, *English History 1914-1945* (Oxford, 1965), p. 79;Middlemas, *Politics in Industrial Society*, p. 254 ff.

19. Croucher, *Engineers*, pp. 9, 46; R.A.C. Parker, 'British Rearmament 1936-39: Treasury, Trade Unions and Skilled Labour', *Historical Journal* (1981).

20. Dwight Rayton, *Shop Floor Democracy in Action* (Nottingham, 1972), pp. 8-9.

21. Croucher, *Engineers*, pp. 37-40; *New Propellor*, June 1936, pp. 8-9; July 1936, p. 8; April 1938, pp. 3, 5-7; May 1938, pp. 5, 8.

22. *New Propellor*, May 1936, pp. 7-10.

23. Ibid., October 1935, pp. 2-3; November 1935, p. 2; March 1936, p. 6; August 1937, p. 7; April 1940, p. 1; April 1939, pp. 6, 9; August 1939, pp. 2, 7.

24. Ibid., January 1936, p. 2; February 1936, p. 1; August 1936, p. 7; April 1938, pp. 6-7; May 1938, p. 8; July 1938, pp. 1, 6.

25. Arthur Exell, 'Morris Motors in the 1930s, Part I', *History Workshop Journal*, no. 6 (Autumn 1978), pp. 67-8; *New Propellor*, August 1936, p. 7; February 1937, p. 6; November 1939, p. 11 (on control of overtime); August 1937, p. 6; December 1937, p. 9; June 1939, p. 6.

26. *New Propellor*, June 1939, pp. 6, 9; October 1939, p. 9; November 1939, pp. 2-3; October 1940, p. 5; 18 April 1941, p. 3.

27. Middlemas, *Politics in Industrial Society*, p. 277; Paul Addison, *The Road to 1945* (London, 1975), pp. 113-43; George Orwell, *The Lion and the Unicorn* (London, 1941), p. 35.

28. Exell, 'Morris Motors, Part I'; Alan Bullock, *The Life and Times of Ernest Bevin*, vol. 2 (London, 1967), pp. 62-3.

29. Bullock, *Bevin*, p. 57; Croucher, *Engineers*, pp. 116-17, for a different interpretation of EWO; Wal Hannington, *The Rights of Engineers* (London, 1944), pp. 73-80; Mass Observation, *People in Production* (London, 1942), p. 103.

30. Hannington, *Rights of Engineers*, pp. 60-6; P. Inman, *Labour in the Munitions Industries* (London, 1957), p. 400; Croucher, *Engineers*, pp. 207-8, 212; *New Propellor*, January 1943, pp. 3, 7; March 1943, p. 1; May 1943, pp. 2, 4; August 1943, p. 4; July 1943, p. 3; November 1943, p. 11; 16 May 1941, p. 5.

31. *New Propellor*, October 1937, p. 5; AEU, *Enquiry into Production Committees. Third Report on Production*, December 1942, p. 44; Bullock, *Bevin*, p. 80; Mass Observation, *People in Production*, pp. 277-8.

32. Mass Observation, *People in Production*, pp. 333-4, 403; J.T. Murphy, *Victory Production* (London, 1942), pp. 97-8.

33. James Hinton, 'Coventry Communism. A Study in Factory Politics in the Second World War', *History Workshop Journal*, no. 10 (Autumn 1980), p. 103; AEU, *Enquiry into Production Committees*, pp. 6, 86; Murphy, *Victory Production*, pp. 99-102.

34. Croucher, *Engineers*, pp. 219-24, 226, 228-30, 237-40; Equity, *The Struggle in the Factories* (Glasgow, 1944); Ken Coates and Tony Topham (eds), *Workers' Control* (London, 1970), p. 197; Hinton, 'Coventry Communism', p. 97; *New Propellor*, 10 October 1941, p. 1; Engineering and Allied Trades, Shop Stewards' National Council, *Report of Conference*, 19 October 1941.

35. AEU, *Enquiry into Production Committees*, pp. 86-8; Inman, *Labour in the Munitions Industries*, pp. 378-9; *New Propellor*, 12 December 1941, pp. 1, 5; Croucher, *Engineers*, p. 155.

36. Croucher, *Engineers*, pp. 171-3; Mass Observation, *People in Production*, p. 331.

37. Bullock, *Bevin*, p. 96; AEU, *Enquiry into Production Committees*, pp. 44-67, 87-8, 91-2; Geoff Brown, *Sabotage* (London, 1977), pp. 280-2; Inman, *Labour in the Munitions Industries*, pp. 382, 388; A. Exell, 'Morris Motors in the 1940s', *History Workshop Journal*, no. 9 (Spring 1980), pp. 93-6; Murphy, *Victory Production*, p. 102.

38. *New Propellor*, September 1944, p. 5 and October 1946, p. 7; TUC, *Interim Report on Post-War Reconstruction*, 1944, pp. 20-3.

39. *Metal Worker*, April 1947, p. 4; June 1947, p. 5; October 1947, p. 1; November 1946, pp. 4-5.

40. For foreign affairs see Alan Bullock's masterly *Ernest Bevin, Foreign Secretary 1945-51* (London, 1983) where a main theme is Bevin's determination from 1946 to work for a close US-British partnership. On the relationship between domestic policy and the reliance on American loans, see Kenneth Morgan, *Labour in Power 1945-1951* (Oxford, 1983), pp. 142-51, Chapter 8, and the stimulating article by Teddy Brett, Steve Gilliat and Andrew Pople, 'Planned Trade, Labour Party Policy and US Intervention: The Successes and Failures of Post-War Reconstruction', *History Workshop Journal*, no. 13 (Spring 1982); see Kenneth

Harris, *Attlee* (London, 1983), p. 333 on Dalton.

41. A.A. Rogow, *The Labour Government and British Industry* (Ithaca, New York, 1955), pp. 41-4; Coates and Topham, *Workers' Control*, p. 197.

42. See *New Propellor*, March 1945, pp. 1, 5, for examples of strikes against redundancies, Croucher, *Engineers*, pp. 309-25, 336-42.

43. *New Propellor*, April 1945, p. 8; *Metal Worker*, December 1946, p. 1; March 1947, p. 1; October 1945, pp. 1, 4; November 1948, pp. 1, 8; December 1948, pp. 1, 8.

44. Croucher, *Engineers*, pp. 342-3; *Metal Worker*, February 1949, p. 1; September 1948, p. 1; March 1949, p. 1; March 1950, p. 1; April 1950, p. 1. Other examples of similar strikes can be found in *Metal Worker*, August 1950, p. 1; November 1950, pp. 1-2; February 1950, p. 3; July 1949, p. 1; November 1949, p. 1.

45. *Metal Worker*, February 1949, p. 5; Seymour Melman, *Decision Making and Productivity* (New York, 1958), pp. 32-9; J.W. Durgan, W.E.J. McCarthy and G.P. Redman, *Strikes in Post-War Britain* (London, 1983), pp. 26, 55, 398-9, 414-5.

46. See Joe Moore *Japanese Workers and the Struggle for Socialism 1945-1947* (Madison, Wisc., 1983); James Cronin, 'Politics, Class Structure, and the Enduring Weakness of British Social Democracy', *Journal of Social History*, vol. 16, no. 3 (1984), p. 138.

8 THE POLITICAL ECONOMY OF INDUSTRIAL RELATIONS 1945-1980

The Past in the Present

Britain's post-war history has been dominated by problems of the economy. A failure to maintain a sufficiently high rate of economic growth combined with the exposed position of sterling as a world trading currency have determined the progressive weakening of British capitalism in the world economy. To speak of decline is somewhat misleading; the real problem is a more complicated failure to adjust to changing economic circumstances – as the inability to match the growth-rates of comparable economies demonstrates. It is generally recognised that this conundrum cannot be understood simply as the function of errors or mistakes in the administration of economic policy. Indeed, it could be argued that economic policy-makers have correctly diagnosed Britain's problems, although with the benefit of hindsight it is possible to point to a succession of tactical misjudgements. What is clear, however, is that effective implementation of these diagnoses has been impeded by behavioural failures in the institutions of British society whose origins lie much deeper than a mere contemporary malaise. The structures that Sydney Pollard has identified as causing 'the wasting of the British economy' or the political contention that Samuel Beer has termed the product of 'pluralistic stagnation' can only be understood through the prism of historical explanation.[1]

The historical circumstances that conditioned Britain's emergence as the leading industrial nation continue to condition the present course of her development. It has long been fashionable to argue that the hegemony of patrician, aristocratic cultural values and norms have come to impede economic growth by their disdain for industry and innovation. Even if this is true, however, it is also the case that for much of Britain's history those same structures allowed growth to occur without social and political disruption.[2] Similarly, Britain's early industrial lead and success in grabbing huge chunks of the world allowed the economic weaknesses that were visible by the end of the nineteenth century to be shielded and counterbalanced by the enormous residual power of the Empire. Thus, the imperatives to social and economic change were neither strong enough, nor the restraints upon change weak enough to alter a comforting, if ultimately unhealthy, stasis in the arrangements that governed economic and social structures and relationships. In retrospect, low growth-rates are typical of Britain's economic history, but they did not become of critical importance until the ability to retreat into empire was closed off after the Second World War. By the end of the 1950s a significant political consensus had come to recognise that the modernisation of Britain's industrial base was a pressing necessity. Determined efforts to achieve this regeneration were hampered at every point by the restraints upon policy and action that derived from two major legacies of the past.

The first lay in the way the priorities and structures of British capitalism were not naturally open to the kinds of changes necessary for a modernisation of the economy. This was more deeply rooted than a matter of anti-growth culture – which, in fact, has been an argument that serves to excuse looking at more basic historical questions. It was more a matter of the historical development of the inner structures of British capitalism and the power relations between its divergent fractions. This question has yet to be properly addressed by historians and, thus, the contribution of the internal features of British capitalism to the difficulties of economic regeneration can only be tentatively sketched here. However, it is an important question not only in its own right, but also because in the 1960s and 1970s the priorities that have historically dominated economic policy conditioned and reinforced the responses to the second major restraint of the past.

That restraint was composed of the dynamic of social relations in production whose history we have been concerned to trace in this book. There was always an abstract contradiction between the restrictive nature and traditions of these social relations and effective economic management, but the dissonances normally remained latent because they could generally be resolved at the local, industry-specific level – as in the late nineteenth century – and accommodated within the structures of economic development. The emergence of national strategies to achieve economic regeneration in the 1960s and 1970s, however, brought this contradiction fully into the open. Each strategy of modernisation was seen to falter upon the pattern of social relations that history had bequeathed. Indeed, ironically, those very strategies tended to reinforce the restraints imposed by the structures of social relations. In addition, unlike past periods when industrial relations had been a problem in politics, the central initiative for policies of economic regeneration was now assumed by the state. Thus, industrial relations became politicised to a level of national significance. By the early 1970s, industrial relations were the central issue around which politics turned and the fate of governments decided. How this came to be is the subject of this chapter.

British Capitalism and Economic Regeneration

It is one of the peculiarities of British capitalism that the distinction between the financial and industrial sectors is sharper and more complete than in other capitalist societies. In Germany, for example, bank and financial shareholdings in industry usually average about 25 per cent of total holdings; in Britain, 1-2 per cent is more usual and holdings of 25% are unknown. The historical reasons for this separation lie in the nature and character of the emergence of industrial capitalism in Britain. Geographically separated from access to the London money-markets, whose main interest in overseas trade was already well established by the time modern industry developed, the growth of industrial capitalism over a protracted period allowed capital formation to be derived from sources internal to industry and to occur at a much lower level than would be the case elsewhere. The gradual and incomplete emergence of a truly industrial organisation of production not only delayed the need for any fusion between the two fractions of capital but also allowed these patterns to solidify and thus increased the difficulties of establishing a relationship when it was desirable. The growth of the large-scale company and the beginnings of attempts to forge a partnership with finance capital occurred about a century after the industrial revolution began. In Germany and the United States, for example, these developments were virtually coterminous with initial industrialisation.[3]

Perhaps the major political consequence of this separation was to ensure that the industrial fraction of capital would play a subordinate role in the making of economic policy. The capital markets were primarily oriented to issues of foreign governments and entrepreneurs, only one-fifth of new stock issues in 1913 were for domestic companies. Neither British industrialists nor the domestic banks that handled their business were admitted to the inner sanctums of the Bank of England. Historically, the same was true of access to policy formation in Whitehall. Industrial diversity and sectionalism between employers reinforced this exclusion. Employers' organisations were traditionally interest-group associations – an early effort to create a general federation of industrial employers in 1873 collapsed seven years later. The Employers' Parliamentary Committee of the 1890s was somewhat more successful, but its focus was to counteract the influence of the TUC in parliament rather than to initiate policy formation. During the First World War, the Federation of British Industries and the British Employers' Confederation were founded but not until they merged to form the CBI in 1965 did a unitary organisation exist to represent the views of industry. Partly as a consequence, it was not until governments created tripartite bodies of consultation in the early 1960s that regularised channels existed for industrial capital to enter into the policy-making process. Employers were, of course, able to react once policy had been announced, but they never seem to have possessed the initiating role accorded to the Bank of England-Treasury axis.[4]

Various efforts to change the priorities of national economic policy failed. The tariff reform campaign led by Joseph Chamberlain was the first to try and shift the balance, but when tariff reform finally did triumph in 1931, it hardly reflected the original agenda of economic and social regeneration. 1931 was a rescue effort to save the pound by creating a sterling area; a final bid to resort to Empire as a prophylaxis against the world economy. Earnings from finance capital had always been of key importance to Britain's economic position. From 1822 the balance of trade ran a perpetual deficit which until the 1880s was covered by the surplus on invisible exports. The strength of sterling did not rest upon the productive capacity of the country, but upon the position of Britain as the centre of a world-wide financial network. By the early twentieth century, the surplus from invisibles had disappeared and a favourable balance of payments was maintained by the earnings from foreign investments – which expanded at an enormous rate from the mid-1890s. The cost of the First World War effectively shattered that dependence – although Britain's relatively good economic performance in the 1920s delayed the balance falling into the red until the 1930s. Thus, from the early twentieth century, financing the deficit fell more and more upon the Empire. Even prior to 1914, India alone covered two-fifths of Britain's deficit with the rest of the world.

In the meantime, as Britain faced competition from Germany and America, trade increasingly followed the flag. From the later nineteenth century exports increasingly came to rest upon the soft markets of the Empire. Whereas in 1872 Europe had taken 43 per cent of British exports, by 1910 it took a quarter and the share of the white colonies and India had risen from 17 per cent to 30 per cent. But the end of the Second World War marked the virtual end of imperial preferences as the Americans insisted upon a liberalised world economy and the independent Commonwealth countries moved to liquidate their sterling balances into dollars. During most of the 1950s, the expansion that accompanied the post-war recovery in world trade disguised the fragility of British economic growth. By the late 1950s, however, the warning signs were writ large: recurrent balance-of-payments crises began to attract attention, and West Germany and Japan began to export the fruits of their economic miracles. Until 1960 Britain's motorcar industry was second only to that of the United States, producing 25 per cent of the world's supply, but in that year Britain was overtaken by West Germany.[5]

The response of finance capital to the demise of Britain's trading position remained unruffled. The City of London's historic association with the movement of capital and its advantageous geographic position allowed it to make an easy transition from an arbiter of capital accumulation to a financial entrepôt oriented now towards Western Europe. Thus, just as in the 1920s and 1930s, when economic policy was based upon the effort to restore London's financial supremacy, high interest and attractive exchange-rates were a main priority for the City of London. On the other hand, this stood in direct conflict with the modernising needs of industrial capital. In the first place, industry was starved of the capital it needed to restructure and, in the second place, the priority of protecting the exchange-rate of the pound made the balance of payments the prime determination of economic policy. This meant that policy was essentially governed by short-term manoeuvres to secure a surplus on the balance and, thus, retain continued international confidence in the pound. The notorious stop-go policies in the late 1950s were one reflection of these conditions. Efforts were made to break out of the cycle. Reginald Maudling 'dashed for growth' in the early 1960s; Anthony Barber deliberately fuelled an inflationary speculative expansion in 1972; and the Labour government presided over their ill-fated national plan from 1964-6. But all were destroyed by severe balance-of-payments crises which demanded immediate deflationary action to protect Britain's financial reputation. This determination of economic policy by the vagaries of international currency movements stood in direct contradiction to the necessarily long-term project of economic regeneration. It was clearly impossible for the state to preside over a modernisation of the structure of British industry if national economic policy was dominated by reactions to exchange crises.[6]

Indeed, the solutions to these crises tended to reinforce this dominance. Each time a balance-of-payments crisis threatened the strength of sterling, deflationary brakes were applied to the economy, imports declined and the balance was restored to surplus. Consumption fell as unemployment increased and industrial output slackened off. But demand was merely pent up to be released with even greater might each time the brakes were released, and the cycle began all over again. Similarly, the increasing necessity in the 1970s to mount international rescue operations in support of sterling further enforced the supremacy of the City and Treasury. The crisis of 1976, for example, was quite explicitly used by hard-line monetarists in the IMF and the United States to cut short government spending on economic and social reform. The strength of monetarist doctrine in Britain in the late 1970s surely owes much to the institutional power of finance capital in that country.[7]

It would be a mistake to assume, however, that the historical predominance of financial interests over the main direction of economic policy was solely due to its unchallenged control of the levers of power. Within industry there were important differences over the direction of economic policy and significant convergences of interest with the City. Given the role of Britain in the world financial markets, any damage to that role was bound to affect Britain's industrial position and there was never a clear-cut choice between the interests of industrial or financial capital. Nevertheless, historically, the question was how to secure a policy that would address the needs of industry without allowing the latter to be buffeted and bumped about by the interests of the financial sector.

In both the post-First World War period and in the 1960s and 1970s, the main alternative policy that presented itself implied a high degree of state intervention and an enhanced power for labour. Understandably, industry has been suspicious of both of these implications. The failure of reconstruction after about 1921-2 signalled not only the revival of finance capital's power after its relative demise during the latter period of the war, but also the unwillingness of industry to accept the social implications of such a policy. During this period concessions to labour could hardly be divorced from the context of militancy. Thus, the restoration of the gold standard and deflation were not only consistent with the financial sector's desire to restore pre-war normalcy, they were also an answer to the social pressures that faced industrial capital. Progressive industrial employers would probably have been willing to try and resolve these pressures, but that segment was never able to establish its dominance over the likes of Evan Williams of the coal-mine owners, or overcome the engineering employers' hostility to the prospect of endowing trade unionism with more power and influence. Similarly, some elements of industry in the 1960s and 1970s were initially attracted to the Labour government's strategy of economic regeneration through increased intervention but only if it could be reconciled with an 'insulation from working class demands'.[8] In all fairness, the Labour government did try to perform this balancing act. Incomes policies successfully held back wage demands; the radical elements of the NEB, the Industry Act and industrial democracy were watered down; Tony Benn was removed from the Department of Industry; and internal pressures from the Labour Party to expand the boundaries of social democracy were consistently evaded. By 1977-8, however, this balancing act had manifestly failed and Labour began the tilt towards monetarism that Mrs Thatcher's Conservatives triumphantly completed.

In order, then, to understand why industrial capital has historically played a subordinate role in economic policy formation, it is necessary to recognise that until the 1960s its interests could continue to be served by the policy of finance capital. Only with the decisive appearance of the long-delayed imperative of economic modernisation did the possibilities for an alternative policy really emerge. The question posed by this imperative was how to attain an economic regeneration that would shoot British capitalism into the twentieth-century world economy. From the early 1960s, the consensus answer was that a more active policy of modernisation was needed which would be coordinated by the state. Policies and strategies of modernisation, however, cannot be achieved in a social vacuum. Just as the legacy of Britain's imperial past impeded the development of a long-term policy of modernisation, so the restraints of Britain's social relations of production conditioned the efforts once they were undertaken. It was in the dynamic thus created that the post-war course of British politics was forged.

The Restraints of Production Relations

The most significant consequence of Britain's participation in the victory of the Second World War was the way it closed off any questioning of the traditional institutional, political and social relationships. Indeed, to a large extent, the viability of traditional structures and arrangements was reinforced. Unlike all the fascist and most of the occupied countries, the British political establishment had not been discredited. The Empire was restored, its glory may have faded but it was largely intact; Imperial pretensions and great-power status were confirmed by the political incapacity of the European countries until 1948-9. The war ratified the essential soundness of Britain and the British class and imperial systems. This was, perhaps, the greatest defeat Britain experienced in her modern history.

The war also served to confirm the traditional patterns of class relations at the point of production. By all the important measurements, British labour emerged from the war with its position enormously strengthened. Labour had escaped the crushing burden of fascism, it had been accorded an equal partnership in political and economic mobilisation, and the political consensus had shifted to a set of 'progressive' presuppositions that reflected its general interests. In contrast to the defeated countries of the Continent, it was not necessary to reconstruct the methods and institutions that ordered and mediated British social relations. Unlike France or Italy, for example, there was no debate or struggle about the nature or bases of political and social relations. In Germany and Japan, as in many of the occupied countries, industrial relations were refashioned from scratch in accordance with the planned rebuilding of society. In Britain, the structures of union government, for example, were left completely unchanged as were the associations and institutions governing employer relations with the unions or the state. Of course, the absence of any attempt to reconsider or alter the basis of industrial relations hardly implied a restoration of employer power and prerogative. Indeed, precisely the opposite was true. If the underlying structures of social relations remained undisturbed, the actual balance of power at the work-place tended to shift in labour's favour and was protected from counterattack by the political circumstances of the time. The Welfare State and the commitment to full employment in Britain entrenched the power of labour in society. Thus, the labour movement was insulated from the kinds of attacks experienced in the USA and Italy where by 1950 militant shop-floor organisation and stewards' movements had been effectively neutralised.[9]

In Britain, however, the growing strength and significance of workshop bargaining structures was the most obvious manifestation of the essential continuity of social relations. As early as 1951, it was noted that 'the centre of gravity in the engineering trade unions has moved more and more to the shop stewards', and between 1947 and 1961 the density of stewards in that industry increased by 50 per cent. During the first phase of the post-war expansion this growth was particularly concentrated in the vehicles sector, but workshop organisation was also evident elsewhere, as in the docks where, even more than in engineering, it replaced official unionism as the prime medium of worker-employer relations.[10]

One indication of the growth of this 'unofficial' system of industrial relations was the emergence of links between workshop organisation in various plants. In Standard Motors in the early 1950s, the shop-stewards' committees were joined together through a system of committees that tried to coordinate action in the various plants. These committees were also able to extend their reach into the supplier companies so that 'details of raw materials, sources of supply and their schedules have become available to the workers' organization in a regular way'. Just how effective these combine committees were in industrial relations must await further research, but efforts to form an industry-wide combine for the motor-car industry in the mid- and late 1950s disintegrated under pressure from the trade-union hierarchies. In individual companies, however, combine committees survived and were successful in coordinating demands, and in calling and running strikes over the heads of the official unions. Some of these committees were well organised and possessed independent sources of income. The BMC Combine Committee, which was formed in 1951, held regular bi-monthly meetings attended by 40 delegates and possessed a formalised structure complete with a constitution. The joint shop-stewards' committee at Briggs Motors linked with other committees, published the *Voice of Ford* newspaper from the mid-1950s and possessed funds totalling £16,000 in 1957. These structures were the precedents for the better-known efforts such as the Lucas Combine Committee which was initially established to advise its members on the complicated industrial pensions structure, later extended its scope to the publication of a bi-monthly newspaper and the development of an alternative plan for the industry as it entered the depression of the mid-1970s.[11]

In the early post-war years this structure of work-place organisation was not associated with a particularly militant industrial posture. From about 1953, however, the post-war pattern of declining strike trends was broken by a strong upward movement which mobilised around a densening matrix of shop-floor organisation and representation and by the mid-1950s a mini-crisis in industrial relations signalled the emergence of the issue as a matter for national politics. Engineering and motor-cars were the locus of this development and the situation at Briggs and Standard Motors provides representative examples of its progression.[12]

From 1952 management at Briggs Motors had endeavoured to persuade the trade unions to bring the stewards' organisation under control, but official trade-union influence was minimal because the company was not part of the national negotiating machinery and, thus, work conditions were determined by shop-floor negotiations. A procedure was eventually negotiated in 1955, but it failed to dislodge this system and, indeed, continued to provide for shop-steward responsibility right up to the national level. There was no stage at which the AEU executive could negotiate alone with the higher officers of the company. At the same time, the company was absorbed by Ford who introduced a tightened managerial discipline as part of a general reorganisation of production. Between February 1954 and May 1955 there were 523 sectional stoppages at Briggs over redundancy, speed-up and time and motion, culminating in the famous 'bell-ringing' strike when a total stoppage was sparked by the dismissal of the stewards' convener.[13]

Parallel tensions were manifest at Standard Motors where changing product markets stimulated an attack upon the relative autonomy of the gang system. The events in this company were very significant because they provided a foretaste of developments that were eventually to characterise the industry as a whole. It has been noted how Standards' managerial policy after the war accepted a wide degree of worker decision-making over work-loads and the organisation of production. By 1956 two major developments combined to undermine the viability of this system. In the first place, a severe slump occurred in the industry, possibly sparked by the removal of the 33½ per cent tariff on imported cars which since 1915 had protected the industry. In the second place, and largely as a response to increased competition, a major phase of re-equipment began. Automatic cycling machines were introduced which diminished labour needs and doubled output. The management of Standard began to adopt a much harder line, arguing that wages were too high, custom and practice too restrictive, work-loads too light, and their right to manage too confined. Custom and practice had accorded stewards informal negotiating rights over the extent and distribution of redundancies, but in 1956, management argued, the depressed state of the industry would not allow this and they denied stewards negotiating rights and laid off 3,500 men.[14]

This signalled the beginnings of a more general attack upon workshop organisation. The dispute at Standard was instrumental in the collapse of the company as it failed to gain sufficient freedom to organise its production to meet competition and was regarded as a test case for redundancies throughout the industry. It was accompanied by the first attempts to undermine the gang system, reorganise payment towards measured day work, and by the beginnings of a diversification of production away from the old centres to avoid the restrictions associated with such things as the tool-room agreement. In general, it must be argued that these efforts failed to reduce the spread and power of workshop organisation; indeed, they served to reinforce its reach.

In the first place, the phase of automation which opened in 1956, like all similar phases, had ambiguous effects on skill. On the one hand, the complexity of transfer machines and the constant attention they required increased the sense of task skill and importance of those who worked them. On the other hand, because these machines reduced the 'margin of managerial uncertainty in work-load assessment and thus also . . . the area within which the effort bargain . . . can operate' they made the question of control over wage-rates, speed of working and work-loads even more acute. Second, automation enhanced fears of redundancy and although the expanding demand for cars did not bear out these anxieties, the issue reawakened memories of the 1930s and heightened car-worker militancy. From this moment the issue of redundancy was to form a constant locus of conflict that helped turn the industry into the archetypal strike-prone British industry; 1956 marked the first emergence of a national agitation over this issue. In the third place, it was after 1956 that the Coventry tool-room agreement began to be used as a standard of national comparison for the whole industry – a stranglehold that was not broken until 1971. Finally, there is a noticeable quickening of stewards' organisation after this date, so that, by the 1960s, peripheral factories like Halewood (originally established partly to escape steward influence) had become new centres of militancy.[15] But the major reason why workshop militancy was reinforced after the mid-1950s lay in the ultimate failure of the Conservative government to endorse a policy of industrial confrontation.

The Conservatives had returned to power in 1951 committed to industrial appeasement. Churchill's Minister of Labour, Sir Walter Monckton, was ordered '"to do my best to preserve industrial peace"', but by 1955 growing economic difficulties and some major industrial conflicts such as a national rail strike put pressure on the government to alter its economic and social priorities. It was urged that wage inflation be controlled by reducing social expenditure and attacking restrictive practices in the cause of productivity. The government toyed with abandoning its attachment to industrial peace. There were discussions in the cabinet about legislating against unofficial strikes by making strike ballots compulsory, and in the spring of 1956 the government decided to impose an incomes policy by holding down public-sector wages. As part of this, extensive discussions were held with industry over a period of nine months which resulted in an apparent agreement to resist increases in national expenditure and wages in return for a promise from employers to hold prices stable. The engineering employers were thus encouraged to resist a new wage claim as 'contrary to national policy' as well as representing a further squeeze on already reduced profit-margins.[16] By 1957 the engineering industry was merely the first in a long queue of pending wage claims which threatened to breach the government norm of 3 per cent. Thus, engineering employers saw this as the time to take a stand and a strike of engineers and shipbuilders began in March 1957. Within a few days, however, it was clear that the government was not willing to stand by its earlier tough words. Fears of an exchange crisis led the government to urge the employers to begin negotiations. A further signal of the government's willingness to buy industrial peace came with the 5 per cent pay award to railwaymen by the British Transport Board in defiance of the government's own guidelines. The engineering employers found themselves abandoned and a court of inquiry was established in return for an end to the strike. In the event the employers gained nothing. Their original demands had included an end to restraints upon productivity and long-term agreements at both local and national levels. Even though the court of inquiry generally supported the legitimacy of their argument, the employers failed to secure these demands and were forced to grant a 6½ per cent wage increase.[17]

This débâcle contained important political implications. It was the first time since the war that the government had contemplated abandoning the consensus policy of full employment and industrial peace, but it had backed down. During 1957 the hardliners in the Cabinet, led by Peter Thorneycroft, Chancellor of the Exchequer, were in the ascendency. The budget of 1957 stimulated a sharp recession and an argument ensued between those who wanted to use deflation to break the inflationary spiral and control wages and those who wished to avoid the confrontation with labour this implied. The hardliners lost and were forced to resign as Macmillan proclaimed his commitment to full employment and presided over a reflationary budget in 1958. At both the political and industrial levels, what Keith Middlemas has called the 'negative veto' of labour was fully revealed in 1957. The search now began for strategies to evade the impediments that industrial relations were seen to pose to economic growth. Before we discuss what those strategies were and their various fates, however, it is necessary to try and give content to the industrial practices that comprised this negative veto.[18]

The fundamental problem of British industrial relations was the obstacles they presented to effective economic management at both the local and national levels. The predominating characteristic of plant-level workshop bargaining reduced the significance and effect of national agreements and foreclosed the stabilising influence which trade-union organisation was supposed to foster. In the 1960s, it was found that trade-union membership in many (not all) occupational categories was an essential ancillary to sectionalist work-group action and solidarity. According to both the theory and ideology of trade unionism, this was the reverse of how class action should have been manifested and it underlay the sociological argument that class and political solidarities were eroding amongst the newly-affluent worker. Furthermore, in the context of full employment, the state's policy of crisis avoidance in industrial relations encouraged the development of particularist interest groups whose autonomous priorities bore no necessary relationship to those of national economic management. Thus, the initiative for determining the content and shape of industrial relations lay primarily at the local level, irrespective of what the state, the unions or the employers might wish. This hardly mattered while there was no pressing need to reorganise either the labour process or the broad lines of economic policy. Indeed, the very real advantage of this system – and the reason why managements were not necessarily disposed to challenge it – was that it could work effectively to maintain industrial peace and production. Standard Motors, for example, does not appear to have had a single strike during the era of 'relative autonomy' (1948-56). And the motor-car industry as a whole was marked by generally placid industrial relations until the later 1950s. Thus, as William Brown pointed out in his study of *Piecework Bargaining*, the growth of custom and practice was an essential part of the reciprocities of the work situation. Managers or foremen would assent to a certain procedure verbally, informally, or merely by not objecting, and it would thus be established as a custom and practice. Similarly, also, managers were often tacitly supportive of the closed shop, especially at times of full employment, because of the stabilising and disciplinary advantages it possessed. Even shop stewards came to be seen in this light.[19]

On a purely formal level, then, the operation of this system of industrial relations was perfectly compatible with managerial authority and, indeed, served to provide the co-operative basis upon which social relations were mediated. As industrial sociologists have demonstrated, this system did not contain any inherent political desire to question the legitimacy of managerial authority, although certain groups such as craftsmen were always much closer to this position than others. In addition, the demands and issues that mobilised work-place organisation and militancy were usually quite modest. As James Cronin has pointed out, the strike wave of 1957-62, which was composed of small-scale, work-place-based actions, revealed how 'the aims and expectations of working people were stable and restrained'. This was reflected in surveys which showed that workers were most concerned to influence issues immediately related to their job and had no pretensions to affect policies on pricing, profits or markets. Thus, if through this uncontrolled and *ad hoc* process of local conflict, compromise and co-operation there developed an increased sphere of worker influence and control over production, it was 'almost certainly by accident and certainly not by design'.[20]

In the final analysis, however, the intent and the dynamic of historical phenomena are two very different things. The important thing about this system of industrial relations was not so much the intent of the actors, about which there was no unanimity, but the fact that its practical operation composed a very real restraint and obstacle to the kinds of strategies that employers and ultimately the government wished to employ in the search for economic regeneration. The reasons for this lay not only in the failure of a largely local autonomous system to respond to central manipulation; nor did they lay merely in the fact that for a long time governments were unwilling to assault its obduracy with mass unemploynent. The reasons lay in the very complexity and denseness which characterised the content of restraints. This was recognised – indeed, it may have been exaggerated – by the Royal Commission on Industrial Relations (1965-8) which became known as the Donovan Commission. The Donovan Commission emphasised the inelasticity of restrictive practices and by use of selective examples (such as the cases of printing and shipbuilding) it argued that such restrictions had not been removed even during the depression but, in fact, had been confirmed as protective necessities. It was further argued that demand policies could do little to affect the pace of wage inflation because the process of wage determination was now so highly institutionalised both at the local and national levels that the reverberations of unemployment hardly extended beyond the sector where it was located. The same characteristics of inelasticity and denseness resulted from piece-work bargaining. Complex rules produced through informal negotiation by fragmented groups were governed by tenaciously applied custom and practice which drifted unguided by conscious will

> towards increasing worker control over work. It is evident, for instance, in the matter of the procedure to be followed in estimating and negotiating piecework values, that custom and practice rules tend to develop to restrict the freedom with which management selects operators to be work studied.[21]

It was very difficult to assess the precise effects of this system on productivity but there is little reason to doubt the wisdom of the time that the opportunities for more efficient ways of working were severely restrained. Naturally, there were other reasons for the marked inability of British capitalism to be as productive as its competitors. The lower level of capital investment per worker as compared to Germany, Japan and the United States reflected, in part, the division between financial and industrial capital referred to earlier. In addition, traditional markets for British goods discouraged long runs, and management was notably unenergetic in seeking new markets.[22] But, equally, it is clear that the social context of industrial relations is one major junction at the centre of a web of historically based structures, policies and attitudes that condition the performance of the economy. It is for this reason that the ideology of monetarist Conservatism emphasised so strongly the necessity of high unemployment and recession as the price to be paid by a country that had 'lived beyond its means' for so long. As Mrs Thatcher constantly insisted, it was social behaviour that needed to change. In any case, by the 1960s there was wide agreement that the restrictions of the system imposed large losses of productivity. And this impression has been confirmed by careful empirical studies of the effects upon production of the pattern of strike activity that characterised this system of industrial relations.

By some measurements – numbers of worker days lost, for example – Britain did not appear particularly strike-prone in the 1960s. But the structure of strikes and their concentrated location in industries of strategic significance to the national economy made them of central importance for economic management. Large plants were particularly vulnerable to strike activity and this tended to induce diseconomies of scale. In plants employing more than 5,000 people Britain lost twice as many days through strikes as the United States and twenty times as many as Germany. Indeed, it would appear that official statistics underestimated the continual disruption caused by strikes by a factor of six. In 1976 alone, British Leyland had 700 strikes which were too short to be recorded in the official statistics. It is quite impossible to argue that such a record was of little consequence for productivity. Indeed, it has been estimated, again in comparison with the United States and Germany, that the productivity differential resulting from strikes and restrictive practices averaged around 30 per cent. In the motor-car industry it has been firmly established that the structure and pattern of labour relations was the greatest single cause of low production and competitive inadequacies. And a survey of 100 companies in different sectors also came to the conclusion that 'behavioural differences do seem to be a significant cause of lower productivity in the UK'.[23]

In the 1950s and 1960s four broad aspects of production relations came to be identified as particular restraints upon economic management. The first was the way local bargaining created a wages drift that was unresponsive to national norms and agreements. The Coventry toolroom agreement was the most famous example of this displacement of wage determination from the national to the local centres. Originally signed in 1941 as an attempt by employers to stop labour-poaching, the employers and union met monthly to agree on average prices that should form the basis of tool-makers' rates. The Humber strike in 1946 established the agreement as the standard for piece negotiations elsewhere and it came to be used by stewards throughout the Midlands to push up wage-levels. Indeed, in Coventry by the mid-1960s two-thirds of the wage increase since 1945 was due to this local bargaining and by the late 1960s it had become the standard on which the demand for parity for all car-workers was based. Wages drift of this kind was implicit in the industrial relations system. In the early 1950s, overtime bans in Manchester and Newcastle engineering shops prefigured the pattern of the 1960s when national agreements were surpassed by local actions to secure advances. Nor was the phenomenon confined to engineering. The wages structure of the docks increasingly came to depend upon local bonuses and special payments. In 1947, bonuses and overtime added 50 per cent to the basic rate; by 1967, this had risen to 300 per cent. But this also served to reinforce the importance of restrictive practices because bonuses, in particular, depended upon the myriad of customs and practices established for the bewildering variations in the detail of the work. Thus, 'the main preoccupation of the men was to manipulate the bonus system to give a *consistently* high surplus'. We should note in passing that it was this entanglement of wage structure and custom and practice that explained the hostility of dockers to decasualisation which threatened to do away with the traditional means of maintaining high wages.[24]

Wages drift also rested upon a second set of restraints to economic management: the capturing of control over piece-rates. As is well known, piece-work was traditionally seen as ideally suited to managerial control over labour. But this was true only when a reserve pool of labour exerted a downward pressure on rates, enabling them to be determined by management. In the 1950s and 1960s neither of these conditions existed. Mutuality of rate-determination was firmly established during the war years and efforts to remove it in the late 1940s and early 1950s were half-hearted and unsuccessful. A week long sit-in strike at De Havilland in April 1950, for example, secured a mutual procedure for timing and where no agreement could be reached provided for a special make-up bonus. By the 1960s, workers virtually made the running on rates and, paradoxically, the Procedure of 1922 (which allowed for adjustments if a job altered) was transformed from its original design of allowing employers wage flexibility to allowing workers the excuse to push up rates. Thus, as Hugh Scanlon pointed out in 1967, the engineers fight to retain piece-work ' 'because with piece work you have the man on the shop floor determining how much effort he will give for a given amount of money' ". Precisely the same point had been made by *Metal Worker* in 1948 when it contrasted American with British engineering. In Britain 'by relating wages to productivity (even partially) they give the lads on the job control over the extent of their exploitation'. Thus, the effort bargain was controlled by mutual determination and surrounded by customs and practices that further impeded the ability of management to secure a firm grasp upon the relationship of the wage to output. As a consequence, by the late 1960s, piece-systems of wage payment over large swathes of industry were in direct contradiction to the imperatives of productivity. The scientific determination of rates had been subordinated to the manipulation of rates to secure a decent wage. Unsurprisingly, there was growing sentiment amongst employers for a return to time-based wages.[25]

A third problem of social relations was that the strike weapon was progressively used for more radical aims. As Cronin has suggested, the belief of the 1950s and 1960s that growing affluence was dissolving 'class' militancy was based upon the mistaken assumption that changing material conditions and social structures were incompatible with class consciousness. The strike wave of 1968-72 dispelled those illusions as the traditional militancy of industrial workers spilled over to white-collar groups who experienced a rapid rise in union membership and began to exhibit tendencies to workshop organisation and control. In addition, the scale and content of strike demands tended to change. Whereas the strike pattern of 1960-8 was essentially a localist, shop-floor movement, between 1968 and 1972 industry-wide stoppages and politically oriented strikes predominated as workers acted to defend themselves against inflationary price-rises by demanding large wage claims. And, finally, there were indications that having firmly established itself as the main determinant of shop-floor conditions, workshop organisation was now beginning to expand its reach. Surveys revealed considerable support amongst stewards for extending the scope of their interest beyond wages to include finance and discipline. Although this was not a totally new phenomenon, it occurred within a social and political context that served to encourage and legitimate such aspirations. Some union leaders, such as Jack Jones, were actively engaged in democratising their own union structures and discussing issues of industrial democracy. Thus, 'workers are participating more deeply in a wider range of managerial decisions than used to be the case. The growing, if not yet clearly articulated demand for greater personal participation . . . seems likely to articulate this trend.'[26] The motor-car industry, where this development has been most thoroughly studied, provides a concrete illustration of this expansion of militancy from a purely economic, shop-floor phenomenon to one that shaded into politics.

Pre-war disputes were likely to be focused around resistance to speed-ups. After 1945, however, conflict was more commonly caused by the internal structure of the wage and the work-load, and, until the mid-1970s, were more likely to be offensive than defensive in character. These developments seemed to mirror changes in the total pattern of strike activity. Thus, by the mid-1960s strikes over 'working arrangements, rules and discipline' composed 33 per cent of all strikes as compared to 15 per cent before the Second World War. Strikes over managerial-control issues grew from 3 per cent of days lost in 1958-61 to 15 per cent in 1960-64. Turner, Clack and Roberts pointed to the emergence of two central motivations for strike activity under conditions of full employment: that wages should be fair in comparative terms, and that workers were increasingly willing to assert their property rights in a job. It is the latter we are concerned to discuss here. The key significance of this was not of course its newness: it had always been an element in craft consciousness, it was the motivation behind demarcation disputes, and there are traces of its assertion by less-skilled workers in the late nineteenth century. What was peculiar about the 1950s and 1960s was the way it shifted beyond the local workshop level to become associated with national militancy. This was particularly the case in the late 1960s when, as Cronin noted, resistance to redundancy was one manifestation of an enhanced sense of workers' rights and dignities that characterised the strike-wave of 1968-72.[27]

In truth, the issue of redundancy had been a continuous aspect of work-place militancy since the war, but the reappearance of trade-cycle insecurity in the mid-1950s reactivated the consciousness of the Depression and brought the issue to the fore as an increasingly important issue of militancy. In 1951, for example, Austin workers had struck over the redundancies of 51 workers and secured the right of consultation with stewards over lay-offs associated with steel shortages. By 1957, the National Committee of the AEU had passed a resolution directing the executive to secure a national agreement whereby 'threatened redundancy in any establishment is resolved by maintaining all workers in their employment until alternative work is found for them, and the introduction of a sharing of work with the guaranteed week applying'. No effort seems to have been made to implement this resolution, but at the local level it may have legitimised efforts to secure mutuality over redundancy decisions at Hoover and Rootes in 1960, Pressed Steel, Ford and Rootes in 1961 and again at Ford in 1962.[28]

The drive to subject redundancy to the same sort of mutual negotiation that characterised piece-rates was almost certainly not accompanied by the same success. In the 1950s and early 1960s, the AEU seemed very reluctant to support local efforts to enforce consultation over the issue, perhaps because it would add yet another reinforcement to steward authority. But it was upon this history of local action that the national prominence of the issue rested in the 1960s and 1970s, and a partial (and temporary) victory for the tradition was secured in the mid-1960s and mid-1970s when Parliament passed laws that limited and defined employers rights to declare redundancies.

The fourth restraint of social relations that of restrictive practices – is familiar enough and we do not need to expound upon it here, except to make some fairly simple points. It is obvious that restrictive practices were not a peculiar condition of post-1945 industrial relations but were deeply entrenched in the historical consciousness and practice of employer-worker relations. As various studies spanning the period from the 1930s to the 1960s showed, the same practices tended to be repeated again and again.[29] Although they were not peculiar to Britain, it is likely that restrictive practices formed a more continuous strategy of resistance to managerial control than elsewhere and their greater visibility in Britain reflected their emblematic representation of social relations generally. The fact was that by the 1960s restrictive practices were to be found everywhere in industry, they were not confined to the craft workers but were bolstered by the myriad of customs and practices that honeycombed most manual occupations. To illustrate this and to indicate, also, the practical effects of their restraints upon management we can take the case of the docks.

In the London docks, for example, it was calculated in 1968 that one-third of working hours were lost to such restrictive practices as the continuity rule which established the principle of one job per gang. Originally introduced as an employers' rule in 1944 to force gangs to remain on unattractive jobs, by 1967 it had become the 'dockers' most treasured possession' as the definition of a job was drawn tighter and tighter until transfer from one job to another during the same work period was banned. Thus, in one case, four cars were carried to North Africa lashed to a hatch cover even though there was a half-empty hold available. Stacking them in the hold would have meant paying a full day's work to a gang and keeping the ship in port an extra day because the half-empty hold had been packed by a different gang. Like the 'welt' in Liverpool, where half a gang worked one hour whilst the other half rested in order to secure the double bonus for overtime, such restrictive practices had long lost their original protective function and had become a means by which the highest price could be secured in day-to-day bargaining. The effects on productivity of such practices were hard to quantify, but it was calculated that, whereas in 1900 a gang of 18 discharged 1000 bales of cotton per day, by 1964 a gang of 24 averaged 500 bales a day – and this with superior equipment. The development of the containerisation of goods threatened to undermine these impediments to cheaper production. Mechanised handling permitted individual instead of gang working, depots were not tied to the place of debarkation and, therefore, unorganised labour far from the unionised port cities could be employed. In order to rationalise dockwork, however, it was necessary to invoke the aid of the state in the form of the Devlin Inquiry which, after protracted negotiations with local and national union organisations, successfully rationalised industrial relations in the docks.[30]

The State and Production Relations

The Devlin Inquiry epitomised the active interventionism that by the late 1960s had come to characterise the state's response to the problem of industrial relations. Until the late 1960s the dominant strategy of those efforts primarily followed the voluntarist approach epitomised by the Donovan Commission (1965-8) whose detailed investigations and researches were largely responsible for informed discussion of industrial relations but whose recommendations firmly endorsed the voluntary course of reform. At this point the role of the government was mainly confined to stimulating change partly through the exhoratory devices of income policies and indicative planning and partly through the jaw-boning of tripartite bodies like the National Economic Development Council. As it became clear, however, that the results of voluntarism were the opposite of what had been intended, the state began to assume a more active posture. Although these two phases were never completely separate strategies either in chronology or concept, they do serve as convenient principles around which the dynamic of events may be understood. As examples of the way the strategies of voluntarism created the contradictions that led to the more interventionist phase, we may examine the cases of measured day work and productivity bargaining.

Measured day work is a form of time-wages which fixes an hourly rate on the basis of performance standards established by work measurement techniques. It represents an attempt to combine payment by results with standardised time-wages. The idea was developed in the 1930s, probably as a variant of Bedaux, and the first British scheme appeared in 1946. But apart from a flourish of activity in the mid-1950s (the most significant being its adoption by Vauxhall motors in 1956) the method did not gain much popularity until the late 1960s. The key adoption was the attempt of the National Coal Board to rationalise production through the National Power Loading Agreement of 1966 after which the system rapidly spread through shipbuilding and engineering and, under the stimulus of Devlin, the docks. Ford – which had never been on piece-rates – was the first of the big motor-car companies to adopt the system in 1967, and a year later British Leyland began an extended effort to introduce it which finally achieved success in 1971-2.[31]

There was nothing new to the purposes or methods of measured day work. Many of its elements were prefigured in the premium bonus system and even its effects – in mining for example – echoed earlier changes in work organisation. The objective of measured day work was to shift the initiative for piece-work bargaining and its related customs and structures away from the work-place, which it promised to achieve in three ways. First, an essential part of the system was the reorganisation of job specifications, a regrading of jobs to fewer categories and the establishment of managerially determined standards of job performance. By these means wages drift would be brought under control and management would secure greater flexibility in manning and setting production quotas. In the car industry, as in the docks, job property rights were eroded by the creation of categories of 'floaters' who could be moved from location to location as they were needed. Thus, in theory, measured day work brought work-loads more under the control of management, and since its details varied from factory to factory it avoided the comparability of earnings under the tool-room agreement that had been a major cause of wages drift. In the mines more continuous working and the expansion of shift work to replace overtime were among the results of measured day work. The old double day shifts were replaced by continuous eight-hour shifts which meant the end of traditional weekend leisure time.[32]

Second, like all systems of direct control by management, an increased managerial supervision followed the adoption of the system. In the North Derbyshire mines, the ratio of officials to workers declined from 1:12 to 1:9.5, and at Chrysler the one foreman per four or five sections under piece-work was replaced by a one-to-one ratio. Third, and as a partial consequence, the system struck at the role of the shop stewards by removing the need for constant bargaining over rates and times. Wages, standards and conditions were now negotiated once a year and disputes over the working of grading systems would be handled by union officials, or, as in the case of the 1967 Ford grading system, by a computer that held the information and results of previous negotiations. The potential of the system aimed at the very heart of the informal structures of industrial relations. Negotiations on measured day work occurred at the factory level, the gang system lost its relevance and the functions of the ordinary stewards were considerably reduced.[33]

But, as this implies, measured day work in the factories (the case of mining was different) also aimed to integrate the factory level of workshop organisation into a restructured industrial relations. The concentration of negotiations at the factory, rather than the gang, level enhanced the role of both senior stewards and union officials in the process. It was partly because of this that surveys noted an increasing acceptance of stewards by management between 1966 and 1972, a concurrent decline in the trust of stewards by workers, and an increase in the importance of foremen in dealing with grievances. It is likely that the growing popularity of schemes for 'participation' during this period was also related to the spread of the system.[34]

The initial effects of measured day work were ambiguous. In order to persuade the work-force to accept the system, management had to offer very large increases in wages and guarantees of stable earnings. The latter was, perhaps, the greatest attraction of measured day work to the worker because it ended the chaotic fluctuations of piece-wages which could vary as much as 100 per cent for the same job. In the docks, the difficulties involved in translating the value of bonuses into weekly wages caused the greatest difficulties in the implementation of the Devlin recommendations. More importantly, it is clear that the strikes and suspicion that accompanied the introduction of measured day work induced management to refrain from insisting upon the full implications of the system. Although the stewards in the motor-car industry were sure that measured day work implied a speed-up, the initial work-loads were so low that it became known as 'leisured day work'. But, in addition, where mutuality could be extended to mobility, job evaluation and overtime, the system could be controlled and workshop organisation maintained. It would seem that where mutuality was already well established this was achieved. Thus, at Longbridge, extending mutuality to manning levels now became the objective in order

> to man the tracks to the highest conditions . . . and we carried over from the piece work days the control we had got into standard day work. We did this on the basis of inclusion in our agreements of a measure of mutuality which whilst on the surface it appeared to be not very great . . . was sufficient for us to exercise the same sort of control and protect workers by ensuring each track was manned to a reasonable level.[35]

The ambiguities of measured day work may have extended even further. It tended to reinforce fears of redundancy, encourage the stewards to expand the range of bargaining issues, and stimulate solidarity. Thus, in the coal industry, the NPLA established national wage and manning standards which shifted the focus of bargaining from local anomalies to national standards and demanded that regional divisions be transcended. By the early 1970s it was obvious that the NPLA had failed in its object of modernising industrial relations in the coal industry. Indeed, a detailed study of this issue argued that 'it is not too much to say that the NPLA transformed work relations, intensified local industrial conflict, reduced productivity, and provided the basis for a national political unity which would defeat a government [in 1974]'. In motor-cars the compression of differentials between skilled and unskilled forced a diminution of group sectionalism which was reinforced by the replacement of gang-based piece-work with factory-level negotiation. Measured day work thus fed into a group of forces that stimulated the emergence of the national parity issue which culminated in the nine-week strike at Ford in 1971.[36]

These ambiguities dominated the early years of measured day work. Workshop organisation and militancy were neither undermined nor thoroughly integrated. In fact, measured day work had added its mite to the intractability of industrial relations. These ambiguities did not begin to be resolved until the mid-1970s when the system began to be applied more rigorously in the motor-car and engineering industries. But the effects of measured day work in accentuating the problem of industrial relations were paralleled by the second of the voluntarist strategies employed during the 1960s – productivity bargaining.

The success of the productivity agreements at the Fawley oil refinery in 1960 – when a 40 per cent increase in pay was bargained for more efficient working practices – established productivity bargaining as an important method of overcoming the restraints of workshop organisation without souring industrial relations. By 1969 something like 5 million workers were covered by such schemes. But it would seem that Fawley was very much an exception to the normal operation of productivity deals in British industry. A true productivity agreement involves a measure of buying out of restrictive practices, the negotiated creation of more efficient means of organising production, and job security for those workers who remain. British productivity agreements never attained these virtues and, therefore, never succeeded in overcoming the restraints that necessitated them in the first place. Ironically, this contradiction was reinforced by government incomes policies in the mid-1960s which were designed, in part, to stimulate productivity bargaining by linking wage increases beyond a flat norm to productivity improvements. But in the context of full employment and a localist work-group-oriented bargaining system, the actual operation of this was the reverse of what was intended. Wage inflation was accentuated as management used increased productivity as the excuse to yield to group pressure and break the norms. William Brown found that very little piece-work wages drift in the late 1960s could be related to increased productivity. Indeed, the association of productivity bargaining with the threatening strategy of measured day work and with the increased redundancies of 1968-72, stiffened resistance to the idea. And, finally, productivity bargaining widened the areas of negotiation, it further legitimated expanded notions of joint regulation and consultation and, thus, fuelled militancy over such issues as redundancy and the limits to managerial rights generally.[37]

The direct relationship between incomes policies and productivity bargaining was but one manifestation of a deepening involvement by the government in the quagmire of industrial relations. This trend to increased interventionism was demonstrated by the shifting nature of income policies. Until the early 1960s, an incomes policy was viewed as a temporary device to meeting passing difficulties – as it had between 1948-50 when the Labour government administered a highly successful wage-restraint agreement with the unions. By the early 1960s, however, incomes policy emerged as essential to government's efforts at economic management by indicative planning, whose success required the control of wage inflation. Thus, in 1961 a National Incomes Commission was established a pay-pause introduced for workers in government and guiding-light wage norms identified for other workers. Basically the same voluntarist policy was followed by the Labour government from 1964-6 as part of the effort to 'talk up' economic growth. In this attempt to mobilise voluntary support for Labour's national plan, incomes policy was absolutely critical. Given the actual rate of growth in the economy, wages should have increased by no more than 2-3 per cent per year; in fact, the actual rate of growth in the early 1960s was around 7-8 per cent. In the summer of 1966, however, the eruption of a major balance-of-payments crisis sounded the death knell of the national plan and voluntary incomes policy. A statutory wage freeze was imposed which successfully forced net earnings down 1.1 per cent in 1966-7, and legislation in 1967 and 1968 enormously increased government power over wages and, less successfully, over prices.[38]

By this time, however, two things had happened. First, the economic situation had deteriorated alarmingly. Devaluation in 1967 and the savage deflation of 1967-9 made the question of wage restraint and industrial relations even more pressing. It was no longer possible to envisage a gradual and easy road to industrial relations reform and, second, these economic policies drove a thickening wedge between the political and industrial wings of the labour movement. The TUC had passively opposed the 1967 Prices and Incomes Bill, more trade-union members contracted out of the political levy in 1966 and 1967 than at any time since 1927, and the government began to suffer alarming losses in local-council and by-elections, including such strongholds as Walthamstow West which had returned Labour members – including Clement Attlee – since 1918. Significantly enough, it is from this point that the secular decline of the Labour vote really begins to be noted. The most immediate result of this crisis however, was the strike-wave of 1968-72.[39]

As we have already noted, the distinctive features of this strike-wave went beyond its economic dimension as a reaction to bottled-up wage claims to include the rapid increase in unionisation, the spread of industrial militancy to white-collar workers, and the expansion of demands to such things as job rights and redundancy. This strike-wave revealed that the problem of industrial relations was becoming more intractable at a time when economic difficulties made worker demands even more critical. Labour costs as a percentage of consumer price increases rose from 1.2 per cent in 1967-8 to 11 per cent by 1973-4 and it has been argued that this triggered a sharp profits squeeze. In addition, a growing closeness between workshop organisation and official trade-union structures and a genuine distaste for the policies of both the Labour government and then those of the Selsdon-man phase of the Heath government (1970-72) led the trade unions to put themselves at the head of this militancy. This conjunction was particularly serious for Labour and it forced the revoking of statutory incomes policy in 1969 which released a further wave of pent-up wage claims and resulted in very high settlements. A final consequence of this chain of events was that industrial conflict and relations became more politicised. In part this was a direct result of government policy as it responded to the failure of incomes policies. The coincidence of the seamen's strike and financial crisis of 1966 led Harold Wilson to speak of a small knot of politically motivated men holding the country to ransom. And by 1969 the Labour government had transformed strikes and industrial relations from a relatively minor public concern into the major political issue of the day, linked in the public mind with the critical question of the balance of payments.[40]

All of this seemed to suggest the need for a different kind of interventionism. Incomes policies seemed to stimulate militancy as their initial period of successful restraint was followed by a wages explosion, and there were growing doubts about their efficacy in conditions of full employment. But even if they could be made to work there was seldom time for their reforming potential to take effect before the intrusion of fiscal crises – as in 1967 – threw them off course. The response of the Labour government to the evident failure of voluntarist or statutory incomes policies was to initiate a further shift towards an interventionist strategy when it proposed to change the law on industrial relations. Rejecting the voluntarist recommendations of the Donovan

Commission, the government's white paper, *In Place of Strife* (1968), laid out a new legal basis for collective bargaining and production relations. The trade unions were offered certain guarantees of collective-bargaining rights in return for legal restraints upon industrial action and greater powers of government intercession. The principles underlying these proposals were more radical than the precise details, for they represented an attempt to dissolve the traditional voluntarism both of free collective bargaining and of the relationship between the state and the trade unions. The central target of the proposed changes was the chaotic structures of workshop bargaining. It aimed to integrate those structures into the official industrial relations system by endowing trade unions with greater legal responsibilities and by granting the state rights to intervene in disputes.

The result, however, was to complete the process of alienation between the political and industrial wings of the Labour movement. The trade-union leadership was forced into opposition by the intense pressure from their membership who tended to see *In Place of Strife* as coherent with management's increasing effort to gain control over work-place discipline. Thus, the negotiating package proposed by Ford management in 1969 reflected the principles of the white paper. Like the government proposals, it imposed penalty clauses for unconstitutional action and required a cooling-off period before a strike could begin. Legal reform was seen to go hand in hand with the efforts by management to undercut and destroy workshop organisation and militancy. *In Place of Strife* was withdrawn, but its significance lay in the way it announced the full entrance of the state into the question of industrial relations, and opened the political possibility of using the law to address the intractable social restraints upon economic management.[41]

This was a precedent willingly adopted by the Conservative government of Edward Heath. There had long been a minority sentiment within the Conservative Party for reforming trade-union law. As early as 1958 a group of Conservative lawyers had argued in *A Giant's Strength* that a new body of law was needed to regulate union power and responsibility. In this spirit, Edward Heath's Industrial Relations Act of 1971 represented an attempt to create a coherent legal framework of industrial relations which included the legal enforceability of collective agreements and the codification of rights and obligations. The protections given to the unions were conditional upon their legal behaviour and the traditional weapons of industrial action were subject to sharp limitations. Restrictions were placed upon the closed shop; a range of unfair industrial practices were defined which made picketing and inducements to breach of contract actionable; the registrar of Friendly Societies was provided with greater supervisory powers over trade-union rules; and the government was granted the right to proscribe strikes considered to be injurious to the national economy.[42]

The Industrial Relations Act represented a decisive reversal of the liberalising tradition of most post-1875 statutes on labour law. It should be noted, however, that the Act built upon a contemporary revival of the restrictive tradition which had always existed in the case law of industrial relations. The Torquay Hotel case of 1969, for example, had found unions liable for secondary breach of contract, and the Act generalised this decision by defining such actions as an unfair industrial practice which made unions subject to prosecution. Similarly, since the early 1960s judges had increasingly adopted a stiffer attitude toward picketing, upholding the tight limits imposed by the police and excluding secondary picketing from the protection of section 5 of the Trades Disputes Act of 1906. The Industrial Relations Act endorsed those rulings and formalised in the statute law the insecurities that already existed in the case law on picketing. Thus, a more vigorous interpretation of the law was encouraged which successfully returned the right to picket back to the limits of *R* v *Hibbert* (1867) and *Lyons* v *Wilkins* (1896) by allowing only the right to communicate information, and not to persuade peacefully.[43] It was hardly surprising that from the early 1970s, picketing tended to become a much more explosive, violence-prone action in British industrial relations.

The major failing of the Industrial Relations Act was that it tried to force a sweeping reorientation of the law in the face of the realities of work-place social relations and the interests of its participants. There was no supporting consensus amongst employers. Indeed, many employers appreciated, for example, the stabilising advantages of the closed shop (which the Act made more difficult to establish) and had encouraged its spread in the late 1960s. Even those who were inclined to favour legislation were soon appraised of its unfortunate consequences as long as workshop organisation remained powerful and self-confident. Similarly, the trade unions were caught by the ambiguities of an Act which, on the one hand, protected the rights of the individual worker over the collectivity and, on the other, insisted upon a strict accountability of officials for the behaviour of their members – the old question of representative action. Finally, in very obvious ways, the Act alienated – and further politicised – workshop militants who stood to lose most by its attempt to shackle industrial action. This was a most inappropriate time to try to formalise the restrictive tradition of case law because it guaranteed a collision between work-place militancy and the law. What was, perhaps, quite remarkable was that labour unequivocally prevailed in this contest.

The new law was discredited by its failure to handle the rash of disputes that were referred to the courts and by the refusal of the unions to co-operate with its provisions. The decisions of the Industrial Relations Court – established to administer the law – were generally ignored, and with few exceptions the unions refused to comply with the registration procedures of the Act. The intervention of the law to resolve the conflict over containerisation in the docks provided the clearest demonstration of the law's ineffectiveness. In order to avert a national stoppage over the findings of the Court, the government conspired in the evasion of its own Act by contriving the intervention of an obscure functionary, the Official Solicitor, to remove the cause of contention.[44] The alienation of the unions was complete. After the government's U-turn in 1973 when it attempted to rebuild tripartite co-operation, the unions refused to cooperate and the government was finally shipwrecked on the miners' strike of 1973-4.

Thus, the fate of both the Wilson and Heath governments had been essentially determined by their failure to handle effectively industrial relations. Heath's attempt at 'free-market' policies between 1970 and 1973, combined with repressive legal intervention, had merely reinforced the restraints of industrial relations. The density and influence of shop stewards' organisation continued to increase; the closed shop showed no signs of withering away, and there were few effects on union organisation. Equally, collective bargaining was no more under control than it had been; individual wage settlements reached enormous proportions during the free-market phase; industrial militancy forced the rescue of lame-duck industries like Clyde shipbuilding; and new tactics of militancy such as the flying mass-pickets reduced the policing of picketing to a shambles. Industrial relations had been drawn into the very heart of politics and the election of February 1974 was essentially a referendum on the question as to who could best resolve the conundrum that industrial relations posed for economic regeneration.

The Failure of Labourism

Labour's bare win in the election of February 1974 reflected the negative judgement that they might deal with industrial relations more constructively than the Conservatives. And there were some grounds for thinking that this time Labour might prove to reconcile economic management with the restraints of industrial relations. Following the defeat of 1970, a considerable rethinking of Labour policies had occurred. Influential intellectuals like Stuart Hall and reflective politicans like Tony Benn allied with the radically-minded union leaders Hugh Scanlon and Jack Jones in an effort to forge policies that would avoid the mistakes of 1964-70. Both Scanlon and Jones possessed a background of shop-floor activism and they encouraged the development of policies that aimed to reform industrial relations by addressing the basic issue of power. Instead of using the trade-union power as a negative veto on local and national economic policy, it was argued that Labourite socialism should aim to transform that power into active participation through the expansion of industrial democracy and accountability.[45] This was to be achieved through a 'social contract' between government and the trade unions.

The stated intent of the Labour Party's programme in 1974 to cause an 'irreversible shift of power and wealth towards working people' was not simply campaign rhetoric. It was the aim and purpose of the major policy proposals that had been formulated between 1970 and 1973. At the national level, trade unions were to be accorded a policy-making partnership through participation in tripartite commissions such as the Manpower Services Commission and the Advisory, Conciliation and Arbitration Service. At the local level, a scheme of industrial democracy would formalise the inroads into managerial authority already achieved by informal workshop action. Collective rights that had been secured by local initiatives were to be given statutory recognition. Economic modernisation was to be forced by new agencies of state intervention. The social contract represented a recognition that the problem of economic management was largely a problem of social relations. The previous ten years had demonstrated that as long as the post-war consensus of full employment and state-supported welfarism was assumed, reform of the economy was impossible without reform of industrial relations. In retrospect, it is clear that the social contract was an attempt to redefine the boundaries of that consensus. Thus, wage restraint was the trade-union contribution to the bargain, but wage restraint was the *quid pro quo* for genuine social reform and not, as it had been in the past, merely a device to fight inflation. At the heart of the idea of the social contract lay the formalisation of the power labour had already acquired through the dynamic of social relations of production. In reality, of course, the social contract was both more complicated than that and its effects more ambiguous, but the stark contrast between its promise and results has tended to divert attention away from the very real challenge that it posed to traditional authority and power relations. This contrast, of course, only accentuates the difficulties of writing a balanced history of the social contract, but there are three areas that would seem to be particularly worthy of attention.

In the first place, the social contract seems to have given a considerable stimulus to the officialisation of the shop stewards' movement. The integration of the stewards was one of the recommendations of the Donovan Commission and, as we have seen, it was implicit in such productivity-oriented strategies as measured day work. Two things seem to have happened in the 1970s: first, the extension of stewards' organisation in those industries (like public service) where it had not existed before; and, second, the transformation of stewards into a quasi-official stratum between the work-force and the union. By the late 1970s, a survey of the changing contours of industrial relations found that it was no longer possible to speak of an 'informal' system of industrial relations. There had been a major transformation from multi-employer bargaining to single-employer agreements covering one or more factories in an industry. This process, stimulated by government intervention, had occurred largely since the early 1970s and, in its turn, had decisively altered the role and place of the shop stewards. Stewards now were more likely to be full-time: 50 per cent of such positions had been created since 1972 and an equivalent percentage of surveyed establishments had formalised their relationship with stewards since that date. Similarly, there had been a very large increase in joint consultation committees.[46] Stewards were no longer separated from the formal negotiating arrangements but increasingly had become 'the principal negotiators and guarantors of clear-cut factory agreements and procedures'. It is possible that this helped to ensure the relative success of the wage-restraint side of the social contract. As Richard Hyman has pointed out, the limited opposition to pay controls until the eruption of mass unemployment in 1979 owed much 'to the new ability of national union leaders to win the backing of major conveners and these in turn to deliver the acquiesence of their own work-place organisations'. On the other hand, this did not imply a new spirit of co-operation; a later study found that

> industrial relations appeared still to be regarded as a zero sum game with only very limited opportunities for mutual benefit. . . . The

> younger stewards (in particular) . . . were most clearly separate from management in attitude and in their desire for change in the pattern of ownership and control of the industrial system. In spite of practical cooperation and the organized steward structure and the involvement of the steward in effective managerial decision making, the stewards remain essentially the representatives of the shop floor, attempting to maintain constraints on the managerial use of labour as a factor of production.[47]

Nevertheless, it is probable that the integration of the older, senior stewards facilitated the attack upon steward organisation that began in earnest in the late 1970s.

The second aspect of the social contract that addressed social relations was the commitment to proposals for some scheme of industrial democracy through the appointment of worker directors to boards of management. Although the Labour Party manifesto had promised legislation on industrial democracy, there was considerable unease at this proposal both within and without the labour movement. But the influence of Jack Jones – who had begun to press the idea in the late 1960s – ensured the appointment of a commission on industrial democracy headed by Alan Bullock in 1974. Although the recommendations of the Bullock Commission were relatively mild, they were received with intense opposition from industry. Industrial democracy was of key significance if the social contract was to work, for it represented – and was so justified by Bullock – an enlargement of democratic rights of citizenship into the area of economic decision-making that paralleled the expansion of the political franchise in the nineteenth century. The case for industrial democracy, however, encountered two impediments.

First, there was a powerful body of opinion within the labour movement that dissented from the extension of these rights into enterprise policy. Opposition was articulated by an unholy alliance between advocates of a narrow, economist definition of trade unionism, like Frank Chapple, and fractions of the extreme left who feared the class-collaborationist overtones of industrial democracy. The resistance was largely based upon the artificial separation between politics and economics that has traditionally pervaded Labourist socialism; but it is arguable that this distinction had become inappropriate, for the problem of politics was defined by the social-relations context of economics. Industrial democracy was relevant because it legitimised the implications that lay beneath the gains of the informal system. Specifically, it legitimised the notion that bargaining rights could be extended beyond wages to include other aspects of management decisions and policy.[48]

This raised the second problem. It was essentially irrelevant that Bullock's proposals for worker directors (elected by trade unions and in a minority on the directing boards) were considerably less than had existed since the late 1940s in other capitalist countries – most notably West Germany. The issue was not the compatibility or otherwise of these schemes within capitalist social relations: the point was the context of the British experience. Industrial democracy was not proposed in a context where the labour movement was in a weakened, malleable state. To the contrary, it was, perhaps, at the height of its political and industrial power. In addition, although it was never expressed in this way, industrial democracy could be seen to legitimate the historical tradition of work-place action and autonomy whose dynamic had made the question of managerial power and prerogative a constant problem. In this context, industrial democracy touched (however indirectly) the heart of social relations as relations of power and authority. The encroachments of the informal system of industrial relations were localist, transient, and received no institutional representation in politics or the wider culture and to that extent they presented no generalised challenge to conventional power and authority relationships. But a statutory scheme of industrial democracy could alter the political calculus of these relationships. It would raise the notion that consent in industry could be secured by altered power and authority relations; it would place these matters on the political agenda; and it would establish the precedent that social relations of production were open to political change and reordering.[49]

There was a third aspect of the social contract which possessed similar implications: the statutory expansion of collective-bargaining rights. Much of the initial legislative programme of the Labour government was devoted to trade-union-supported measures of social reform. In what may come to be regarded as a quite remarkable burst of reforming legislation, the government repealed the Industrial Relations Act, passed a new Trade Union Act, an Employment Protection Act, legislated on equal pay and sexual equality, and established a large number of trade-union-influenced 'quangos' to regulate and intervene in the labour market and industrial relations. It was, perhaps, in this area that Labour came closest to fulfilling its promise to achieve a shift in wealth and power towards working people. This was particularly the case with the Trade Union and Labour Relations Act and the Employment Protection Act which together redefined the legal status and collective-bargaining rights of the unions.

The Employment Protection Act was especially significant, for it embodied in legislation many of the issues that had mobilised workplace militancy over the previous two decades. Redundancy was now brought within the scope of collective bargaining. Employers were obliged to consult with trade unions over lay-offs, to disclose relevant information and to negotiate alternatives. The Act also established industrial tribunals to which appeal against various managerial decisions on dismissal, for example, could be made. It would be unwise to exaggerate the scope of these measures: collective bargaining was not extended to pricing or investment policies; the obligations to disclosure were not backed up by legal penalities for failures to comply. Equally, however, it would also be a mistake to underestimate their potential significance as legitimising a redefinition of managerial prerogatives. This was one of the few times that labour law was specifically biased towards a reordering of managerial authority. To find adequate parallels it is necessary to go back to the emergency legislation of the War years. The Employment Protection Act addressed itself to formalising and extending bargaining rights that represented 'the substantive aspirations which have emerged through the spontaneous growth of workplace bargaining since the 1960s'. It was this connection, of course, not the legislation itself, that distinguished such measures in Britain from similar reforms elsewhere.[50]

However, these reforms were destined to have a very short half-life; their advancement was conditional upon a self-confident and assertive labour movement and, as the economic and political climate darkened, they began to be eroded. Thus, until 1976, the 'general direction of case law at the [industrial] tribunal level was to impose more exacting requirements upon employers' on such issues as unfair dismissal, but after 1976, High Court decisions shifted the balance back towards managerial freedom. In *Lesney Products* v *Norton*, for example, Lord Denning pointed out that ' "nothing should be done to impair the ability of employers to reorganize their workforce and their times and conditions of work so as to improve efficiency' ". Further decisions by

> the employee appeals tribunals and by industrial tribunals strongly [implied] . . . that an employer may fairly dismiss an employee who refused to accept a change in hours or conditions of work providing he has convincing economic reasons for insisting on the change in question.

Similar themes marked the treatment of redundancy. It was decided in 1976, for example, that a tribunal could not investigate the circumstances that led to redundancy, only that the employer followed his obligation to consult. In addition, the obligation on the employer to find alternative employment was diluted, as was the warning period that a redundancy was pending.[51]

The shift towards a conservative interpretation of the limits of this legislation reflected the wider demise of the social contract. By 1977 at the latest it was clear that, for a variety of political and financial reasons, the radical implications of the Labour government's programme were in retreat. Although it is too early to provde a full explanation for this, certain developments are clearly marked. We can draw attention to fate of both the Industry Bill and the National Enterprise Board as symptomatic of the deradicalisation of the government's programme. Both measures were originally conceived as key instruments of economic modernisation which would combine a competitive restructuring of industry with an expansion of the power and responsibilities of the unions and the state. Intervention by government was to be predicated upon the industrial priorities of society and was to be used to ensure that industrial decision-making (over investment planning, for example) was more accountable to the unions and the state.

In the event, neither measure was used as an instrument of economic regeneration. Their interventionist and directive aspects were systematically gutted and their main purpose turned out to be the funnelling of large chunks of state capital to private industry in support of managerial rationalisation. Too often nothing was gained in return. Chrysler was the classic case. The company bail-out in 1976 was accompanied by 8,000 redundancies and two years later the company was sold to Peugeot without even the government being informed. By 1976, the National Enterprise Board – whose job it was to acquire an interest in companies judged to be of vital national interest – had not purchased a single share in a major company, nor had it negotiated any planning agreements. One company was eventually taken over by the Board but was then handed back once it had been made profitable.[52]

It is, perhaps, appropriate to identify three major elements that help to explain the reasons why this effort to combine economic regeneration with restructured social relations failed. The first was the intense opposition from industry to the interventionist aspects of the legislation. To take one example, a major campaign against the National Enterprise Board was launched by the CBI when the Labour government arrived in office. Attention was drawn to the Board's lack of accountability to Parliament and to the 'unfair' competitive advantage it would provide for the firms under its control by its ability to cross-subsidise units within its portfolio. The government allayed these fears by staffing the board with industrialists like Lord Ryder of British Leyland and by redrafting the legislation 25 times to meet industry's objections.

Such pressure undoubtedly reinforced the second element of explanation: the hesitancies that existed within the Labour Party and particularly within the leadership. Between 1970 and 1973, the policy-making committees of the party had been controlled by the left; it was under their influence that these proposals had been formulated. Their guiding strategy for economic modernisation was to combine a constructive intervention in industry with an extension of democratic control in an attempt to break with the pure statism that had traditionally characterised Labour Party socialism. The left's control of policy-making did not secure automatic acceptance of its programme, however, and as the election of 1974 drew nearer the more conservative elements of the party began to regroup. Once in office the pre-eminence of the right was assured. Thus, there was consistent, if varying degrees of, resistance within the Labour Party to the radical implications of its policies. Harold Wilson, for example, repudiated a 1973 National Executive Council resolution to nationalise the top 25 companies, and as the original proposals for the National Enterprise Board and the Industry Act passed through the policy-making committees of government they were progressively denuded of their radical elements. The Cabinet committee chaired by Wilson removed the proposal for compulsory planning agreements from the Industry Bill and relied upon Conservative and Liberal votes in the House of Commons to pass the final Act.[53] It should hardly need to be said that this opposition to the leftward drift of the party was not a function of the 'betrayal' mentality. It was based upon a different assessment of what was electorally feasible and upon the different ideological assumptions of traditional Labourism. In that tradition socialism was defined as the efficient management of the economy through statist means, not as a strategy for attacking the bastions of established power in society.

But the third reason for the failure of the party's original programme and the events that spelled the dissolution of the social contract was clearly the most important. In 1976 and 1977 the intervention of financial crises once again revealed the vulnerability of social and industrial reform to the fluctuations of the money markets. The most important aspect of this particular crisis was the irresistible pressure it created to bring public expenditure under control. Indeed, it was a condition of the IMF rescue operation in late 1976 that £12,500 million be slashed from government spending. It was at this point that the government decisively changed direction. Whilst the Labour Party conference was demanding even more radical measures to meet the crisis and an 'alternative economic strategy' began to be offered by some economists, the Labour government slithered down the slippery slope to monetarism. Cash limits and then cuts were imposed on public expenditure. An increasingly restrictive pay policy undermined the social contract on wage restraint. By 1978-79 the familiar pattern recurred of intensified industrial conflict breaching pay norms and an alienation between Labour and its supporters. But this time mass unemployment had made its appearance and monetarism had been established as the hinge of social and economic policies. The promise of the social contract had been shattered, but so, too, had the policy assumptions that had governed politics since the Second World War. In 1977 James Callaghan signalled Labour's abandonment of its own history when he announced that the option of a reflationary protection of employment no longer existed.[54]

The emphasis so far has been on how the 1970s were marked by an expansion of labour's power in society and how this was represented by an admittedly qualified attempt to entrench a new political economy through the agency of the social contract. Even once the qualifications have been admitted – such as the diminishing influence of the trade unions in Whitehall after 1976 – this does describe one reality of the decade. Trade-union density increased from 51.6 per cent of the occupied work-force in 1974 to 57.8 per cent in 1978 for example. As late as the winter of 1978-9, as mass unemployment was deepening, it was still possible to mobilise a strike-wave that caused more working days to be lost at any time since 1926. From another angle of vision, however, there were important ambiguities present in the 1970s that laid the groundwork for the emergence of the policies of monetarism. In this process, politics played a leading role. The policies of the Labour Party in government served both to sever the already weakening allegiances of its traditional voters and to diminish its credibility as a party that could control both unemployment and inflation.

It is not proposed to enter here into the much debated question of the relationship between changing class structure and the political dealignment that struck Labour in the 1970s. It is enough to point out that the most persuasive explanations of Labour's crisis were those that linked the ideological disputes, the diminished electoral appeal, and the decline in voter loyalty to the performance of the party in office.[55] Apart from the 1945-51 government, there has been an enormous gulf between Labour's programme and its policy implementation. The major policy failure in the 1960s and 1970s was in the area of economic management which Labour had come to power with programmes specifically designed to address. In particular, it would seem that Labour never really managed to come to terms with the changes that had occurred in class structure and working-class expectations since the Second World War. On the one hand, there were the enormous increases in material well-being within the working class and the legitimate demand that they continue. On the other hand, surveys taken in the early 1970s revealed that a sense of class and opposition to the inequalities of class society remained deeply rooted in the consciousness of working people. The steady defection of the instrumentally-oriented working-class activist and voter followed growing evidence of Labour's failure adequately to address either of these questions.[56]

All sorts of arguments may be deployed to explain this failure, but its key effect was to dissolve Labour's political and programmatic credibility. It is fruitless to argue whether more or less radical programmes would have retained or increased the political appeal of Labour. The central obstacle to the continued mobilisation of political support for Labour was the contrast between its promise and performance in office. This explains, for example, the declining support for nationalisation as a policy: as it was actually experienced nationalisation was revealed to have changed relatively little for the worker. Similarly, the eroding support for the Welfare State can in large part be attributed to the way tax policies (especially under Labour) became increasingly regressive with large transfer payments coming from the less wealthy themselves.[57] Perhaps the most serious failure, though, was the seemingly cyncial abandonment of the 1974 programme soon after Labour had taken office, when its rapid retreat into conventional and conservative economic and social programmes revealed its ultimate political bankruptcy.

In their turn, these policies served to legitimate and reinforce the growing neo-Conservative orthodoxy that economic modernisation could only come from unleashing the traditional forces of liberal capitalism. It was under Labour that the boundaries of the politically possible shifted to the right. Thus, levels of unemployment that had been politically unthinkable ten years before came to be accepted under a Labour government. The more positive side of the social contract also assisted in this shift. It is probable that attitudes towards redundancy changed in the mid-1970s as the shake-out of labour instigated by various measures of rationalisation was eased by state-supported redundancy payments.

Similarly, at the factory level, the Labour government's policy both encouraged the integration of the workshop organisation into the industrial relations system and endorsed managerial rationalisation that could be used to undercut that organisation. After 1974, for example, British Leyland began to breach the mutuality agreements on measured day work and to attack stewards' organisation. This offensive was made easier by the growing gap between the stewards and the work-force noted earlier and by the increased economic insecurity that made any management offer seem generous. Under the Thatcher government, of course, such policies received positive endorsement. Between 1979-81 there was a wholesale removal of stewards' negotiating rights and of mutuality. New working practices at British Leyland in 1979 and 1980 denied consultation over changes in the work organisation and job timing; a new disciplinary code at Fords, introduced without consultation, provided for dismissal for refusal to follow foremen's orders. Leading stewards – like Derek Robinson, the convener at BL who had been a major supporter of the Ryder Report's participation scheme in the mid-1970s – were fired and, unsurprisingly, the numbers of stewards declined precipitously. Strike movements called by stewards – against, for example, the 3.8 per cent wage offer at BL in 1981 – failed disastrously, reflecting and reinforcing their weakness. And the failure of union-led strikes – like the one in the steel industry in 1980 – mirrored the growing inability of labour to resist the hostile economic and political environment that surrounded it by the early 1980s.[58]

A further element of that environment that we may note by way of conclusion was the renewed use of the restrictive tradition of case law as a weapon against labour action. The prior experience of both Labour and Conservative governments did not deter Mrs Thatcher from proceeding to use the law in this way. And with good reason. The possibilities of trade-union resistance were much diminished by the early 1980s and, unlike Edward Heath, the chances of Mrs Thatcher's reverting to a tripartite policy of co-operation were always minimal: she did not need union assistance in the implementation of her economic policy. There was no sweeping legislation like the 1971 Act, but rather a series of specific measures aimed at reversing the bias of the statutes of the mid-1970s towards the trade unions and reinforcing the restrictions of the case law. The code of picketing practices, for example, gave added support to aggressive policing of picketing and harsh judicial attitudes, even though it was a code and not a set of legal requirements. Legislation in 1980 and 1982 prohibited the secondary boycott and picket, exposed the closed shop to attack and removed trade-union immunities from tort. In addition, legislation was promised to replace contracting in for contracting out of the political levy, to make strike ballots compulsory and to open the way for unions to be sued for commercial damages resulting from breach of contract.[59]

The changes in the law, however, were not at the centre of the politics of industrial relations as they had been in the early 1970s. They were merely one aspect of a much wider attack upon labour extending across the whole front of government policy. It is indisputable that the main aim of that policy was to weaken the role of labour in the political economy, to remove the trade-union influence from market determination. The changes in the law obviously assisted those ends and, together with mass unemployment and the determinedly anti-Welfare State, privatising inspiration of government policy, these elements represented a radical attempt to alter on a long-term basis the structure of power in production relations. In this effort it was inevitable that there should be constant resonances of the past – the recurrence of the familiar themes of the law, for example – because the crisis of labour in the late 1970s and early 1980s was, in part, the moment when the legacies of the past were at last confronted in the present.

Notes

1. Sydney Pollard, *The Wasting of the British Economy* (London, 1982); Samuel Beer, *Britain Against Itself. The Political Contradictions of Collectivism* (New York, 1982). It is impossible to keep up with the literature on Britain's 'decline' and equally impossible to list here all the books and articles that have contributed to my thinking on the subject. A very useful and stimulating summary of the problem is Andrew Gamble, *Britain in Decline* (New York, 1982).

2. Martin Weiner, *English Culture and the Decline of the Industrial Spirit 1850-1980* (Cambridge, 1980), Chapter 1.

3. S.J. Prais, *Productivity and Industrial Structure* (Cambridge, 1981).

4. This section on finance capital follows directly the arguments of Richard Rosecrance, 'The Pax Britannica and British Foreign Policy' in Issac Kramnick (ed.), *Is Britain Dying*? (Ithaca, NY, 1979), pp. 217-25, and Frank Longstreth, 'The City, Industry and the State' in Colin Crouch (ed.), *State and Economy in Contemporary Capitalism* (London, 1979), pp. 159-88. See also William Keegan and Rupert Pennant-Rea, *Who Runs the Economy*? (London, 1979), pp. 126-37; Andrew Yarmie, 'Employer's Organizations in Mid-Victorian Britain,' *International Review of Social History*, vol. 25 (1980) and Yarmie, 'British Employers'

Resistance to 'Grandmotherly' Legislation, 1850-80', *Social History*, vol. 9, no. 2 (1984).

5. Rosecrance, 'Pax Britannica', pp. 218, 221, 223; Gamble, *Britain in Decline*, pp. 52-63; Sean Glynn and John Oxborrow, *Interwar Britain: A Social and Economic History* (London, 1976) p. 69; Longstreth, 'City, Industry and State', p. 172.

6. Longstreth, 'City, Industry and State', pp. 178-84.

7. Paul Whiteley, *The Labour Party in Crisis* (London, 1983), p. 153.

8. Longstreth, 'City, Industry and State', p. 188.

9. On the European situation generally see Anthony Carew, *Democracy and Government in European Trade Unions* (London, 1976), pp. 57-75, 158-98; Pierre Dubois, *Sabotage in Industry* (London, 1979), pp. 134-7, 189-200. On Italy see, for example, Paul Ginsborg, 'The Communist Party and the Agrarian Question in Southern Italy', *History Workshop Journal*, no. 17 (1984); B. Savalti, 'The Rebirth of Italian Trade Unionism, 1943-54' in S.J. Woolf, *The Rebirth of Italy 1943-50* (London, 1972), pp. 198-203, 206-11. On the US see Nelson Lichtenstein, 'Auto Worker Militancy and the Structure of Factory Life 1937-55', *Journal of American History*, vol. 67, no. 2 (1980).

10. F. Zweig, *Productivity and Trade Unions* (Oxford, 1951), pp. 222-3; A.I. Marsh and E.E. Coker, 'Shop Steward Organization in the Engineering Industry', *British Journal of Industrial Relations*, vol. 1, no. 2 (1963), p. 176; H.A. Clegg, *The Changing System of Industrial Relations in Great Britain* (Oxford, 1979), pp. 215-20.

11. Seymour Melman, *Decision Making and Productivity* (London, 1958), pp. 74-8; Shirley Lerner and John Bescoby, 'Shop Steward Combine Committees in the British Engineering Industry', *British Journal of Industrial Relations*, vol. 4, no. 2 (1966), pp. 155, 160-62; Tony Cliff, *The Employers' Offensive* (London, 1970), pp. 188-9; H.A. Turner, Garfield Clack and Geoffrey Roberts, *Labour Relations in the Motor Industry* (London, 1967), pp. 218-20; *Report of a Court of Inquiry into the Causes and Circumstances of a Dispute at Briggs Motor Bodies (Ltd.)*, 1956-7, Vol. XIV (Cmnd. 131), pp. 8, 24; Ken Coates, *The Right to Useful Work* (London, 1978), pp. 2, 14-15; Hilary Wainwright and Huw Beynon, *The Workers' Report on Vickers* (London, 1979).

12. J.W. Durcan, W.E.J. McCarthy and G.P. Redman, *Strikes in Post-War Britain. A Study of Stoppages of Work Due to Industrial Disputes, 1946-73* (London, 1983), p. 90.

13. *Report of a Court of Inquiry into Dispute at Briggs Motors*, pp. 9-26.

14. Andrew Friedman, *Industry and Labour: Class Struggle at Work and Monopoly Capitalism* (London, 1977), pp. 214-15; Melman, *Decision Making and Productivity*, pp. 112-13, 154-8, 178-80, 188-90. Wages were as much as 60 per cent higher at Standard than in other companies.

15. Turner, Clack and Roberts, *Labour Relations in the Motor Industry*, pp. 90-2, 127; Friedman, *Industry and Labour*, pp. 219-31, 243.

16. C.J. Bartlett, *A History of Postwar Britain 1945-74* (London, 1977), p. 95; Stephen Blank, *Industry and Government in Britain. The Federation of British Industries in Politics 1945-65* (Lexington, KY, 1973), pp. 127-8, 134-5; H.A. Clegg and Rex Adams, *The Employers' Challenge: A Study of the National Shipbuilding and Engineering Disputes of 1957* (Oxford, 1957), pp. 46-59.

17. Clegg and Adams, *The Employers' Challenge*, pp. 78-91, 114-40.

18. Blank, *Industry and Government*, pp. 138-9; Keith Middlemas, *Politics in Industrial Society* (London, 1979), pp. 400, 407-9.

19. Turner, Clack and Roberts, *Labour Relations in the Motor Industry*, p. 222; I. Boraston, H. Clegg and M. Rimmer, *Workplace and Union* (London, 1975); John Purcell and Robin Smith, *The Control of Work* (London, 1979),

pp. 136, 134; John H. Goldthorpe, David Lockwood, *et al.*, *The Affluent Worker: Industrial Attitudes and Behaviour* (Cambridge, 1968), pp. 103-7; William Brown, *Piecework Bargaining* (London, 1973), p. 98; Alan Aldridge, *Power, Authority and Restrictive Practices* (Oxford, 1977), pp. 68-70.

20. Theo Nichols and Huw Beynon, *Living with Capitalism* (London, 1977); P. Armstrong, J.F.B. Goodman and J.D. Hyman, *Ideology and Shop Floor Industrial Relations* (London, 1980), pp. 84, 112; James Cronin, *Industrial Conflict in Modern Britain* (London, 1979), p. 141; Purcell and Smith, *Control of Work*, pp. 140-1; Brown, *Piecework Bargaining*, p. 115.

21. *Royal Commission on Trade Unions 1965-68, Research Paper no. 4*, 1966; Brown, *Piecework Bargaining*, pp. 21-3, 88-93, 111; Kevin Hawkins, *The Management of Industrial Relations* (Harmondsworth, 1979), p. 68.

22. In 1973 BL had £1,600 worth of fixed assets per man, Renault, £2,300, GM £4,300; see Kevin Hawkins, *British Industrial Relations 1945-73* (London, 1976), p. 167.

23. Prais, *Productivity and Industrial Structure*, pp. 60-5, 80, 163, 261-2; C.F. Pratten, *Labour Productivity Differentials Within International Companies* (Cambridge, 1976), pp. 53-4, 55-64.

24. Croucher, *Engineers at War 1939-1945* (London, 1982) pp. 342-3; Cliff, *The Employers' Offensive*, p. 3; Friedman, *Industry and Labour*, pp. 219-24; *Metal Worker*, February 1951, p. 1; March 1951, p. 1; April 1951, p. 1; May 1951, p. 4; David Wilson, *Dockers. The Impact of Industrial Change* (London, 1972), p. 225.

25. *Metal Worker*, April 1950, p. 1 and October 1948 p. 4; Geoff Brown, *Sabotage* (London, 1977), p. 314; Wm. Brown, *Piecework Bargaining*, pp. 88-91; Friedman, *Industry and Labour*, pp. 219-20; Wilson, *Dockers*, p. 232.

26. Cronin, *Industrial Conflict*, pp. 141-4; Cronin, *Labour and Society in Britain 1918-1979* (London, 1984), pp. 159-60, 169-72, 200-1 for the most effective critique of the embourgeoisement thesis; Turner, Clack and Roberts, *Labour Relations in the Motor Industry*, pp. 234-5; R.O. Clarke, D.J. Fatchett, and B.C. Roberts, *Workers Participation in Management in Britain* (London 1972), pp. 134-8.

27. Turner, Clack and Roberts, *Labour Relations in the Motor Industry*, pp. 115, 334-6; Cronin, *Industrial Conflict*, p. 144.

28. *Metal Worker*, July 1951, p. 1; April 1959, p. 4; July 1960, p. 1; November 1960, p. 1; Turner, Clack and Roberts, *Labour Relations in the Motor Industry*, pp. 278-85.

29. See John Hilton, *Are Trade Unions Obstructive?* (London, 1935); Zweig, *Productivity and Trade Unions*, pp. 222-3; J.A. Lincoln, *The Restrictive Society* (London, 1963) which also discusses restrictive practices in the professions.

30. Wilson, *Dockers*, pp. 215-17; Clegg, *The Changing System*, p. 142.

31. Cliff, *The Employers Offensive*, p. 50; Brown, *Sabotage*, pp. 326, 353. On the NPLA see Joel Krieger, *Undermining Capitalism. State Ownership and the Dialectic of Control in the British Coal Industry* (Princeton, NJ, 1983).

32. Cliff, *The Employers' Offensive*, p. 88; Brown, *Sabotage*, pp. 335-6; Friedman, *Industry and Labour*, pp. 232-5; IWC Motors Group, *A Workers' Enquiry into the Motor Industry* (London, 1978), p. 17; see Krieger, *Undermining Capitalism*, pp. 16-17 on the NPLA and control over manning in the mines.

33. Anthony Barnett, 'Politics and the Shop Floor', *New Left Review*, no. 80 (1973), pp. 31-2; Brown, *Sabotage*, p. 336; IWC, *Workers' Enquiry*, p. 16; Huw Beynon, *Working for Ford* (Harmondsworth, 1973), pp. 164-73.

34. M.G. Wilders and S.R. Parker, 'Changes in Workplace Industrial Relations, 1966-72', *British Journal of Industrial Relations,* vol. 13, no. 1 (1975), pp. 16-19;

Hawkins, *Management*, p. 118.

35. Wilson, *Dockers*, p. 187; John Bloomfield, 'Interview with Derek Robinson', *Marxism Today*, March 1980, p. 5.

36. IWC, *Workers' Enquiry*, p. 14; Barnett, 'Politics and the Shop Floor' pp. 33-4; Cliff, *The Employers' Offensive* p. 227; Clarke, Fatchett and Roberts, *Workers' Participation*, pp. 52, 179; Hawkins, *Management*, pp. 95-7; John Matthews, *Ford Strike* (London, 1972); Krieger, *Undermining Capitalism.*

37. Allan Flanders, *The Fawley Productivity Agreements* (London, 1964); Hawkins, *British Industrial Relations*, p. 65; Hawkins, *Management*, pp. 30, 35-44; Brown, *Piecework Bargaining*, pp. 48-9.

38. Leo Panitch, *Social Democracy and Industrial Militancy: The Labour Party, The Trade Unions and Incomes Policy 1945-74* (Cambridge, 1976), pp. 47-8, 113-29; Michael Stewart, *The Jekyll and Hyde Years* (London, 1977), pp. 39-41.

39. Stewart, *The Jekyll and Hyde Years*, pp. 86-91; Panitch, *Social Democracy*, pp. 138, 144-5, 155.

40. Colin Crouch, 'The Intensification of Industrial Conflict in the UK', in Colin Crouch and Allessandro Pizzorno, *The Resurgence of Class Conflict in Western Europe since 1968* (London, 1978), pp. 208, 215; Andrew Glyn and Bob Sutcliffe, *British Capitalism, Workers and the Profits Squeeze* (Harmondsworth, 1972); Panitch, *Social Democracy*, pp. 173-9. Until the government began to treat strikes as a major political issue – and especially to identify them with economic problems – only 17 per cent of the public (in the autumn of 1968) saw them as the most urgent problem facing society.

41. Panitch, *Social Democracy*, p. 173; Hawkins, *British Industrial Relations*, p. 69; Middlemas, *Politics in Industrial Society*, pp. 440-3; Beynon, *Working for Ford*, pp. 243, 246, 250, 255.

42. John Elliott, *Conflict or Cooperation? The Growth of Industrial Democracy* (London, 1978), p. 10; Hawkins, *British Industrial Relations*, p. 121. For a full account of the 1971 Act see O.H. Kahn Freund, *Labour and Law* (London, 1972); and A.W.J. Thomson and S.R. Engleman, *The Industrial Relations Act* (London, 1975).

43. Secondary breach of contract is forcing somebody not involved in a trade dispute to break his contract. For details of these cases see K.W. Wedderburn, *The Worker and the Law*, 2nd edn (Harmondsworth, 1971), pp. 355-8, 324-37; Brian Weekes, *Industrial Relations and the Limits of the Law* (London, 1975), pp. 195-6; *Tynan* v *Chief Constable of Liverpool* (1965) 3 All ER; *Piddington* v *Bates* (1960) 3 All *ER; Broom* v *DPP* (1974), *Industrial Court Reports*.

44. Between 1962 and about 1978 the closed shop had increased its coverage from 25 per cent to between 31 and 39 per cent of all workers, and over 70 per cent were supported by employers: see William Brown (ed.), *The Changing Contours of British Industrial Relations* (Oxford, 1981), pp. 55, 57-8; Thomson and Engleman, *The Industrial Relations Act*, pp. 70-2, 100-9; Weekes, *Industrial Relations*, p. 95; Middlemas, *Politics in Industrial Society* pp. 440-4.

45. Elliott, *Conflict or Cooperation?,* pp. 28-40. Trade-union influence on Labour Party policy-making tends to increase at times of political crisis. But what was unique about this period was that the weight of that influence was tilted towards radical, not conservative, policies.

46. Brown, *The Changing Contours*, pp. 63-4, 78-9, 118-19; Hawkins, *Management*, pp. 125-30.

47. Richard Hyman, 'The Politics of Workplace Trade Unionism', *Capital and Class*, no. 10 (1979), p. 58; Tony Shafto, 'The Growth of Shop Stewards' Managerial Function' in Keith Thurley and Stephen Wood, *Industrial Relations and Management Strategy* (Cambridge, 1983), pp. 47, 48, 52.

48. David Coates, *Labour in Power? A Study of the Labour Government 1974-79* (London, 1980), pp. 137-9; Paul Hirst, 'On Struggle in the Enterprise' in Mike Prior (ed.), *The Popular and the Political* (London, 1981), pp. 56-61; Jim Tomlinson, *The Unequal Struggle? British Socialism and Capitalist Enterprise* (London, 1982), pp. 38-46.

49. This is why some commentators argued for the social contract on the same grounds that G.D.H. Cole had justified encroaching control. The context of the 1960s and 1970s did afford some justification for that argument. See David Purdy, 'The Social Contract and Socialist Policy' in Prior, *The Popular and the Political*.

50. Hawkins, *Management*, pp. 31, 157-8; Coates, *Labour in Power?* pp. 133-4; see Brown, *The Changing Contours*, p. 58, on the expansion of the closed shop associated with these measures. The precedents for this legislation were more complicated than we have allowed. An Act of 1965 established the principle of redundancy payments; the code of practice of the 1971 Act emphasised the need for consultation on redundancy.

51. Hawkins, *Management*, pp. 160-1.

52. On the Labour government's strategy generally, see Coates, *Labour in Power?*, Chapter 3; Geoff Hodgson, *Labour at the Crossroads* (Oxford, 1981), pp. 97-8; 129.

53. Hodgson, *Labour at the Crossroads*, pp. 84-7, 97-8.

54. Ibid., pp. 110-13, 118, 123-4; Keegan and Pennant-Rea *Who Runs the Economy?*, p. 181.

55. Sensible statements and arguments about this matter can be found in: Eric Hobsbawm *et al.*, *The Forward March of Labour Halted?* (London, 1981); Goran Therborn, 'Britain Left Out', *New Socialist*, May-June 1984; Whiteley, *The Labour Party in Crisis*, Chapters 1 and 3; James Alt, *The Politics of Economic Decline* (Cambridge, 1979); Ivor Crewe, 'The Labour Party and the Electorate' in Dennis Kavanagh, *The Politics of the Labour Party* (London, 1982).

56. See Cronin, *Labour and Society*, p. 201 and Chapter 11 generally for the argument that the heightened material expectations of the working class in no way betokened a decline in class consciousness; C.W. Chamberlain and H.F. Moorhouse, 'Lower Class Attitudes towards the British Political System', *Sociological Review*, vol. 22, no. 3 (1974); H.F. Moorhouse and C.W. Chamberlain, 'Lower Class Attitudes to Property: Aspects of the Counter Ideology', *Sociology*, vol. 8, no. 3 (1974).

57. Whiteley, *The Labour Party in Crisis*, Chapter 7; *New Statesman*, 30 October 1981, pp. 6-7.

58. IWC, *Workers' Enquiry*, p. 7; Brown, *Sabotage*, pp. 361-2; *New Statesman*, 2 January 1981, p. 7; 3 October 1981, p. 5; 6 November 1981, pp. 10-11, 27 November 1981, pp. 16-17. 5 March 1982, p. 4; *Manchester Guardian Weekly*, 8 November 1981, p. 3. By 1982 the number of stewards at Cowley and Longbridge was about 80 per cent less than in the early 1970s.

59. *New Statesman*, 22 February 1980, p. 272; 27 July 1979, p. 127; 14 December 1979, p. 925; 21 January 1981, p. 5; 24 April 1981, p. 4. See Peggy Kahn, Norman Lewis *et al.*, *Picketing: Industrial Disputes, Tactics and the Law* (London, 1983), which is mainly concerned with the 1980 Employment Act.

9 CONCLUSION

As Britain entered the last third of the twentieth century, its present continued to bear the indelible legacies of its past. The ghost of Empire continued to haunt the formulation and operation of economic policy in the importance of sterling as an international currency. It was in the domestic arena, however, that the deposits of history were thickest and nowhere was this more true than in the heritage bestowed by the history of British social relations in industry.

Since the industrial revolution, a tradition of labour action and organisation in the work-place has been integral to labour's history and to the history of British capitalism. How far this is a distinct peculiarity of British labour might be a matter for debate. It is clearly true, however, that in Britain the choice of how to deploy labour in production has been powerfully restrained by the existence of this tradition. The origins of this characteristic of British production relations do not lie in some immutable essence within the working class. They were a product of its history and, more particularly, they derived from the course of economic and social change during the industrial revolution.

The economic process of industrialisation was dominated by the methods of the past. Thus, a pattern of social relations could survive that combined a paternalist representation of class relations generally with a sphere of autonomy from capitalist authority at the work-place. The unique supremacy of British productive capacity for much of the nineteenth century allowed this particular construction to remain viable, and, until the late nineteenth century, it was a force for social stability. But it ceased to perform such a function once the world dominance of British capitalism itself began to erode. Collective organisation of interests replaced the informalities of mid-nineteenth-century class relations. New imperatives of economic change were incompatible with the traditional indeterminancy of authority at work, and, thus, the structures of production relations were transformed into a source of instability. At this point a far more complicated picture of the relationship between labour and society began to emerge – which has been reflected in this book by the densening of its analysis and the shift of emphasis to politics.

In the first place, the potential for a fully-fledged crisis of social relations at the end of the century was avoided by the qualified nature of the economic imperatives to change. Britain had her Empire to fall back on and this retreat tended to reinforce the traditional economic and social structures in society. In the second place, work and politics became entangled by the partial admission of labour to an organised presence in industrial and political bargaining. Ever since the collectivity of artisan politics had been dissolved by the demise of Chartism, Labour politics had basically been those of an unorganised individualism. Labour now attained a collective status in the national polity and the question arose of how that presence should be articulated and represented. In the third place, this new status set loose tensions over the correct strategy of action and stimulated debates about policy both at the local and national levels. And, finally, the necessity to integrate labour into a directed national policy during the First World War forced these matters to a climax. That integration did not countenance the full contribution of Labour to policy-making, but it did elevate the issue of how labour politics were to be represented from a purely local matter to a national concern.

The end result was a contradictory tension within labour's relationship to society. On the one hand, the political integration of the Labour Party posed no particular problems or dangers after 1918. On the other hand, the tendency of political radicalism and industrial militancy to reinforce each other presented an obstacle both to that integration and – most crucially – to the direction of national economic policy. Neither could be safely assured until the structures of political radicalism were discredited or tamed and the presence of industrial militancy had been dissolved.

This complex series of events decisively changed the political significance of production relations. In the early and mid-nineteenth century, the character of production relations was integral to both artisan radicalism and later liberal individualism, and was coherent with the paradigms that governed the place of labour in the wider politics. In the later nineteenth and early twentieth centuries, however, production relations were deeply implicated in the political debates within labour and to the developing relationship between labour and national politics. The defeats of the early 1920s decoupled those linkages. In the short run this fracture allowed the economic restructuring of the Depression to run its course unhindered by serious political and industrial challenges. But the full implications of this separation only became evident in the post-Second World War era.

The necessity to secure a voluntary war mobilisation led to an enormous accretion to labour's industrial and political power. After the war, political protection for the restraints of production relations on economic management to flourish undisturbed was afforded by the Keynesian consensus of full employment and the Welfare State. Politically, this represented an unspoken partnership between the labourism of the Labour Party and the tradition of labour action at the work-place. The party would take care of the politics of welfarism while the trade-union presence took care of gains in industry. This consensus was so strong that even the Conservative Party accepted its implications: hence the convergence between Labour and Conservative policies epitomised by 'Butskellism'. It is hard to see how materially different the history of the 1950s would have been if Labour had continued in power after 1951. But this balance between the two powerful traditions of labour's presence in Britain could not survive the imperatives of economic regeneration, and from around the mid-1960s industrial relations once again became politicised.

During much of the 1950s and 1960s, industrial peace had been secured at the expense of management strength and initiative. Similarly, the state refused to move away from a policy of industrial appeasement. But only the state possessed the requisite authority to enact policies that would modernise the British economy. Thus, the trick of government became the ability to navigate an economic policy that would answer the imperatives of economic regeneration, cope with short-term fluctuations that were the legacy of a world imperial role, and ensure the full employment and the protection of the Welfare State that were considered to be essential to political survival. The dominance of the Labour Party in the 1960s and 1970s rested upon the diminishing promise that it was most likely to carry that suit. However, every effort government made to reconcile these constraints stumbled into the thickets of industrial relations. As a result, by the mid-1970s Labour's political action was paralysed by three forces: first, it could not escape the tightening noose of international economic fluctuations; second, the growing demand in the party for a strategy that sought economic regeneration through an expansion of political and economic democracy, third, the suspicion aroused in the country and the party by this tendency to recouple work and politics in the redefinition of labourist socialism. Thus, a political and ideological void was created in the centre of politics which was filled by a resurgent Conservatism fuelled by the doctrines of monetarism.

Mrs Thatcher's government was one of the products of the history recounted in this book. The policies of the Thatcher governments represented an attempt to erect a political economy of power relations between labour, the state and society which would impede the possibility of the balance of power that came out of the Second World War ever recurring. The justification for this policy lay in the promise that it was the only way to ensure a new phase of economic growth. How far the aspirations of Thatcherite conservatism were realistic will be known only in the fullness of time. It does seem reasonable to suggest that the era of Mrs Thatcher will be seen to mark a new phase in the history of British labour, but exactly what will be the future shape of labour's relationship to society can safely and thankfully be left to future historians. My purpose has been to offer an interpretation of labour history that can help us understand how it has been shaped by, and also has shaped, the history of British society.

INDEX